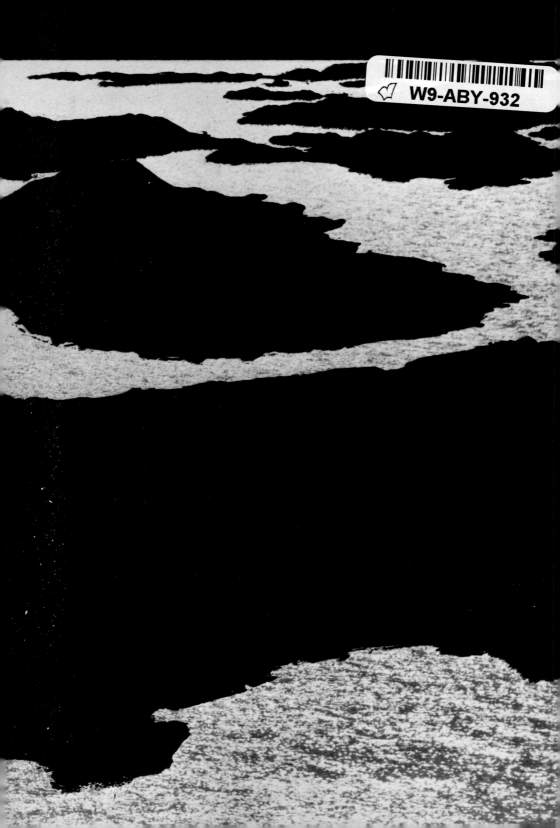

The Inland Sea

THE INLAND SEA

by Donald Richie

WITH PHOTOGRAPHS BY YOICHI MIDORIKAWA

NEW YORK · WEATHERHILL · TOKYO

First edition, 1971

Published by John Weatherhill, Inc., 149 Madison Avenue, New York, New York 10016, with editorial offices at 7-6-13 Roppongi, Minato-ku, Tokyo 106, Japan.
LCC Card No. 78-157276   ISBN 0-8348-0063-2

FOR MEREDITH

Contents

LIST OF PHOTOGRAPHS

The Inland Sea

I hear they are building a bridge
To the island of Tsu.
Alas . . .
To what now
Shall I compare myself?
                    —*an old Japanese poem*

The Inland Sea is a nearly landlocked, lakelike body of water bounded by three of Japan's four major islands. It is entered through but four narrow straits, three opening to the south into the Pacific Ocean and one—called Kammon or Barrier Gate—to the west into the narrow sea that separates Japan from Korea and the rest of Asia.

By Japanese standards it is a long sea. At approximately the same latitudes in other parts of the world it would stretch from Little Rock to Dallas, from Cyprus almost to Crete. But, like the land of Japan itself, it is also narrow.

Traveling westward along its length, one feels the shores pressing close, as though it were a large river rather than a small sea. On the right are the mountains of Honshu—in the foreground, low hills ranged one behind the other and then, behind them, the snow-capped spine of the country itself, the Japan Alps. On the left are first the sharp and Chinese-looking mountains of the island of Shikoku, so different that it appears another land, and then the flat coasts of Kyushu. This shallow sea is a valley among these mountainous islands.

It has been called the Aegean of the East. There are, however, differences. The Greek islands are few, and they stand from the sea as though with an effort, as though to indicate the water's great depth. The islands of the shallow Inland Sea are different. They are small, and there are many—hundreds of them, so many that a full count has never been made, or certainly not one that everyone can agree upon. They rise gracefully from this protected, stormless sea, as if they had just emerged, their beaches, piers, harbors all intact. Some have springs, most have wells; many are covered with forest, almost all have trees or bushes. A castaway, given the choice between a Greek and a Japanese island, would swim toward the latter. It looks like a place where it would be nice to live.

Grandeur is missing, the precipitous hard-rock climbs of Santorin. But, in place of vertical magnificence, there is the horizontal majesty of the panorama. Wherever one turns there is a wide and restful view, one island behind the other, each soft shape melting into the next until the last dim outline is lost in the distance.

This sea, flat as a meadow, looks domesticated. From its surface rise the

13

islands, *fingers and noses of some shallowly submerged range, but softened and rounded—female mountains of unexampled loveliness, all loins and haunches, skirts of sand of purest white, fields of deepest green, and black, black bushes. These islands, even those on which no one lives, seem civilized, or at least as though waiting for civilization.*

The Japanese call this part of their country the Seto Naikai, a name that might be translated as a sea within straits; and though its beauty is famous, it is perhaps significant that the Japanese have long thought of it mainly in terms of navigability (a sea within straits) because—lying at the mercantile crossroads of the nation—it has always been something to get across rather than merely to enjoy. Consequently, to this day, though widely known, it is little understood and, except for those few islands where the larger steamers pause on their way between Honshu and Shikoku and Kyushu, little visited. It extends from Osaka and Kobe to Shimonoseki and Moji, but when most people speak of the Inland Sea, they mean the more scenic and heavily islanded part that begins at the island of Shodo and ends just past Hiroshima.

The people of the Inland Sea have been called backward. And so they are. Living in island towns, cut off from each other and from the mainland, they are like mountain villagers separated from the next village by whole ranges. They know much of their own island and nothing of the next, though it is framed daily in their bay. Island-bound, or else wild to leave; distrustful of all new information, or else possessed of a wide and curious knowledge—these people's lives are circumscribed by the placid, lakelike sea. If their lives have little width, however, they do attain depth. A good catch of fish, the spring festival, a fine tangerine harvest—such events evoke a feeling and a response with which the mainland city-dweller in Japan is now largely unfamiliar.

So the people are indeed backward, if this means a people living eternally in the present, a people for whom becoming means little and being everything. At the same time, living on their history, treasuring it, they are distrustful of mere novelty. Their present is their own and not that of frantic Tokyo or Osaka. The froth of novelty pouring continually into the country casts barely a ripple around these islands, where the headman remains the headman because his father was, where nicknames last for generations, where life is so much slower than in the cities and—since it still follows the round of the seasons—so much more natural.

The islands of the Inland Sea are among the last places on earth where men rise with the sun and where streets are dark and silent by nine at night. Here is the last of old Japan, this valley-like sea where the waters turn green or blue with the season, where the islands stand black against the horizon or lie like

14

*folded fur under the noonday sun, where the blue and silver of towns and vil-
lages merge with the rich yellows, browns, and greens of the patchwork land.*

*These islands are extraordinarily beautiful, and a part of their beauty is
that it is passing. Already the modern mainland is reaching out, converting
each captured island into an industrial waste; already the fish, once so abun-
dant, are leaving their annual paths, maintained over the centuries, and seeking
clearer depths. When this paradise, this ideal sea garden—310 miles long,
40 miles at its widest and 4 at its narrowest—when it goes, devoured by the
land, so will the people who inhabit it, the race of the Seto Naikai that these
islands have created.*

*But not quite yet. A few islands have been captured as Honshu pushes its
factory-littered shoreline into the sea, but only here and there. The great bridges
that will inundate Shikoku and, eventually, all the larger islands in between
with buses and motorcars are still only on the drawing boards. Though fish
have been driven from the shallow shore waters, they continue to live farther
out. In a few decades, however, the ruin will be complete.*

It is to this Inland Sea that I am bound.

*   *   **

Kobe, from where I have just come, is indication enough of Japan's
sad future. It has become a large, overgrown, unfinished-looking
city. It contains big new hotels shouldering out shrines and temples,
big new banks pushing away parks and gardens, big new parking lots
where the gracious old inns of the city once stood. Yet enough of the
old remains to spoil the effect of a new Los Angeles. The city is a
hybrid. East and West have collided here and the wreckage is strewn
at large.

Kobe looks like Manila, that city which is neither one thing nor
the other. It is like the gentle tiglon—no teeth, no claws, the strongest
characteristics of each parent having been canceled out. In the abject
Philippines the resemblance to this unhappy animal is stronger in
that such has been the fate not only of the city but of the countryside
as well. In Japan the symptoms are, as yet, mainly visible only in
the larger cities.

It is at Kobe, or at Yokohama, that the sea-borne traveler gets
his first glimpse of new Japan. A single look, one would think, would
be enough to send him back home again. Nor does the air-borne
traveler fare better with the airports of Tokyo and Osaka.

15

Even here at Himeji the destruction is already well begun, though the results are less unsightly. I am sitting in front of the new railway station, all 1960-ish modern with square windows, escalators, free-form counters, a playground on the roof, probably a bowling alley in the basement. In order to construct this gleaming building all the old trees around the station were cut down, and here the station sits baking in dusty sunlight.

New Japan does not like trees. Its totem is the bulldozer. Whole stretches of park are razed, healthy trees ripped out like sound teeth by this voracious machine, and then, eventually, the whole is land-scaped with grass that cannot grow without shade and with bushes that wither in the eternal glare.

I squint into the sun and watch the people as I wait for the bus that will take me to the port of Shikama. It is morning and the people are mainly farm women who have carried their produce into town and are now resting, squinting, wiping the dust from their faces. They wear traditional farm-woman garb—padded trousers, straw sandals, their bundles caught in great squares of cloth. So dressed their mothers and their mothers' mothers. Yet, as I watch, one of the younger suddenly draws from her pouchlike front pocket a shiny compact from which she powders her face. Back to the farm? On to the cabaret? Either seems likely.

I look around. There are still local faces in Japan. It has been only a century since the opening of the country, only decades since people began to move freely from region to region. Before this, for hundreds of years, people lived where they were born. High moun-tains, a lack of roads, a martinet government kept people in their place. Even now one sees a kind of eyebrow, a cast of nose, that is sure Ibaragi, certain Kyoto.

Japan continues to give this unexampled view of history. It also offers the excitement of watching change. Old and new in these small provincial cities continue to exist side by side, and the new is often built directly beside, rather than directly on top of. One may, for a time, compare; for a space, see history in the gap. Very attrac-tive to a heritage-starved, history-parched American.

I stand up. My bus is coming.

I look eagerly for the sea. On the trip from Kobe to Himeji I saw little enough of it. A glimpse of its eastern reaches, as yet islandless, on the other side of factory chimneys, fertilizer plants, salt works, and

the belching fogs of heavy industry. Now the bus trip to the harbor gives no indication that the sea is anywhere near. The port is like a deserted lot, piled with rusting refuse, boilers, wrecked autos. All of this, I tell myself, is typical of the mainland whose dust I am about to shake from my feet, as I spend the next days and weeks touring the Inland Sea. I lean forward, impatient for the horizon.

The islands of this sea will be my steppingstones, out, far away from the smoking land, onto the formless water. I will continue into history, island after island, far to the west, far to the south.

The ferryboat shudders, whistles blow, people shout. A magical moment. One is sea-borne. The distant city grows dim. A sudden sun-struck ground mist spreads out from the land but cannot catch us. The open sea is ahead and from somewhere above comes the cry of a sea bird—a long, lonely, piercing cry, different far from the chirrupings of land. And then, as though in answer, a sailor in some corner of the ship, already hard at work, begins a song—a folk song, perhaps, from the islands that I shall visit.

I turn toward the sea. I don't care if I never come back.

*   *   *

A JOURNEY IS always also something of a flight. You go to reach, but you also go to escape. I am going to see the islands and all that they seem to promise, but, at the same time, I am going to escape the mainland and all that I already know it contains. I find less fault with Japan than with the century that is destroying this country along with all the others. Now, to escape is no sentimental gesture, it is survival.

Anyone coming to Japan is, in a way, already escaping the worst— as glimpsed in other countries, mainly in America. But I have lived for a quarter of a century in Japan now and have watched the growing blight whose traces might well be yet invisible to those coming from more fully corroded capitals.

And it is not just the pollution, the smog, the death of forests and oceans that I seek to escape from. It is the future. In Japan, for the moment, the past still lives. But already in the larger cities one is aware of the pressures of affluence and overpopulation, those twin ogres, one seemingly benign, the other already wrathful, that are killing the world.

21

Along with too many people and too much money have come the ills that now afflict America, Europe, Japan alike. And while I can accept the crowds, the autos, the television, I cannot accept the diminution of humanity that follows—the sensationalism, the cynicism, the brutality.

Though I am not interested in the humane disciplines, not interested in humanity itself, I am interested in people, some of them, and I believe in them, a few of them. This may not make me a humanist. It certainly makes me a romantic. Perhaps that is why I chose this land to live in. Certainly this is why, now that it is too crowded for me, too unhealthy, too like the land I came from, I want to move onward.

Or rather, perhaps, backward. As one leaves the city now, one moves backward in time, back to places no more crowded and only slightly less spoiled than they were a hundred years ago, places where history lives and superstition is truth. It is no paradox that this is the only progress now.

In Japan one feels, even now, cut off from rampaging history. One is in a still backwater that modern civilization has not yet had time to consume. One feels, more and more, the impermanence of such few places as the Inland Sea, and consequently, one feels their beauty more strongly because in another quarter of a century they too will have disappeared.

To talk to other people, to make pleasant acquaintances and perhaps friends, to learn something of what is now so rapidly vanishing, to become close, if only for a moment, with someone, anyone—this is my quest. I'll be satisfied with even less. I want to observe what people were like when they had time and space, because this will be one of the final opportunities.

I think of hot, crowded, smog-covered Tokyo, of steaming Osaka, of poor fragmented Kyoto, and I know that even there, right now, there are carpenters and stonecutters who take pride in their work, taxi drivers who polish their cars, salesmen who believe in the company, housewives who believe in happiness, disinterested politicians, students who have faith in the future, and waitresses who manage smiles for each of their hundreds of daily customers. And I know that such things have largely vanished elsewhere. And I wonder what depths of humanity the Japanese must contain that, even now, despite everything, they remain civil to each other, remain fond of each other.

And so I want to go to the font of that humanity, to this still and backward place where people live better than anywhere else because they live according to their own natures.

*   *   *

THE BOAT IS going to Iejima, a group of islands an hour by boat from Himeji. Some say there are forty-eight islands in the group, some forty-four; but in any event, only four are inhabited. Among its early visitors was Jimmu Tenno, the first and, some say, legendary emperor of Japan. If not mythical he would have been an almost exact contemporary of Zarathustra and only several years older than another celebrated Asian personality, Siddhartha, known as the Buddha, and he would also have come to Iejima. His fleet was blown north by one of the rare typhoons that sometimes manage to hurdle the natural barriers protecting the Inland Sea. They sighted these islands. Once inside the harbor of the largest, the emperor is supposed to have remarked that here, though the typhoon blew, you were as safe as in your own house. Hence the name, *ie* meaning "house" and *shima* (or sometimes *jima*), "island."

Though little visited, at least one of the islands has been caught by the times. A grand tourist hotel has just been built. After telling me how the emperor found the harbor snug as a house, my informant — one of the hotel's maids coming back from a happy outing in civilization — tells me all about it:

"And we're building a big beach right now, just tons of sand from some place else, but you have to take a bus to get there from our hotel or else it's a very long walk because it's some little distance, and there are jellyfish there, but we'll get rid of them before long, and then we're thinking of this baby golf course." Then, seeing my expression, mistaking my consternation as concern over lack of accommodations: "But the hotel is all done, really. You can move right in."

She rattles on, sprinkling her conversation with bits of modish slang, garnered presumably from this and other trips to the mainland. The hotel is eventually going to be really great (*saiko*, maximum), but the island is dreadful (*saitei*, minimum); the hotel is, in

23

fact, going to be real *ikasu* (groovy). She then hands me a picture postcard showing its exterior.

It is grand indeed, all in the plyboard-and-stucco style of quick-profit tourist architecture, a common enough sight, a travesty of everything useful and beautiful in Japanese design. In my mind I can see it all:

Every room has a real and traditional tokonoma alcove, but the walls are some plastic composition, or else thin laths sprayed with a furry material smelling eternally of fish glue. The traditional having been taken care of, there are some modernities: an electric fan, a radio, a large doll in a glass case, plastic flowers stuck into an octopus-covered vase. Though the tatami mats may still be real, the shoji doors are covered, not with paper, but with a plastic that is supposed to look exactly like paper and looks exactly like plastic.

Dominating this scene, hung in tokonoma or on fish-glue-smelling wall, is one of those modern-painting pastels so prized by these hotels. Violently pink carp in Paris-green water; or lovely Kyoto geisha leaning heavily on sill, looking sadly out to sea; or another lovely Kyoto geisha in attitude of despair, biting towel; or famous priest on back of renowned ox; or beloved animals such as turtles, cranes, white foxes, peacocks. All of this completed in bright water-color pigments, elaborately and illegibly signed and sealed by some locally famous decorator who creates these objects by the dozens, is bowed down to, addressed as maestro (*sensei*), and makes a pretty penny.

Then there is the bath for two. My informant produces a picture of one in the garish hotel pamphlet she also happens to have with her. Two people are in the bath. Both are girls and both are heavily clad in towels though immersed to the chin. Neither seems to be enjoying the experience. In actuality, such baths are for two of opposite sex, such grand hotels being constructed mainly for couples on a holiday, with or without wedding rings. No man should attempt to stay at such a place by himself. The loneliness is stupefying, and the maids are virtuous.

Then there are the game rooms—the other side of the pamphlet—and though I cannot see them too well, I can imagine them. Ping-pong table with broken net; television set that, this far from the city, records only the more florid of patterns; near it, empty bar with lined-up bottles of creme de violette, crème de banane, creme de

24

green tea, with which such things as violet fizz and grenadine flip and orange blossoms are concocted by one of the local fisherboys who on weekends gets out his bartender's guide and into his white jacket. Surrounding these attractive rooms, and not shown in the pamphlet, is a wilderness of corridors always covered with green linoleum and seldom containing any people. Couples are engaged with each other in the privacy of their chambers, and there is never a village nearby. One is at the mercy of the maids and oneself. The boredom is truly astonishing.

"A quite unusual place," confides the girl, concluding, pulling tighter a modish white straw hat. She is pleasant in her adenoidal hotel-maid kind of way, but when it becomes increasingly clear that I have no intention of going near the grand hotel nor the island it dominates, she offers me information, most of it discouraging, about the island where I have decided to disembark.

"Oh, yes, there's a town—well, a kind of town, anyway. Oh, it's large enough, but not, you know, not very nice. It's really dreadful" (*saitei* again), "but, after all, it's only a fishing village." This daughter of a fisherman continues with: "Yes, there are, I do believe, several inns, but I would never answer for them. Dirty? Well, no, not dirty, but they are not made for tourists, you know. I don't believe the Tourist Organization recommends any of them. It does ours."

*   *   *

THE PORT OF the main island of Iejima, despite or because of its lack of tourist recommendations, is instantly attractive. Houses tumble down the hillsides, fall over each other, and all but end in the water. Their gray-tile roofs almost touch, and small and narrow alleys swarm in all directions. The mud walls, straw showing through, are so close that it would seem the inhabitants move crab-fashion. The port is filled with fishing boats, strange, junklike ships with high prows and raked sails, and around them, on the docks, are bales and coils and baskets and boxes. On all sides there is the most glorious confusion.

In modern Japan one becomes so used to a special kind of order that such visible disarray—surely a relic from some earlier, happier time—is exhilarating. New Himeji is hopelessly orderly; even Tokyo is, in its muddled and messy manner, fairly systematic; and Kyoto is

25

positively methodical. Compared with this order, the dirt of this port—and it is very dirty—is refreshing. Dust, cinders, shavings, ashes; the unwanted, unused, discarded objects that collect around a harbor; stones and bits of wood to kick, piles of earth to step over, holes to avoid; all the castaways of the sea—whole tree stumps, curious bottles worn thin by the waves, fruit bleached and rotting, a whole boat on its side as though gasping—these, unlike the empty rusting autos at the deserted Himeji dock, are products of an active, disordered, human life.

I have come to the right place. How different, how warm and human this port, from the definitely *saitei* hotel happily invisible on a neighboring island. Here is where people live.

Congratulating myself upon this fact, I was at once accosted by one of the island people. An old man who had apparently been waiting approached, hailed me, asked how I had been and why I had not come in June as I had promised, told me that he had waited and that the fishing season was over, almost, and that it was a shame. He then stopped and told the small boy beside him that he had forgotten I did not speak Japanese.

I assured him that I did, and that this fact might prove that I was not the tardy foreigner he had been expecting all this time. He looked at me narrowly, as though distrusting, then stared into my eyes, looked at my nose, shook his head, and sighed as though it were past all comprehension, while the little boy pulled his sleeve and whispered that I was the wrong one.

Hearing this, I said that it is well known that all foreigners look alike. The old man nodded in agreement. Then he added that since I did speak Japanese—though with a rather strong foreign accent—and since the other spoke not a word, this might be interpreted as an argument against my actually being he. Still, foreigners were rare on the island. Indeed, the last had been myself and that had been a whole year ago. Didn't I remember that we had caught a shark—a baby one? Didn't I remember even that?

The little boy, old enough to be self-conscious, pulled his sleeve and whispered.

In order to extricate us all, I asked for an inn. By this time several women, large, open faced, heavy armed, carrying fish, had gathered around to nod and smile. They knew, it would seem, that I was not the right one. The old man was not so certain. He kept glaring at me, as though suspecting a trick, not a nice one seeing as how he had been waiting all year.

The inn was right around the corner, one of the plain, friendly women told me. But which corner?—there were so many. That one, indicated the woman, pointing simultaneously to five different corners.

Well, how far was it then? Here the old man, finally convinced that I was myself, said that it was two. Two what? My question amused the watching women, but he had used *hon*, the counter for, among other things, long, thin objects, such as umbrellas and cucumbers. After it was explained, I realized that the people on this island do not reckon length in terms of meters but something else. Just as the natives of Mexico divide space into the time it takes to smoke a cigarette, these island people reckon by the relatively recent innovation of electric-line poles. My inn was two poles away.

*   *   *

BEFORE SUPPER I decided to walk along the sea road to the small shrine—high, isolated on a long spit of land—that I had seen from the boat.

The streets of the town, so narrow that my arms brushed either side, stretched past open doors, open windows, through which I saw families sitting at dinner; mothers in kitchens busy with fish, pickles, rice; two young boys flat on their stomachs doing their homework, one with his trousers pulled down to his knees to enjoy the late-afternoon cool.

At one turn I blundered directly into someone's house, was met with smiles and laughter, told to take the next crossing but one, then turn right until I reached the carpenter shop, then past the sakè store, turn left when I saw the place where ice-candy was sold, then right to where the children had chalked a large picture of a cat, then straight on, and I couldn't miss the sea road.

It was almost sundown when I finally found it, a path overlaid with drying fish nets, and in the far distance, around the edge of the empty bay, on a spit of land, there was the shrine, its stone-torii gateway tiny, white and glowing in the declining sun. Along the way a few late fishermen were mending nets, and some women and children were returning home.

27

In Tokyo the foreigner is rarely stared at except in out-of-the-way places where he is a rarity. In towns where foreigners go but are not common—Himeji, for example—they are commonly stared at and usually regarded as great curiosities. But in places like this, here in the real country, foreigners are so rare, so curious, that they are not stared at at all except by the youngest children. In Tokyo we are too common to be looked at; in deep country we are too strange to be looked at.

Yet, though the islanders will not stare, there is a slight shifting of the eyes as one walks past, as though they are purposely keeping their gaze from wandering naturally over to you. Once past, however, if you turn and look, you will find that the other is doing the same. Perhaps politeness prevents the open stare, perhaps a kind of fear of the novel, the unknown.

Two old women carrying baskets on their heads saw me from a distance, stopped, consulted, then passed, one in front of the other, both looking straight ahead. A young boy gave me one instant glance, then, eyes on the horizon, walked soberly past. A girl was fixing her bicycle at the edge of the sea and did not see me until I was almost upon her. She sensed me, turned, and for a second I saw surprise. But at once her eyes narrowed. Having turned toward me, she did not turn away. She looked through and past me. I smiled; she smiled back, though vaguely, tentatively. Then I spoke.

Words make you visible in Japan. Until you speak, until you commit yourself to communication, you are not visible at all. You might travel from one end of the country to the other and, unless you open your mouth or get set upon by English-speaking students, be assured of the most complete privacy. Just as in small country inns where you are never visible until presentable—after the face-washing, the brushing of the teeth, the combing of the hair, all often performed just outside the kitchen, from where the same maid who will presently formally wish you good-morning will stare straight through you—so, in traveling, you are invisible until you announce you are not.

In the inns, where you must march all unkempt through corridors to bath or toilet, this is a civilized custom. But alone and lonely in the country, you come to long to be spoken to, you wish for the spontaneous and unbidden sign that you truly exist. It rarely comes. Rather, you speak first and, just as though you had handed out your

28

namecard, that truly magical piece of paper with arcane symbols on it that invests you with identity, you become real.

I asked the girl if the shrine was old. Oh, that she didn't know. Well, was it still used, did people go there? Oh, she couldn't say. Polite, naturally polite, she improved on nature in the manner of many other young girls her age. One should not be too knowing. Ignorance—real or feigned—never gets you into trouble. It is considered seemly for a young girl to know nothing at all. The well-brought-up maiden insists upon this.

I too insisted. Did she ever go there? Since this question was about herself and not about the outside world, she felt free to answer. Oh, yes, often. She had just been there. The other answers then fell out. It was an old shrine and people hardly ever went except people like herself who had nothing else to do. Oh, yes, there were big crabs there. I was to take care.

The shrine lay in the path of the declining sun. The shadows were beginning to lengthen, the light was growing horizontal. The open-mouthed shadow of the stone torii that marked the approach to the shrine stretched into the dark of the trees at the base of the hill. The sand of the beach was still gold, but inside, beyond the gateway, all was a mass of thick black trees and bushes. On the beach, it was still day; inside the grove, it was already night.

Many Shinto shrines lie on heights. One goes up and up and up to worship. The steps lead straight into the sky and are always steep. It is work to reach such a shrine. The faithful must arrive puffing, gasping, senses reeling. This is as it should be. One arrives as though new born, helpless, vulnerable. One's panting sounds in the ears because a shrine is very quiet, quieter than a church. A church is hushed because one is made to be quiet; a shrine is simply quiet. It is so far away that noise does not reach.

You yourself may be as noisy as you please. Gasps for breath, eventual shouts and laughter, are quickly swallowed up. You speak in a normal voice as you walk about, investigating everything, peering behind this door, into that box. The reverent, the hushed, the awed—these have small place in a shrine. If there is any restraint, it comes from nature itself. You may lower your voice, just as you naturally lower your voice in a grove or a gorge. If you feel like it, you impose a willing silence upon yourself.

29

Shrine prayer is not communal prayer. It is solitary and spontaneous. No one says when to begin or when to stop. You choose your own time. You speak to the gods in the way you might greet your hosts at a party. It is a discreet, friendly, happy, polite prayer.

Apparently no one came to pray any more in this small shrine. The stone steps had been forced apart in places by roots of trees grown large after the shrine was built. The only motion in this tangle of bushes and weeds were the large red crabs that, looking already cooked, refused to move, menaced with waving cleft claws, and denied being afraid.

At the top one is ready for the god. One is reeling, fainting, panting. And there, as though for reward, spread out like a banquet, is a view of the other side of the bay, the sea, the distant farther islands, all gleaming in the setting sun, as though cast from bronze and floating on lacquer.

Here at the top it was still day, though below, back toward the village, the sea was clouded and the beach was darkening. The shrine, seen through a line of trees, gleamed a rich yellow, the color of cut wood in sunlight. It was silent. I heard the cicadas the moment they ceased.

Walking through the clinging weeds I crossed to the shrine and stood before the votive box. The god was just inside the closed doors in front of me. I pulled the rope of the god-summoning rattle. The sound was like that of a dry husk shaken. These gods have no bells—the only sound they know is this dusty sound of dried reeds shaken by the winds.

Shinto is nature. Perhaps animism—and Shinto is the only formal animistic religion left—is the true religion. It has roots deep in all of us. One recognizes this. It is the only religion that can inspire the feeling children know when the wind or a rock is made god for a week or a day. Its essence is unknown and unknowable, yet this unknown does not exclude us because we too are unknown. This religion speaks to us, to something in us which is deep and permanent.

Once I had sounded the rattle, once its rasping cry, like the quiver of a cicada, had died, once the god was looking from his trellised doorway, I was afraid not to give. The votive box looked hungry, its slats like teeth.

The Shinto gods are near us. They prefer money. I dropped a coin; then, not knowing what else to do, shook the rattle again. A dark shape stood for a second against the sky, whirled about me, was a speck of black in the darkening sky, was gone. It was a bat.

The sun was sinking behind the farther mountains behind me. Its final rays fell on the shrine as the distant shadows began climbing nearer, toward me. The farther sea was a sheet of gold, which, as I watched, faded at the edges, the deeper blue becoming black while the sky, still azure at zenith, faded slowly and a single star appeared, quite suddenly, opposite the disappearing sun.

*   *   *

Climbing slowly down the shadowed stones I thought of Ise, the greatest shrine of all, the mother shrine, home of the Sun Goddess herself. A visit to any shrine, as humble and forgotten a one as this, leads one to consider such imponderables as life, death. Thoughts of ancient Ise led me to consider another—time.

Time for the West is a river. Down its changing yet forever unchanging length we float. In the East, however, the river is more a symbol for life, our earthly span, the *ukiyo*, than it is for time itself.

Time has no symbol in this Asia where almost everyone, at least formerly, lived in a continuous and unvarying present. If it had one, it might be a symbol as startlingly up-to-date as the oscillating current. The reason this occurs is Ise—not only one of the great religious complexes of the world but the only answer yet discovered to man's universal wish either to invent the perfect perpetual-motion machine or, else, to stop time entirely.

The way to stop time, the Japanese discovered, is by letting it have its own way. Just as the shape of nature is observed, revered, so is the contour of time. Every twenty years—and for over a thousand years —the shrine at Ise is razed and a new one is erected on an adjacent plot reserved for that purpose. After only two decades, the beam-ends barely weathered, the copper turned to palest green, the shrine is destroyed. Only twenty generations of spiders have spun their webs, only four or five generations of swallows have built their nests, not even a single blink has covered the great staring eye of eternity—yet down come the great cross-beams, off come the reed roofs, and the pillars are carted off to be reused in other parts of the shrine grounds.

On the adjacent plot is constructed a shrine that is in all ways similar to the one just dismantled. More, it is identical. Something dies, something is born, and the two things are the same. This ceremony, the *sengushiki*, is a living exemplar of the greatest of religious mysteries, the most profound of human truths.

And time at last comes to a stop. Forever old, forever new, the shrines stand there for all eternity. This—and not the building of pyramids or ziggurats, not the erection of Empire State Buildings or Tokyo Towers—is the way to stop time and thus make immortal that mortality which we cherish.

*   *   *

THE SEA ROAD was still faintly light, a ribbon of gray between the black forest and the blacker sea. Then, light against the sea and near, I saw two men, one larger than the other, their clothes white in the dark. They were folding their nets before going home. I spoke and they answered.

They were father and son, both fishermen. They had not gone out in their boat but had spent the day repairing their nets. The old man was sixty-one; the young man, the larger, was twenty-two. They had lived all their lives on this island.

Then they asked about me. I said that I had always wanted to see the Inland Sea, that I had a liking for old-fashioned island people, that I wanted to find out more about Japan, that I liked history.

At once the older man told me about the emperor's finding the island as snug as his own house. After I had thanked him, he said that he knew another story. He had heard it from his father, who had heard it from his, who had, probably, heard it from his, and that even if the ending had somehow gotten lost during the years, he would be pleased to tell me as much of it as he knew. We sat down in the dark by the invisible whispering sea on the still-warm sand and he began:

"A long time ago on the other side of this island, and you may still see the place, there lived an old man and an old woman and a priest."

"All together?" I asked.

"That I don't know. Perhaps. They were happy but they had no son. But this was a good priest and one day he brought the old woman a peach. Peaches are rare. They don't grow around here. So this was a strange thing to her and so she didn't eat it, but kept it in her kimono sleeve, and carried it about with her, because it was a strange

32

object to her, and so she did just as I've said. Well, one day her husband looked at the peach and he thought it would be good to eat and he said that was what he wanted to do. He brought a knife and he said he was going to cut it open. And she agreed because she also wanted to taste it. And so he cut it—and out stepped a little baby boy."

I realized that I was hearing the story of Momotaro—the little peach boy—Japan's most famous fairy tale, but that I was hearing some local variation that had existed, perhaps, for generations, passed on from father to son, different from the one everyone knew. In the standard version, there is no priest, for example, and the peach is found in a stream.

The old man was sitting back, observing the effect that this surprise—a small boy coming out of a peach—was having on me. "What happened next?" I asked, wanting to hear further folkloristic differences when Momotaro called the animals together and they all went to attack the ogres.

"Oh, that I don't know. I told you that I didn't know the ending, that I'd forgotten it. No, it wasn't me. It was my father who was the first one to forget, I guess."

"But what about the priest then?" I asked, anxious to hear more.

"He was a good priest. He gave them the peach, didn't he?"

"But what happened to him?"

"Now, that I don't know. I wonder who forgot about him first. Not my father, because he never told me anything about that priest. His father perhaps, or his grandfather maybe."

He laughed, rocking on the sand. It grew darker. A night breeze blew past us. His son spoke, his voice deeper than his father's.

"If you want to see the island, I could show it to you," he said.

*   *   *

HE HAD PUT ON a clean white shirt and stood in the doorway, tall, his hair cut short, in the manner of all the island fishermen, so that it stood straight from his head. He stood blinking in the light, large hands at his sides, self-conscious under the electric bulbs.

When I asked him to come into the room, he bowed from the waist, the quick, dignified bow of the country Japanese, held up one hand, fingers closed, to signify his intent of entering, and then stepped inside the room and stood there until I ask him to join me on the mats. It was beginning as a very formal visit.

Once we were sitting on the tatami however, with the big table between us, sipping cold beer, he relaxed. He took his ease but kept his reserve—that warm, smiling reserve which is so attractive in rural Japan.

The familiarity of some city people—particularly the English-speakers who are convinced that instant intimacy is the custom of my country, as I suppose it is—this presumption is rarely seen in the country, where people elevate reserve into a kind of respect, a respect that includes both giver and receiver. It is seemly, a kind of decorum, a natural dignity.

At first he is self-conscious. He has never before spoken to a foreigner. In this he is, of course, like the majority of Japanese. I am inured to this particular kind of self-consciousness. I also think it stupid. Reserve, yes; but a kind of bashfulness in adults, no.

To him I must seem a different species. Foreigners in Japan are annoyed when treated like idiot children, or when they are spoken to in baby-Japanese. This, however, indicates merely the loss at which the Japanese finds himself. How to treat this white- or black-skinned creature with his strange eyes and stranger language? I have had grown men approach me with the tentative yet daring gestures, timid, well-intentioned, a bit afraid, that people show in the zoo when they come near an animal marked dangerous. This island boy is far too assured for such a primitive reaction. Nonetheless, he is conscious of himself in a new situation. He is perspiring lightly, his forehead is damp, the reaction of many Japanese to not being completely at ease.

We talk. He has been on the island all of his life, and since his elder brother is now married and living in Himeji, he must stay with his parents and undertake the duties of the eldest son. He will marry whomever they choose and his life on the island will continue. At present there is talk of his marrying a cousin. I ask if this is allowed. He looks surprised. Oh, yes, almost everyone on the island is some kind of cousin.

Every day he gets up at five and is in the boat by six. He and his father have favorite fishing spots on the far side of the island. Since the chemical plants began their work at Himeji, there are not many fish on this side of the island anyway. Even far out at sea, working their big basket-like nets, he and his father now gather only about thirty pounds of fish a day. When he was a boy it was four times that.

They return about three in the afternoon and mend nets or scrape the boat. After five or six o'clock he may do as he pleases. Since he doesn't drink and no one here owns television, except at the big hotel on the other island, he either listens to the radio or plays the guitar. He saved and bought himself that guitar. He cannot read music and so he plays by ear—folk music from the island, or popular music from over the air. He is usually in bed by nine. Yes, he would like another bottle of beer.

Here in the country there is little of the holding back that characterizes city Japanese. Reserve, yes, but acceptance as well. In the city it can be infuriating, particularly with girls who have been taught that an assumed timidity is somehow virtuous. They stand in the entryway and must be urged time and again to come in. This reluctantly accomplished, they will not drink their tea, or lemonade, or whatever you have put out. It sits there growing cold, or warm, and all references to their perhaps refreshing themselves with it are met with that animal sound of assent, a kind of grunt, which is, they have been taught, the proper way to respond. It is neither positive nor negative and has all the grace of the English "uh-huh."

I once counted. Five times I urged a city girl to drink her Coca-Cola. She mumbled and grunted, left it successfully untouched. When she went home she was quite elated, smiled charmingly. She had behaved in a particularly gracious manner and was pleased with herself. She had not once said either yes or no, had done nothing at all, had been unexceptional to a degree, and this is the way that proper city-bred young Japanese ladies are supposed to behave.

Not country Japanese, not this young man. He drank his beer, held out his glass for more, poured my beer for me. Smiling, friendly, now much more sure of himself, he remained, at the same time, reserved. This was not formality, it was natural politeness. City people reserve their actions; country people reserve themselves.

This had its effect upon me. I found myself using words larger than usual, observing polite forms of address I never used in Tokyo. This he saw and so he brought our conversation down from its meaningless heights by showing me something concrete—some photographs and picture postcards. He had apparently brought them to show me. We had been sitting on the cushions, our legs sprawled

35

out under the table. Now he drew his politely under him, sat on his haunches. I did likewise. This looking at pictures was to be marked by a certain gravity.

The first politely handed me was of some local figure who had died fairly recently, judging by the statue pictured on the postcard —bronze frock coat, bronze cravat, bronze laced shoes, bronze spectacles. His name was Hamakichi Hosono and I never discovered why he was famous—not understanding the single and apparently only word that described him. There he was, official, imposing, standing life-size on his pedestal.

Another picture showed him before his apotheosis, peering myopically behind his glasses into some ancient camera, mouth judiciously pursed, the petulant baby mouth of the Japanese states-man. What was it he did, now? Why was he so famous? Again I was told. Again I failed to understand the word.

The next picture, handed me after I had shown a restrained enthusiasm for the first two, was of another fat man. He was naked except for a rope girdle over a loincloth. His arms were held palms out away from his massive sides. A sumo wrestler. Little pig eyes set deep in fat, stubborn face; concentrated stupidity, in part the result of a lifetime of pushing other fat men out of a ring.

The young man smiled fondly. Sumo wrestlers are popular. Per-haps it is because of their fatness. In Japan, when a person says that you have gotten fat he means it as a compliment. What he implies is that you have become rich enough to afford fatness. In the same way, mice and rats are welcomed as attractive beasts. If your house shelters them, it means you are rich enough to draw these engaging rodents to you.

This particular fat wrestler is named Hosumiyama and he came from these very islands and went on to become a grand champion. Very famous. Now all the schoolboys are wild for sumo and are for-ever pushing and pulling each other all over the island. And he—does he engage in sumo? Oh, no. He is far too thin. He looks sadly at his own well-made, hard, smoothly muscled body. He is not nice and flabby at all. He looks again, with affection and presumably envy, at the porcine Hosumiyama, and we go on to the next picture.

It had been taken at the port. The ships were bunted and flagged and looked more than ever like Chinese junks. There were lanterns and sprays of bamboo. It was a picture of one of the local festivals. Standing in front of the camera were a number of young men holding boys on their shoulders. The young man in the middle, strong, strapping, was holding another grown man on his shoulders—this one carrying a staff and wearing a red-lacquer lion mask with long string hair.

"That is our festival. But you missed it. It was last month. There is a big procession to the shrine and back and then there is a dance. I dance—that's me." He pointed to the man in the middle holding the lion on his shoulders.

"Isn't he heavy?"

"Oh, at first, but I'm used to it now. Five years ago when I was only seventeen, I carried a twenty-four-year-old. This year I'm twenty-two but the man I carried was only twenty-one, though he was a big twenty-one. And the dance takes about half an hour and we do it a number of times so that everyone can see it. Sometimes I do get a little tired."

"Do you ever drop him?"

He smiled at the thought. "I can't. All the boys are watching me. They'll be doing the same thing in a couple of years. If they remembered that I dropped someone, then they might get tired and drop someone too. No, no matter how tired you get, and you get very tired, you don't drop anyone."

I admire this, coming as I do from a country where such exertion would be thought cruel, a permissive land where you naturally drop things when you get tired, where you do not think of the next generation looking on.

These thoughts were interrupted by his showing me a map. He pointed to where he and his father usually fished. He indicated the various places and named the fish they caught there. In the winter, with smaller nets, they get sea bass, some kind of crab, and a fish I don't know named *meibaru*. In the spring, with large nets, there is the esteemed sea bream, a fish named *sawara*, and squid; in the summer it is mackerel, sea pike, and horse mackerel; in the fall, *hamachi, bari,* the long squid, and more crab again. There is octopus the year round.

"Are there many?" I ask, having had octopus for supper.

"Many—you catch them with pots, or else with spears."

"Aren't they fast?"

37

"Yes. You have to trick them. You look down into the water and see one, either asleep in front of his cave, or else just looking around, you know. Then you put down a pole with a red flag on it."

"To make it angry?"

"Oh, no. Octopuses are gentle creatures. They never get angry. You put down the red flag because the octopus loves it. He just loves red. He will reach out to get it, then he'll hug it, and won't leave loose because he likes it so much. Even when he feels himself being pulled up, he won't let go. He loves red that much."

The octopus is occasionally eaten on the spot by the fishermen or, more usually, taken back to land either to be eaten at home or sold to the local dealer. The non-fishing islanders do not buy directly from the fishermen, nor would the fishermen sell directly to them: that would be unkind to the fishmongers, who have already invested in their carts, knives, and boards, and who have to make a living, just like everyone else, don't they? Right now, at the end of August, horse mackerel is the cheapest and sea bass is the most expensive and— Oh, he had forgotten the well.

This well is the local wonder. It seems that Kobo Daishi, that indefatigable and widely traveled Buddhist priest, a contemporary of Charlemagne, came here in the ninth century, as he also went almost everywhere else, and made a magic well, which is still used. He simply struck the ground with his staff, and waters flowed. It was later folk who built the curb and put the shed over it. Even now, no matter how much water you take from it, next morning you go there and there it is full to the brim. It is only across the town if I would like to go see it.

It is past nine. The town is all but asleep. Near the boat station is a big red-paper lantern, a small shop. Inside a few men are eating shaved ice with red fruit syrup over it. Occasionally, outlined in a window, some child is still doing schoolwork, some woman is busy with yarn. The air is fresh, the night breeze is continuing. The stars overhead seem brighter than the few lights of the village.

The road was light before us in the night; his legs were black against it. He would guide me when he remembered a hole, or when I strayed too near the edge, taking my hand in his, rough, calloused, holding me lightly with thumb and two fingers. A polite familiarity, helpful but not presuming to grasp the entire hand. I stepped into a

38

hole he had forgotten, steadied myself against his shoulder. He stopped at once, politely, observed that it was a big hole, waited until I had rubbed my shin for a time, then led me on. A dog barked, the sound carrying in the night. Though the sea was far below, its lappings sounded near, just off the edge of this light road. The smell of kelp was carried to us by the breeze. We stopped: we were at the well.

I lighted a match and peered in. The water was at the top. He turned, smiled, his face bright for an instant in the light of the match. "There, see?" he said. "Just as I said. It is filling up."

He found a bucket, lowered it carefully over the curb and into the darkness. The rope rasped on the edge of the stone. He drew the bucket up full. I bent and drank from it. It was good water—slightly sweet and very cold.

The well had a name. It was Habu no Ido—the Well of the Viper.

"Are there any vipers around?" I asked, looking about in the dark.

"No, just blue racers and some other harmless snakes."

"Then, why is it called the Well of the Viper?"

"I don't know. Would you like another drink? It's very good for you."

"It makes people healthy?" I asked.

"Not us. We drink it every day. We're used to it. But you come from far away and this is the first time for you to drink here. It should be very good for you."

Again I drank from the bucket, which he held while I put my face into it, like a watering horse. The water was black, sweet, and so cold that my teeth began to ache.

"That's enough," he said, gently. "It is good for you I am certain, but too much of anything is bad."

This last sounded like a proverb. But it also sounded like what this sweet, serious young man would say. He had been a good son and would be an equally good father. Among his ancestors there must have been many serious young men just like him. Among his progeny, continuing the line, I hoped that there would be many more.

"There, there, that's enough," he said again and put his hand on my shoulder, drawing me back as though I were a child. Then, his hand on my arm, he guided me back, pointing out in the dark various remembered holes, drops, steps.

Back at the lighted entryway—the hotel maid had stayed up until I returned—we bowed and then shook hands, and he said that, if I wanted, he would take me to Bozè tomorrow.

*   *   *

Bozè is the island to the south, small, uninhabited. We left his father on the beach mending nets. The boat's small motor stuttered, blew several smoke rings, and we moved slowly over the waveless sea, our wake spreading behind. We passed the harbor, the spit, the shrine, its torii gate now in shadow.

He was talking about fish again, and ended cheerfully with: "I'll probably spend all of my life here with the fish."

"Won't you ever go to the city?" I shouted above the racket of the motor.

"I can't. I'm stuck here with my father. There's only us, you know."

Now that we were meeting for the second time there was no need for formality. Before, he had been using the standard Tokyo dialect, taught in all schools all over Japan, and a formal, respectful delivery. Now he dropped into island dialect, heavily influenced by Osaka pronunciation, and used ordinary contractions and pronunciation. Last night I had been the respectful *otaku*, today I was the standard *anata*. I could have responded by calling him the familiar *kimi*. I was, after all, older and richer. But I have never felt at ease with *kimi*. In the same way I will call myself the formal *watakushi*, the standard *boku*, but I don't feel right using the familiar *ore*—much less that lowest of all you's, *omae*.

Rather tricky this pronoun business in Japanese. The grammar books tell us that the words for "you" and "I" come in pairs. Leaving aside the extremely polite forms, now increasingly rare, the standard I-you combinations, in increasing order of intimacy, are *watakushi-anata*, *boku-kimi*, and *ore-omae*. But it never works so smoothly. For one thing, the pairings presume an absolute equality between speakers, a state that I as a foreigner can never hope to achieve.

If someone is angry with me, I sometimes become *omae* for a time. Otherwise I am *anata* forever. Rare indeed are those acquaintances who bestow me with the familiar and accepting *kimi*. Being American, I am very anxious to be called *kimi*. It would mean I was one of

40

the bunch, that I belonged. Being foreign, however, I can never belong—hence I rarely hear someone casually call me *kimi* unless they are exasperated with me for some childish remark or action. Since I am not to be so favored, I don't feel right about using the word myself in speaking to Japanese friends.

"Don't you ever want to go to the city then?" I asked, calling him *anata* in turn.

"The city is boring. Fish are very interesting, you know."

"It's very nice here," I agreed.

"That's only because it's strange to you. You live in the city."

The Japanese make a great distinction between urban and rural life—it is almost eighteenth century in its intensity. The Japanese think of the City in the way that Englishmen used to think of Mighty London. It is either one or the other. Rice paddies or the Ginza.

"I thought you liked it here," I shouted.

"I do. I like it here." He looked around, hand on the tiller. "I like that."

He pointed to a small island to the south, the island we were approaching, and over the noise of the motor told me its story.

A long time ago a fisherman lived there, on a headland on the other side. He had a lovely daughter and the two of them were very happy. Then one day he made a big catch and this pleased them very much. But just then a great storm came up and the waves crashed on the land and the sea mist descended.

The daughter, thinking the sea angry, threw all the fish back. This angered the father, and she, seeing this, said that since one action had so angered him, another might pacify him.

Might what? Might pacify. Oh.

At this, typical Japanese maiden, she threw herself into the sea, which swallowed her up and instantly quieted. The bereaved father and the grateful villagers built a shrine to her that we would see any moment now. Her name? It was Benten.

Benten. A favorite deity. A willful goddess, one of the seven deities who came from China, the only female one. They all came in a boat and took up residence. One by one the others became identified with good things—one with agriculture, one with fishing, one with wisdom. But Benten remained aloof—a foreigner. And, in fact, she also behaved badly. She was jealous, lustful—insatiable, in fact—and shared with Japanese womanhood only pride and occasional vin-

41

dictiveness. An Oriental Cybele, she came to have a bad name and even now her shrines—she occupies that peaceful no man's land which exists between Shinto on one side and Buddhism on the other—are carefully avoided by married couples and by young couples while courting. She is the closest Japan ever came to personifying the Great Earth Mother, and, like Kali, a possible relative, she demands complete and exclusive faith and is interested only in her male worshipers. Oh, she may accept the homage of women, particularly those involved with music or other performing arts, but her real interest is with the men. So much so that once in Kamakura she slipped out of her shrine and seduced a handsome young general who had taken her fancy. Truly democratic, she also developed attachments for palanquin bearers and horse drivers.

Her amorous activities are chronicled in careful detail in the early writings, and one of the more famous of her statues—the one in a cave on Enoshima—emphasizes her considerable charms. This shows the goddess with outstretched arms—to embrace? to beseech? Originally the statue is said to have held a lutelike *biwa* between her legs, which would have modestly hid what is now the object of public gaze—her wooden vulva, half-open and painted a delicate, shell-like pink.

I have always been fond of Benten, a woman who knows her own mind, but I doubted that this typical-sounding maiden of whom I was hearing could be she.

"Was she nice, this Benten girl?"

"Yes, very nice. But she's dead, you know."

This was obviously not my Benten, known under other names but always her disciplined self, always the eternal foreigner in a land she seemed to like. It was interesting that islanders would have appropriated her, localized her, made her one of their own.

"She liked men a lot, this Benten did," I ventured.

"Oh? I hadn't heard that about her. But, in any event, she's dead now."

While talking, he had taken a limp, dead squid from a small box and tied a line to it. Now he threw the squid far into the sea and, jerking the string, began pulling it back. The squid jetted through the water with little leaps as though it were still alive.

"What does it catch?"

"More squid usually. Or else a big fish. But there aren't any more

42

big fish around here. The chemical plants have driven them all away."

His large, broad, brown fingers worked the white string as it coiled between his legs, falling from his fingers. The squid jumped. Benten's island loomed. The sun poured down. I leaned back, closed my eyes, happy.

"There!" he said suddenly. "That's what I like best."

The boat had rounded the spit. There, on the other side, was a tiny island, high, a rockery, the kind of rocks one sees in Chinese Sung paintings. At the very top, surrounded by wind-bent pines, was a small shrine.

The entire prospect was superbly beautiful, even if one remembered gossip about its presiding goddess. The scene was made of so little—the horizon of the sea, some rocks piled high, a pine or two, the little shrine, the sky. Views are rarely this simple. This one was so right, so appropriate, that it seemed ideal. And like all ideal things it did not seem real, but more like a mirage floating on the surface of the sea.

If I had seen a picture of it, I would have said it was pretty—a postcard view, typical Japan. But coming upon it in a boat under a summer morning sky, I was startled into beholding its simplicity. It was accidental, this beauty. And it is difficult for us to believe or remember or admit that the greatest beauty is always accidental.

And this accidental quality is to be captured only if the full context is shown. Japanese scenery is like Japanese poetry. Both its beauty and meaning depend upon a context of things perhaps incongruous. One observes a relationship that had always hitherto escaped notice but which, once seen, becomes inevitable.

Such an island as this exists, but its beauty exists in the morning sky, in the endless expanse of sea, in the light that hovers and bathes. Japanese scenic beauty is a whole beauty because it requires this context before it can be recognized. Since it is whole, it creates in the viewer a sense of wholeness, however fugitive. Travelers from our fragmented West are ravished by the vision of such wholeness, such natural inclusion of everything in the world. I gaze. The beauty lies not in the single lovely object standing alone. It is in this combination that slides into and out of its background. The shrine is not beautiful, nor are these pines. It is their being so much a part of the sea and the sky that makes them beautiful.

I sit in the boat, rest against the warm wood, the sun raining upon me, and I am happy—happier than I have been for weeks or months. I am marvelously invaded by this perfect beauty before me. And I am happy because I am suddenly whole and know who I am. I am a man sitting in a boat and looking at a landscape.

Its simplicity moves me. In the midst of my happiness I know that I will remember these rocks, those pines, this sky and sea that have calmed and enriched me. This I will remember and I will also keep the knowledge that in these islands there are people who, like this fisherman's son, will raise their eyes, forget the trailing squid, and gaze upon the beauty of this shrine, this sea.

*   *   *

"WHAT DO YOU THINK of Japan?" This is the first, the salient question that one is asked. Every acquaintance, every friendship, every love affair is begun with: *Nihon wa do omoimasu ka?*

How to respond? I think the most honest answer is: I like myself here. There are places—Calcutta is one—where you can come to loathe yourself. I never knew I would be ready to kick children from my path, to strike out at cripples, to compose a face apparently contemptuous at the sight of misery so great it seemed almost theatrical. And all because of sheer terror.

I, along with most of my richer Western brothers, had believed that such qualities as disinterested politeness, trust, friendship, even love are necessities. It had never occurred to me that they are luxuries until India showed me that this is so. Such attributes—the pride of Western man—are but accouterments, like well-cut clothes. They are removable. One can go naked and miserable. No, not *one* could —*I* could.

Japan, at times suffering as great a misery as India, found another solution. Going naked was not enough for the Japanese. They developed a civilization that partially conceals the more ferocious facts of life. Floods, typhoons, earthquakes, grave financial debacles— these are not to be hidden and they are therefore treated as imponderables, acts of God. It was in this way that the Japanese, originally at any rate, regarded the bombing of Hiroshima and Nagasaki; it is this feeling for the unexpected evil that accounts for that pessimistic-seeming phrase forever on all Japanese lips, *Shikata ga nai*, "It can't be helped." Seemingly pessimistic, it is actually quite hopeful. This, perhaps, indeed can't be helped, but at least one's mind is cleared, and it is understood that whatever comes next will not be so bad.

The Japanese keep up appearances. Even the poorer are relatively well dressed. The best suit or dress is worn every day. The West in its more hypocritical moments has condemned this. Keeping up appearances is hypocritical. But to believe this is to disregard a great truth that all of Asia knows: appearances are the only reality. To wear your best suit daily implies a degree of self-respect but, more important, it also defines a reality that one chooses for oneself. If one looks like and acts like a certain kind of person—then one *is* that kind of person.

This truth, so simple, so basic, has evaded the West for centuries. Both church and psychiatry—not often so perfectly aligned—have mutually condemned it, the one finding in it the seeds of freedom, the other discovering in it the seeds of anarchy. Yet common sense—which is about all the Japanese have in way of transcendental values—indicates the truth. The only way to get prosperous is to look and behave in a prosperous manner; the only way to get out of an emotional funk is to shake your head and think of something else. You become, as near as possible, what you think you ought to and would like to become.

The Japanese is thus freed from his own history. Simply because he was a certain kind of person does not mean that he must continue to be. Perhaps it is just this freedom that allows the Japanese to make so much of history, to learn from it, to play with it, since it has no power otherwise to control his actions or to hold him back from whatever he might want to do.

In the same way he does not have to hide completely from himself the more horrid of the facts of life. They are there—suicide, murder, insanity, death in all its hundreds of forms—but they are no more insisted upon than they are denied. Japan seems to be the ideal compromise between India's undressed open wound and the West's open wound suppurating behind a bandage. The Japanese disclaims nothing and, at the same time, really hides little.

For this reason, the Japanese mind has always reminded me of the Japanese garden, which is a place that nature plainly made but which man has just as plainly ordered. The insipidity of nature tamed, as seen in the Western garden, is missing, but so is the awesomeness of the jungle. It is a wilderness but not a chaos. There are many paths, and if they turn and double in a curious manner quite different from the grand promenades of the Western park, it is because the Japanese observes and preserves the natural lay of the land.

It is this quality, then, that makes one like oneself here. One is close to nature in all ways, and nature is also one's own nature. At the same time, one is not lost in the natural of which one is only a part. Japan is a good place for the foreigner to live.

Not for all, however. You either love Japan or you loathe it. Like Lafcadio Hearn, you gasp and press it to you heart, for a time at any rate, or else, like Bernard Shaw, the place rubs you so wrong that you even forget your manners, refuse to take off your shoes while treading tatami mats. Writers like Somerset Maugham or James Michener like it; writers such as Aldous Huxley and Christopher Isherwood do not care for it.

And it is also true that Japan has seldom appealed to the exceptional Western mind. It is perhaps too comfortable a land for that, given to few of the extremes with which greatness is associated. At the same time, it is natural that an original mind would not find the place attractive. Not only is it, in its way, too reassuring, it is also a country that has found means to call a truce, if not a halt, to the great war between aspirations and actuality—and it is just this disparity that has always sent great writers off to glorious battle.

This could be one of the reasons why the Japanese do not have a particularly vivid or even meaningful literature—at least, not if you think of literature as composed of Shakespeare, Cervantes, Tolstoi, Dostoevski, Conrad, Melville, the great searchers of the soul.

But I am not of that mind. I prefer Fielding and Jane Austen, Turgenev and Chekhov. And I also like Natsume Soseki and Tanizaki, Nagai Kafu and Kawabata. It is not so much their civilization that appeals to me in these writers, it is their wisdom and —perhaps more important—their way of imparting it. They know that only in appearances lies the true reality. Jane Austen was quite right to leave out the Napoleonic Wars. They were not her reality because they made small appearance where she was. Consequently perhaps, she, and the others with whom I have grouped her, do not need to tell. They are content to show. The natural life they lead

46

and write of is so much a part of them that, whether they approve of it or not, it allows them the freedom of tact and irony.

This said, one would hope that the Japanese would admire Jane Austen above all others and honor their own masters as well. This is, however, not true. The heavier Russians (not Turgenev) are admired above all, as is whatever they understand of Shakespeare, though Cervantes is regarded only from the safe distance of *Man of La Mancha*. That the Japanese have spiritual inclinations is not to be doubted. I doubt very much, however, that such inclinations have ever come to anything.

The commonest Japanese way of exercising these inclinations is to read *The Idiot* or to go far away all alone or to climb a convenient mountain by oneself. The Japanese is too pragmatic, too empirical, too common-sensical, however, for such excesses to last long. Drugtaking, the modern equivalent of reading Byron or wandering ancient glades forlorn, would not, I believe, have become a national pastime in this unromantic land even if the police were not so righteously persistent in their endeavors to eradicate its slightest manifestation. The Japanese does not become an addict because he is not ready to trade actuality for the artificial reality of continual inebriation.

The Japanese are resolutely of the here and the now, and this, to be sure, limits them. In the same way, one of the ways they have learned to survive in a sometimes quaking, occasionally flooded, and always overcrowded archipelago is to prepare themselves, daily, continually, for the worst. If it does not come, they have had a good day. I have always wondered why Seneca is not a best seller here. His stoic admonitions would find, I should think, one hundred million pairs of willing ears. Do not fear the future—if it is too terrible, you will die; if you do not die, it could not have been too terrible. Such thoughts, so very Asian-sounding, might, one would believe, find a ready audience.

That they do not is largely because the Japanese—different in this from the Indians, from the Chinese—are not self-conscious except in the lowest and most social sense. They are literally not conscious of self and they literally have no conscience—Western man's pride and pain—at all. Thus Ruth Benedict's conclusion that they have an abundance of social shame but not a shred of private

47

guilt is probably true. A thing is not a crime unless you are caught; nothing is bad except something that fails—and even then there is always the sense of *shikata ga nai* to fall back on.

One can imagine what a Dostoevski or a Melville would have made of such a place. Here the very conflict that gives all meaning to Western life does not exist. It is not merely ironed out or hidden. It quite literally does not exist, has never even been imagined. Its mysterious attractions may be felt in whatever little a Japanese derives from a reading of *Crime and Punishment*, but, unless he is so awed by the idea of Literature that his mind numbs, I can imagine him first asking himself what was the matter with Raskolnikov, to carry on so about his crime when no one but himself knew anything about it and it would never have been known if only he had kept his mouth shut.

One can imagine, with more pleasure, what a Henry Fielding or a Jane Austen would have made of the country. Both would have criticized. He would have exposed, in the midst of laughter, the most awful discrepancies and she would have observed with her loving but cutting irony many an abyss between intention and fact. He would have come to love Ihara Saikaku, whom he so resembles, and she would have passed her afternoons reading, for pure pleasure, Sei Shonagon.

Japan, then—to answer this perennial question—allows me to like myself because it agrees with me and I with it. Moreover, it allows me to keep my freedom. It makes very few demands on me—I am considered too much the outsider for that, a distinction I owe to the color of my skin, eyes, and hair—and, consequently, I become free. I become a one-member society, consistent only to myself and forever different from those who surround me. Our basic agreement permits an amount of approval, some of it mutual; our basic differences allow me to apprehend finally that the only true responsibility a man has is toward himself.

But it is just this quality that I now find threatened. In a decade this Japanese sense of difference will have perhaps disappeared and with it—along with much that is jingoistic, insular, and certainly xenophobic—will disappear other precious Japanese qualities. "One world" is becoming a hideous possibility and I wish to celebrate our differences for as long as is possible. Romantic my present quest may be, but quixotic it is not. The world I search for still remains. A part of it I know—my life in changing Tokyo where (even where) Japan remains a nice place to be. At the same time I wonder now about the other part, the vanished part. It must be somewhere around.

My search is for the real Japanese, the originals, the ur-*Nihonjin*. In this I am not to be put off by doubts, by fears, nor by such reasoned observations as that private remark by one of the most popular of writers on Japan: The soul of the Japanese is like the heart of the onion; you peel off layer after layer, then expectantly, hopefully, you peel more; finally you reach the center, the heart, the core: the onion has none.

Somewhere—somewhere near the sea, I believe—I will find them: the people the Japanese ought to be, the people they once were.

*   *   *

THE BOAT THAT will take me to Shodoshima backs up apologetically and leaves the just-waking town. A number of children are going for an outing and I sit facing them in the large mat-covered cabin.

A young mother is nursing her child, a sight not usual in the cities any more. Even more unusual is the fact that the child appears to be at least three years old. He is heavy. The mother has trouble holding him, arms wrapped around him as though he were a large bundle. He strikes out with his strong boylike arms and the mother winces. Still an infant, greedy, he nuzzles, half-asleep, one nipple in his mouth, the other in his hand. In the country, babies are nursed longer than in the cities. I have heard that not so long ago, in the north where food was still scarce, children were not fully weaned until nearly school age, but this I am inclined to doubt. How could the mothers carry them?—or did they just set the children in front of them?

A more apparent difference is that the children of islands are smaller than children of the mainland. The latter now eat meat, bread, and potatoes and drink milk. Island children are still on rice, tea, fish. On the mainland, fewer and fewer families live on tatami, fewer mothers carry their babies strapped to their backs—two practices thought to stunt growth. On these islands, however, everyone still squats on tatami and infants are still carried papoose fashion.

Whatever the sociological reasons, physically the Japanese are short only because their legs are short. The young man who was nice

49

to me, who took me to Boze, was about my height but was built to be taller. If his legs had been longer, he would have towered over me. His proportions to his hips were those of a large, powerful man. The legs were short.

We, brought up on Greek canons of proportion, find long legs attractive. So, indeed, do most city Japanese now. There is another aesthetic, however, that of the traditional Japanese, which finds short thighs and slightly bowed legs attractive. In women this results in a sinuous walk, in men a walk that is firm and masculine—the kind of movement that looks so good in Japanese classical dance and is so disastrous to ballet. It makes a people who belong to the earth upon which they walk, who need not bother with tiptoe standing, with aspirations to the skies. They know who they are. They are a part of the landscape. Content, at home, they do not find necessary the straining postures of the West, which seem to suggest that being of the earth means being earth-bound.

Busy with such thoughts, I turn and survey the rest of the passengers. Directly opposite me on the tatami-floored cabin are two little boys with their father. They are dressed in identical navy-blue shirts and shorts and both wear the inevitable gabardine hat. Almost every child in Japan wears a hat, at least when traveling, usually with an elastic band beneath the chin to hold it on.

These little boys are well behaved. They sit with their legs tucked under them, presumably growing shorter by the minute. One begins to lean, is evidently going to lie down, but a sharp word from his father, busy with the sports section, brings him up again. They do not sprawl—so good for the legs—in the manner of city children. Deportment is observed, even on an outing. They sit side by side, good little children, delighted to be going some place, showing this by sidewise glances at each other, little secret smiles and—father now engrossed in the classifieds—a few furtive pinches.

Next to them a baby is sitting all by itself on the tatami. My eye is attracted to it. Something is the matter with the baby. I look at it, try to figure out what's wrong. Then I realize what the trouble is. The baby doesn't have a hat on. Strange child, to be going on a journey without a proper hat.

A few days ago, sitting in the station plaza at Himeji, I had noticed a group of relatives who were seeing each other off, among them a voyaging baby on a bowing mother's back. Suddenly one of the relatives had an idea. A hat, a hat—the baby must have a hat. At once one of the older women hurried off to find one. In the meantime the bus was starting for the port. Returning just as the bus was pulling out, the woman ran after it for a considerable way, waving a large white gabardine hat. She laughed and smiled as she puffed alongside the bus, dust rising. Inside, the departing relatives also laughed and smiled as do most Japanese when disappointed, embarrassed, or in serious trouble.

Perhaps this deprived infant now in front of me is the same baby—still hatless. It is impossible to say. All babies look identical and Japanese babies look even more so. This one certainly has an unfinished look, though.

Next to the baby sits a girl with a guitar case at her feet. She looks pleasantly at me from time to time, too polite to speak but ready enough to talk once I begin.

Yes, as a matter of fact, her hobby is the guitar and because today is her day off—she works in the local emporium on Iejima—she is going to take her lesson. Once a week, on her day off, she goes to Shodoshima, has her lesson, then perhaps sees a movie before returning to her island and the general store.

I ask her what she is studying now. She tells me, and, surprised, I ask her to repeat it, to make certain I have not misunderstood. No, it is the Fauré "Pavane".

Here, where the lion dance is an annual event, where they have magical wells, and children suckle until too big to carry—here, someone is learning Fauré.

But this is Japan, land of incongruity. Once on Sadogashima, which the Japanese themselves think of as being the end of the earth, I wandered into the local store. It was filled with odd, unknown, straw-wrapped objects, a few iron instruments, savage-looking, the use of which I could not determine.

Since I was waiting for a bus, the helpful young lady in charge, wearing an exotic country-checked kimono and odd-looking sandals, asked if I would like some music to pass the time. I said I would, thinking to hear some local songs. She put on a battered but still quite audible recording of Mozart's "Les petits riens."

The bus was late; we listened to the entire suite. During it she

51

snapped her fingers and moved her sandaled feet to its strains, motions that probably also accompanied the flute and drum during the summer festival of the dead.

I questioned her about the recording. Oh, they had a few records. She showed me. Folk music, popular Japanese singers, Jessica Dragonette, Benny Goodman, and the Mozart. All of these were played in turn, one after the other. No discrimination was made because no discrimination was necessary.

Now, back on the boat to Shodoshima, I asked the girl with the guitar if she heard any other Fauré. She had not. Indeed, up to now she had not known that Fauré was the composer. She had thought that the name of the work was "Fauré Pavane," like "Für Elise," that perennial Japanese favorite.

I told her that the "Pavane" was Fauré's opus fifty. I also hummed the piece to show her that I knew it. I was pleased with myself. After all, how many people know this work?—one in a thousand? A liberal estimate. She was not surprised, hummed along with me, corrected me when I got the melody wrong. When we finished she observed that it was a pretty tune. And did I know "Banjo on Knee"?—this in English—which was another pretty tune?

She had first heard the Fauré over the radio, thought it attractive, and listened for the number of the recording and the name of the company releasing it, Japanese radio stations usually giving information of this sort. She copied down the name and number and eventually saved enough to buy the recording. (She does not have a record player but a friend does.) Repeated listening inspired her to ask her teacher to get the music.

The teacher was busy teaching his pupils "Banjo on Knee," to be followed by "Happy Farmer" and "Moonlight on Ruined Castle," but agreed that the tune was pretty enough and so sent to Tokyo for the music. Tokyo did not have it, not for the guitar at any rate. They did, however, have a piano version and this was eventually sent. Teacher took the piano version and, by cutting out notes here and there and playing it very slowly, managed to adapt it for the guitar. It was this version that the girl had practiced this week. Next week was "Swanee River," another pretty tune, and wasn't Foster a good composer though? Already interest in Fauré was dying away. After all, she already knew it now. When asked to play for company it would make an appearance flanked by "Moonlight on Ruined Castle" and, possibly, "Old Gray Mare."

I wanted her to play me the "Pavane" —I had not heard it for years. It was not the kind of music one expected to find on a boat going to Shodoshima. But she became shy, clutched her case, said that if she did, then she would become nervous and not be able to play it properly for her teacher.

Later, we stood together in the bus, all the seats having been taken by the outing children. The bus was to take us from Kusakabe, where we had landed, to Tonosho, another of the island's small ports, where her teacher lived. I had stopped to buy a ticket, but she told me not to, took a book of tickets from her purse, with a smile gave the bus girl one for each of us. Then she smiled again.

This kind of disinterested kindness is common in Japan, at least if you stay away from the cities. It is not ostentation, as it might be in Tokyo, in the tow of some loudmouth determined to pay for everything and consequently denying your own generosity entirely. This was hospitality. I was a stranger in parts where strangers seldom came. And it was courtesy too.

I asked her to the coffee shop at Tonosho, or what passed for one, and we had a tepid cup in the half-hour before her lesson. She talked about her life on the island. She apparently saw it as a series of happy weeks punctuated by the even happier weekly visit to the guitar teacher.

A plain girl, her hair pulled back in schoolgirl fashion, her face scrubbed, her fingers square, nails long and clean. She was wholesome as a farm girl but her movements had the agility of someone who, from childhood, has skipped and balanced on seaside rocks. There was nothing of the stolid mountain maiden about her. A large, full-breasted girl, her pink suit cut fully, like a student's uniform, she would make a good wife, a better mother, and would, I imagine, keep up with her guitar as well. She would have a happy life.

When we rose to go, this pleasant, round-faced, nice girl picked up a box of matches from the table. All coffee shops give away boxes of matches with the name of the shop, its location, telephone number. She held them out to me. I said I already had some of my own.

"Take them anyway," she said. "It will be a nice memory of the

53

place." She smiled because she meant our meeting, our talk. I put the matches in my pocket. How typical the gesture. Sentimental Westerners put things in their pockets to carry home as souvenirs. Sentimental Japanese give things to people going away as souvenirs.

*   *   *

SHODOSHIMA IS the largest of the islands of the Inland Sea and stands between Shikoku and Honshu near its eastern end. True, Awajishima, which forms one side of the Bay of Osaka, where the Inland Sea begins, is still larger, but, separated from Honshu by only a thirty-minute ferry ride, it is so near Osaka and Kobe as to seem a part of the mainland. Don't think the engineers haven't already noted its position, haven't already planned the two short spans that will make it nothing but a highway between Honshu and Shikoku. Only the deep channel and the great whirlpool of Naruto temporarily delay this monstrous dream that will quite steal Shikoku from the sea as well and surrender it at last to the touristing hordes with their buses, loudspeakers, children, and car-sick old ladies.

Shikoku is still somewhat protected from the Japanese tourist because it is such trouble to get there. All the lovely spots of Honshu—Izu, Kinki, Chiba—lie helpless before him. His depredations in Nara during the last five years must be seen to be believed. All of this will come in time, but, as yet, the whirlpool whirls, bridges are difficult if, alas, no longer impossible, and for the moment Shikoku and its neighboring islands are saved.

Shodoshima looks rather like the mainland, like Honshu, but since it is cut off from the kind of progress the mainland is at present entertaining, it looks like the mainland of the last century. It is all bays and inlets, headlands and peninsulas, filled with examples of old Osaka architecture.

It looks very nineteenth century, like the scenes one used to see on plates and fans, and in late-period, bad woodblock prints. One looks across these small intervals of land and water as one looks across them in Oriental pictures in Western restaurants. There is an example in Munich like this, a Chinese restaurant wall with a completely imaginary landscape by some talented Bavarian who had never heard of Shodoshima but captured it perfectly. It looks like a

54

verismo set for *Narcissus*. One expects that peculiar shade of blue found in inferior china.

Otherwise the place is very middle Japan with roofs of gray tiles laced with white, mud walls, low and dusty vegetation, lots of paddies, narrow roads. It is an agricultural island. One fishes only for one's table. The towns are inland villages, their backs turned resolutely to the sea. They all look inward. These lovely Victorian seascapes are visible only from attic or bathroom windows.

I see a graveyard facing the sea. The grave markers look out over the waves, shaded by pines. Here, as elsewhere, the dead are put where no one else wants to go—high in hills, deep in valleys, facing the uninteresting sea. The Western idea that a cemetery should be beautiful—the grave-island of Corfu, the heights of Père-Lachaise, the smiling amenities of Forest Lawn—is unknown. Happy dead. To be facing this slate-blue sea, to be watching the waves as the centuries turn. Unhappy living, crowded cheek by cheek with only the dusty road for view.

The bus passes some pilgrims walking along the road. They are making a grand tour of the forty-eight temples of the island, a route patterned after a similar eighty-eight on the large island of Shikoku. There the distances are so great that the faithful once took half a year to do the whole thing. The temples of Shodoshima can be done in a matter of days and are consequently the more popular.

The pilgrims, dressed in white, used to march from place to place, begging along the way, later cooking whatever they received. Nowadays they carry lunch boxes and thermos bottles. Even so, the walking pilgrim is rare enough that everyone cranes to see. Much more common these days is the bus-riding pilgrim or the pilgrim on motor bike, who can do the whole course in mere hours.

In the middle of the island, fitfully glimpsed in the dust rising from the road, is the mountain known as Kankake. Kobo Daishi, the priest who made the well at Iejima, came here too. So did the emperor Meiji, who himself climbed, for what reason I do not know, to the very top. In any event, the top is sacred and, being such, is extremely troublesome to reach. At the top is a gate, Kankakemon, built right into the stone and distinguished for the extraordinary difficulty of its construction. From here one can, it is said, see the valley named Kankakei, where the rocks are famed for their beauty.

55

Stones and temples, these are the two attractions of this attractively backward place. It was from the Shodo quarries that stones used in building Osaka Castle are said to have been taken. The temples are not noted for beauty but, after all, the eminent Kobo Daishi came here. Visiting all of them is good luck, ensuring a long life and good health. I should think so, at least in the old days. The exercise alone would set you up for years.

There is another attraction, as I discover, following in the bus the path of the pilgrims and ending up at the boat landing of the port of Tonosho. This is a statue of the movie actress Hideko Takamine surrounded by children, all in bronze and nearly life-size. It commemorates the filming of *Twenty-four Eyes*, a 1954 picture, made here in Shodoshima, about a poor schoolteacher and her terrible life. Actually, the book upon which the film was based was the near-autobiography of a local teacher, Sakae Tsuboi. But Miss Tsuboi is not immortalized in bronze; Miss Takamine is.

She is hereabouts something of a heroine. Pictures of her are sold in this and other roles, little fans that open up to reveal her, little lockets that, when opened, present her smiling face. She is becoming immortal. Long after the negative of this film has begun to bubble in its can, the statue will remain—our Hideko facing life, already turned into folklore.

The Japanese mind is so quick to immortalize, to idealize. The past that we would consider recent is thought already ancient. "A long time ago" turns out to be a mere five years; "an old-time movie star" means, not Valentino, but Gary Cooper. Japan lives intensely in the present. At the same time, and perhaps consequently, it needs a rich and varied past, which is itself forever under reconstruction.

On the island of Sado I once saw this past in the process of becoming. There was a multipart 1953 film called *What Is Your Name?* Its plot was that hero and heroine should miss each other by inches all over the islands of Japan. In obedience to the script, one of the more unlikely places chosen for this non-occurrence was this tiny northern island of Sado, the Japanese idea of ultimate distance. Cast, crew all assembled, and the sequence was shot. Again the two failed to meet.

Now the film is forgotten by everyone except the islanders. They alone remember, and they remember every detail, though they have forgotten that it was a film.

There, on the suspension bridge, I was told, she had come. "Poor thing, little dreaming that he was only minutes distant, and on his way. And half a minute after she had left—just imagine, only half a minute—here he came, poor thing, little dreaming that she had just left, that he might have called or run after her if only he'd known that she'd been there. Oh, it's a sad story."

"When did this happen?"

"Oh, long, long ago. Poor things."

Not two decades have passed, yet all vestiges of crew, camera, lights have vanished. All that remains are the names of the two lovers—Haruki and Machiko—already passed into folklore. A rural Romeo and Juliet, only more tragic because, you see, they never met.

*   *   *

FROM SHODO the islands begin. They stretch westward, hundreds of them, almost as far as the large southern island of Kyushu.

The sea is like a lake. The wind ruffles the surface; the water looks shallow. The islands ride upon its lightly broken surface. The boats move back and forth, lines of choppy waves diverging, the wakes like furrows after a plow.

It is late afternoon. The port islands catch the sun. Each detail—a rock, a tree, a stretch of sand—stands out clear, sharp-edged. The starboard islands, the sun behind, are outlines. The nearest is almost black, those farther away a dark gray, the ones behind them purplish, until—islands piled like low thunderheads—the farthest pale into a watered blue, deepest toward the crest, almost white where their far shores meet the horizon.

In between, upon this lake, as though upon the baize of a billiard table, the toy ships churn their ways, their courses marked for minutes as they pass. Fish jump, reflecting silver in the sun. And in the distance, lit by the slowly sinking sun just beside it, I see a single island, perfectly shaped, so far away that it is but a breath of color against the sky, so far that it could be the very crown of some enormous triangular island with all but the apex of the pyramid hidden by the earth's curvature.

*   *   *

57

ONE OF THE CHARMS of Shikoku's Takamatsu, to which the boat from Shodo has now brought me, is that, though it is a small city rather than a town, you can walk practically anywhere you want to go in it. Boat station, railway terminal, downtown—each is not too distant from the other.

Most Japanese towns, like those in Calabria, have railway stations miles from anywhere else. Matsuyama, Shikoku's largest city, is almost a parody of the pattern. The docks are in another city, and the place where you might want to stay, at the hot-spring hotels of Dogo, is an equal number of miles on the other side.

Another attractive quality of Takamatsu is that trees have been planted and there is a plaza for sauntering. One rarely finds such a plaza in Japan. The general idea is that we Japanese are so busy that we have no time for strolling. In the same way, bars and coffee shops close up at midnight because we Japanese are such early risers. In point of fact, the Japanese are almost Turkish in their love of a leisurely and aimless walk; and in the cities they also rise later than any other people I know, and no one is ready for any kind of business until ten in the morning. Due, however, to such discrepancies between fact and fancy, any town will have some hidden all-night places for a drink or a snack and at least an occasional park tucked away somewhere. Takamatsu is different only in that it openly admits the Japanese fondness for strolling: on every hand there are gardens and plazas and arcades designed for leisurely perambulations.

The city was almost completely destroyed during the war, and when it was rebuilt, for once someone sat down and thought about how best to do it. While there are no outdoor cafés, no public places in which to sit down and read in comfort—that would be asking too much of the image Japan has of itself—there is at least a leisurely air about Takamatsu that reminds one of some provincial European city.

It is elegant as well. The shops are well designed, smart. There are covered arcades in which no motor traffic is permitted. The city buildings are beautifully designed from the native stone, and there is more public art—murals, sculpture—than I have ever seen in a Japanese city. The stores are equally modern, except for an occasional brick front left over from the Meiji period and hence fairly inde-

58

structible. And there are the coffee shops, great harbingers of modern culture.

The role of the coffee shop in contemporary Japan should excite the interest of some social anthropologist. Here is where one first glimpses the foreign innovation that will shortly become Japanese. In the musical coffee shops you first heard Schoenberg, in the artistic coffee shops you first saw the picture of a Giacometti. Here also were observed the first signs of that great innovation, the miniskirt. For years the only place I could ever find the *Partisan Review* was in a coffee shop I used to frequent. Copies of the latest *Vogue*, the latest *Evergreen Review*, lie scattered in coffee shops all over Japan. There is no attempt at discrimination, but many of the pieces of various foreign cultures are lying there, all brand new and ready to be put together, like pieces of some giant and scattered puzzle. The Japanese coffee shop is the Japanese avant-garde.

I go into one here in Takamatsu. It is all abstract, a kind of softened cubism: wire chairs, bent-iron tables, solid units of primary colors, acute angles, and a mobile in the form of a bird cage holding two baffled finches. This is not a modern shop. It is, by Japanese standards, coffee-shop standards at any rate, quite traditional. It is very Léger-like, it feels of the thirties, and yet is quite obviously Japanese.

In a way international style in the thirties happened to coincide with the traditional Japanese style. Module architecture, shoji doorframes, tatami rectangles—all very much like Mondrian. Japan was never more in fashion because the fashion had never been more Japanese. What early books had called nude, unfinished, primitive suddenly became spacious, clean, sophisticated. When the functional came into vogue, the Japanese interior, always functional, began to be noticed.

This particular coffee shop, however, looks the way it does because Mondrian and Léger are still fashionable in Japan. In the nineteenth century, for example, Hiroshige prints reached Europe, where one was seen and copied by Van Gogh; his copy became very famous, and recently I saw a Japanese painting that was a copy of the Van Gogh copy of the Hiroshige print.

Or take the case of Japanese impressionism. Japan's love for Monet is extreme. They do not realize that it was, in part, through Japanese art that the impressionist school became what it was. Both the nine-

59

teenth-century Frenchman and the twentieth-century Japanese are noticing the same things in the same way, but the Japanese are unaware that it was their great-grandfather's vision that is partly responsible for their own.

I sit sipping excellent coffee in this near-parody of the twentieth-century sensibility, thinking about, wondering about, what it is in the Japanese that makes them so naturally appropriate whatever is new outside them. I look about for the latest issue of the *Hudson Review*, fail to locate it, pick up the new *Harper's Bazaar* instead, leaf through it. The Japanese have a nose, I decide. A nose for the new, a nose for fashion, a nose for interior decoration—those antennae through which society first senses its intentions and what it will become. Japan is the most modern of all countries perhaps because, having a full and secure past, it can afford to live in the instantaneous present.

My musings were interrupted by the entrance of a troop of boys whose finery would have put Tokyo, New York, and Paris to shame. The very latest fashions—pink and chartreuse checkered caps, carefully faded dungarees, sharp summer shirts, pearl-white stripes on gray, red checks on light tan, a fashionably old-fashioned touring cap, and, of course, the Japanese touch, now that it was getting toward dusk, dark glasses.

At the same time I saw that they were country boys, very dressed up, but country boys nonetheless. Big, wide, honest faces; big pink ears; large wrists; solid wide feet; enormous hands. There they sat in their wide-lapelled jackets, their tapered trousers, some even indulging themselves in the ultimate of country elegance—never seen in the city—white cotton gloves. I had hit upon the haunt of the local young bloods.

At least, so I thought. One can never be sure. It is one of many peculiarities of Japan that such extremes of fashion also appeal to the criminal classes. No one is more elegant than the young Japanese gangster. One would think he spent all his time poring over back issues of *Esquire*. Consequently, it is sometimes difficult to determine whether one is speaking to a young person of fashion or to what the Japanese are pleased to call nascent criminals. The well-to-do in many countries now affect the styles of the proletariat, but only in upside-down Japan, I believe, are hoodlums fashionable.

It takes Japan to produce a really elegant young criminal, a dandy with fawn trousers, moss-green jersey, dazzlingly white shoes and—just a touch of brutality—a silver chain lying lightly across the instep. The unwashed common criminal of other cultures might look to his Japanese counterpart. He is worth copying.

These boys are not, I decide, criminals. They are not nearly so assured as their garments would indicate. Also, they are too lively. Young hoods cultivate, the world over, a careful impassivity; they strive to appear indifferent. Not these boys. There are several careful looks at the foreigner, some chatter, a few stifled giggles, then a hollow hello, loud but tentative, tossed in his direction, to see if he will respond. He does.

My attempts at lively and sophisticated conversation were not, however, successful. They were not at ease, giggled, smoked too much, and when I asked if they were students, they spoke up like children, gave their ages, their names, their hobbies.

What they really wanted to know, I eventually learned, was whether or not Indians continued to roam the great West. Recently they had begun to doubt, and no amount of viewing American Westerns had eased this growing suspicion. I ended the fantasy forever by telling them about reservations and the poor mass-producing Zuni. To underline my explanation I said that the American Indian was just like the Japanese Ainu, once a proud and independent people living in the northern part of Honshu, now decimated and pushed into the wastes of Hokkaido in the far north and reduced to carving wooden bears in department-store windows.

At the mention of something known, however, of something belonging to their own country, the boys lose interest. Instead, tell us about New York, tell us about the latest designs in automobiles, what about Jane Fonda, how did President Kennedy really die, and so on. I answer as best I can, aware—as one is always in Japan—that I have ceased being myself. Rather, I have become—once again—a Representative of My Country.

I cannot begin to describe the sensation except to assure you that it is both tempting and disagreeable. I find myself, quite suddenly, a spokesman, and my every word seems accepted as literal truth. At the same time I realize that these boys are not looking at me as another person more or less like themselves, and that their friendly questions contain no friendship for solitary me. Like all Americans, like all romantics, I want to be loved—somehow—for my precious self alone. I don't want them to pay so much attention to what I say. I want them to pay more attention to me.

Under the strain I become didactic, and eventually petulant. I know what it looks like, having seen the nicest and most well-intentioned foreigners turn themselves into nit-picking, narrow-minded pedants as they attempt to explain:

"Well, of course, I said that, but, actually, what I mean is that the Americans never—well, I can't say never, perhaps hardly ever would be better—hardly ever go to the extremes you suggest—you didn't suggest, of course, you implied, still, perhaps there is some truth, however, in what you seem to be saying, namely that..." And on and on and on, trapped in their doubts, asea amid their convictions, at a loss in this new, baggy, and completely unattractive role.

At such times I want to strike the table, stand up and bare my breast, strike attitudes, shout loudly that I am myself—take me or leave me. But I do nothing of the sort. I am patient, I pause, I consider. I become what every American longs to be—a teacher.

They nod, earnest, as I lay bare the secrets of the world, with particular emphasis upon the workings of American democracy and the love life of Jane Fonda. I try to be honest about both but soon lose impetus among the shards of my rhetoric.

They eventually tire of such concentration and, now that I have told them all about my country, are pleasantly anxious that I see something of theirs. Have I seen the famous beauty spots? The names are reeled off and I nod, pleased that I am widely traveled. Kyushu, Hokkaido, too? Yes, yes. Well, then, perhaps something more local. Have I seen the Ritsurin Koen? No, I don't even know what it is—a park of some kind? So it is, and one of them, the largest, wearing the touring cap and the red and tan shirt, the darkest sun glasses, seems to know all about it. Such being the custom of the country, he offers to take me. Not the next day. He, being a butchershop employee, must work that day. But the one after that, Sunday.

*   *   *

CONSEQUENTLY, the next day I decide to go and see Yashima, a straight-rising rocky promontory, a miniature Diamond Head but deeply wooded, stretching away from and above the city. Here, toward the end of the twelfth century—the beginning of the House of Plantagenet on one side of the world, the completion of the Great Temple of Angkor on the other—was fought one of the many battles between the Heike and Genji clans, two enormous families that seem to have spent a third of a century chasing each other about in the complexities of Japanese history.

They fought along the beaches below these cliffs. The Heike had thirty thousand, what with women and children; the Genji had considerably fewer, but they won.

The killings must have been dreadful, but, all the same, I imagine that the massacres were held according to rules. The enemy must not get too far from sight; battle lines must be drawn up; if women and babes in arms are to be slaughtered, this must be agreed upon ahead of time. I cannot imagine the Japanese fighting otherwise, not among themselves, just as they cannot drink a simple cup of tea without an elaborate etiquette.

The battles were probably somewhat formal, showing elements of an intricate choreography. In later centuries the Japanese were also able to fight successful battles with the Chinese, who also understood this military formality, and again with the Russians, who did not, but who had their own ritual of battle. And this is perhaps why they fought unsuccessfully during World War II and lost. The American method of personal initiative and improvisation, of rushing right up and firing, was disconcerting to soldiers taught more formally. Later on, the Japanese soldiers, mainly new recruits, were encouraged to use the same tactics. The cry of the samurai as his sword flashed down became the scream of attack. It contained as much terror as determination. The shouting, leaping, fanatical Japanese soldier was a late development. He was born from despair. These single, foolhardy individuals, though alarming, were dangerous only if lucky. The Americans, who knew all along that this was no formal battle, scoured the underbrush, shelled the sea, pressed in with flame throwers—and the grand Heidelbergian army of Japan was destroyed.

Japanese civil wars were different. Here everyone knew the rules and obeyed them. Leaders knew each other well, and often they were closely related. The carnage was there, but it must have been of the kind pictured in Flemish war paintings or in the cyclorama at

63

Nashville. It was decorous, even picturesque—all, that is, except the dying.

One can see what it might have been like from the screen paintings of a later period. Warriors scrambling about in orderly fashion, each neatly labeled with name and rank; men in heroic attitudes; ladies in a faint, sliced babes at feet; a horse running away dragging its rider by a single foot caught in the stirrup as in a circus turn; higher up, men in undress setting fire to the pavilion; then—next panel—pavilion in flames, ladies in underclothes—most elegant, all red and white silk—running out and into the arms of irreproachably armored, intelligent-looking ravishers; finally—last panel—the remnants escaping, climbing industriously up the mountain or sailing serenely over the sea.

Whether any of the battle was actually fought on these heights I don't know. I doubt it. It is difficult to ascend: a trolley ride, a cable car, then a long walk, after which one finds the usual—temple, kind of museum, big hotel-restaurant with neon and pinball machines.

Though the height is famous for the battle and its remains, these linger only in the wrapping papers on the souvenirs—samurai on horseback in the water pointing the way—and in a small booklet, badly printed, eclipsed behind piles of "Views of the Inland Sea" in full color and "Views of Gracious Takamatsu in Cinerama." The view has superseded the battle. Which is as it should be. I cannot imagine any Japanese, even two warriors engaged in a life-or-death struggle, not stopping to admire the view. Nor do I want to suggest that the tawdriness of the souvenirs, their vulgarity even, is due to any recent decline in aesthetics or craftsmanship. From earliest times the Japanese have—along with the perfectly worked stone, the joint carpentered precisely right—produced deceitfully ornamental objects. Indeed, the Japanese seem always to have had a liking for the meretricious.

I go around a corner and there are three girls who have stopped to admire the view. They are on a holiday, all dressed up—handbags, high heels, smart hats. They see me and hold immediate council. Obviously they have been waiting by this view for someone to come.

With a charming and apologetic smile, the eldest approaches, holding out her camera as she might hold out a cookie to a tame bear, and in slow but exquisitely polite Japanese asks if I would not be so very kind as to do them the great favor of perhaps taking their picture. She asks with that winning blend of dignity and hesitation one finds in girls of eighteen. Younger, they giggle and are silly as they ask; older, they do not ask at all. The manner, both hesitant and assured, is winning.

I am happy to comply, working the levers, pressing the buttons, moving the knobs this way and that. Japanese cameras have become so professional, so complicated, that I am not certain I have taken their picture at all. Neither are they, and so, to make sure, I am to stand with the other two while the prettiest takes our picture. Then, with politeness, dignity, they thank me and move off, hand in hand.

*   *   *

FORMERLY THE SITE of the rural retreat of the Matsudaira family, several of whom were daimyo of this region during Tokugawa times, the Ritsurin Park, an expanse of well over one hundred acres, is one of Japan's finest landscape gardens. That is, the finest of its genre: big, grand, official, imposing—the answer to Versailles. This far I read in the guide book before going off to our meeting.

The young man who offered to show me the park is waiting at the same coffee shop, which we have designated as our meeting place. He is, surprisingly, alone. Though the invitation was his, it is common for Japanese to bring friends along. Many are the times when I have prepared dinner for two and discovered I am expected to feed five. This young man, however, now sat all by himself, though in considerable splendor.

He wore a navy-blue open-necked shirt with enormous red dots on it, a matching neck-scarf, white-suede shoes, a white Panama hat. He had left the white gloves at home but still wore his sun glasses. His hair was freshly combed, the long sides plastered above his ears in the style known, for some reason, as the Regent in Japan, and he smelled of breakfast pickled-radish, of pomade, and of what I eventually identified as Old Spice cologne. His name was Saburo—which indicated that he was the third son. If his brothers had been named in the same fashion, the eldest would have been Ichiro or Taro and the next Jiro. His younger brothers would have been Shiro and Goro. But, no, he has no younger brothers. He is the youngest. His father owns the butchershop where he works.

The park is very large. There is a small admission charge, and he

65

insists upon buying the tickets since, as he points out, it is he who has invited me. He does so with such an air of assurance, seems to know his way around so well, that I assume he has come here often, that this is somewhere young people usually come of a Sunday afternoon.

It was hot as we trudged the gravel paths among the pines, the shimmer of a lake far ahead of us. "This belonged to the Matsudaira family, I believe," I observed, having read this in the guide book that morning.

"Yes, the Matsudaira family," he answered, but did not seem very interested in the fact, seemed to be thinking of something else. Eventually it appeared. "Have you ever *met* Jane Fonda?"

I told him that unfortunately I had not. And, no, I had never met Elizabeth Taylor, nor Susan Hayward. He was silent again. This unlikely triumvirate were his favorite movie stars, it turned out, and he had thought that surely I must have known at least one of them. He would stay up late to watch Miss Hayward in old movies on television, and occasionally Miss Taylor as well. Miss Fonda he had to pay for at the motion-picture theater.

Had I seen *Barbarella*?

Yes, I had seen *Barbarella*.

He had not. Was it true that she took off all her clothes?

"Well, it seemed to be true, but it was right at the beginning of the film, when she takes off her space suit, and it is under the titles and the lettering gets in the way and I couldn't be sure."

"Well, how much of her did you get to see?"

"Well, you got to see pretty much."

"Oh."

He seemed so upset by the news that I turned the conversation to the garden. "Is this the kind of garden you are supposed to see by walking through, like the Katsura Villa garden in Kyoto, or will we come to a place from which we look at it all spread out in front of us?"

"Oh, you can look at anything you like here. They aren't strict."

"No, that's not what I mean. Is there a special place for viewing it, or is the garden supposed to be an experience, one that you create while walking through it?"

"A lot of people walk through it."

"Well, do any of them stop at a certain point?"

"I don't know. Let's watch and see."

He stopped and turned around, good-naturedly humoring me,

looked in this direction and that. "There," he said, "two people have stopped over there."

"I see."

We walked on. Soon it was my turn to humor him.

"Well, even if you haven't met them, you're a foreigner, so you would probably know, since they're foreign too."

"Know what?"

Drawing this out took some time. We looked at the famed iris bed, empty now in August, at the famed wisteria trellis, at the place where a famous boat had been built, at several pavilions with cut-rush roofs, and what remained of a famed rock garden; and finally he asked me if they went to bed with people.

"Well, each has been married a number of times so I would suppose so."

He supposed that being foreign and all they were rather, well, large.

"If you mean big boned, I think that Miss Taylor is. She has wide hips, wider at any rate than Miss Hayward and Miss Fonda have."

"That's true. I guess they are probably big all over."

They all seemed of a height, I remarked, if that was what he meant.

"Are all foreign women so big then?"

"Oh, no, there are all sizes. You must have noticed that much in the movies and on television."

He became exasperated. "No, no. I mean—well, down there."

"Oh, well I don't know about Miss Fonda and Miss Taylor and—"

"I know you don't know about them. I mean in general."

I stopped to think. It was where a famous general had stood to ward off something or other, but I was busy thinking and so did not read the placard.

I told him that in general I thought women were small down there no matter how large their bodies. Men as a rule weren't, it is true, but on the other hand you could never tell how big a man was down there by just looking at him. Big men were sometimes small and small men sometimes big, wasn't that true, now?

He nodded, deep in thought. "Yes, that's true."

"But women," I said, "seem to be different."

We walked on, nearing the big central pavilion by the lake, once the home of the daimyo presumably. It was very pretty, this park, with its deftly shaped shrubs, judiciously spaced trees. The pavilion rode the water, low, decorative. It looked like a large boat.

I could imagine an antiquarian daimyo having built this for himself. He purposely chose the architecture of another, earlier, better age, that of Heian-kyo, with its T'ang influenced roofs, its elegant verandas stretching into the waters. Like the Ashikaga shogun Yoshimasa, he was sick of his own times, of the wars and the police-state government. Like Beckford or Horace Walpole, he built this anachronistic pavilion, surrounded it by acres of woodland and high walls with guards on them, and created the kind of life he thought he ought to have.

I gazed at the splendid rooms, at the marvelous sleeping platform, half in one chamber, half in another. One could open the elegant sliding trellis and fall into one room or the other as he willed. He could have someone in one room, someone in the other, turn busily left and right all night long.

Saburo was apparently following a similar line of thought. "They had lots of girls, these rich old daimyo had," he observed. "They didn't even have to buy them, they just clapped their hands and out they came."

"Saburo, I imagine you don't have a girl friend. Is that true?"

"Yes." He did not shuffle or hang his head while delivering this information. It is quite proper for Japanese young men not to have girl friends.

"And I imagine that you are still a virgin and have no knowledge of girls whatsoever."

This caused some embarrassment. One ought to have had *some* experience at his age.

"How old are you?"

"Nineteen—but I'm going to get some experience soon."

I looked at him. It would be difficult. He wasn't bad looking but he was big, ham-handed, inclined to be hulking, awkward and hence overly assertive, unpolished, and not too bright—all qualities which I esteem but which the well-brought-up young Japanese lady does not. Her ideal, like that of the majority of well-brought-up young ladies all over the world, is initially someone who is older and wiser and kindly. Later she settles for someone who is serious and hard-working and thoughtful.

Even now in Japan the female standard for male beauty resembles that of ages past—the somewhat fair, somewhat round faced, somewhat aristocratic-looking, somewhat effeminate young man who is found around Kyoto—the kind of face that Kazuo Hasegawa, the movie actor, has. I imagine that this is changing, as is everything else in Japan, but in backwaters such as Takamatsu the beau ideal of the young and eligible lady probably remains the same as that of her mother and her mother's mother before her. A rough, peasant-like, salt-of-the-earth type of young man such as this doesn't have much chance.

"What about marriage?" I asked.

"Fun first," he said, "marriage later," quoting what I presumed to be a proverb.

"Well what about whores?" I ask—knowing that there are always whores, in every country. In Japan they are always in back alleys and must be searched for.

They were too expensive and all had social diseases. It wasn't like it was before.

Indeed it wasn't. I remember with pleasure the licensed quarters of Japan, closed more than ten years now: the enormous and pleasure-loving Yoshiwara, the little red-light district of the Chiba part of Choshi, the elegant houses of Nagasaki's Maruyama. The pleasure, like all real pleasure, was in the atmosphere. The strolling men, the smiling girls, the ubiquitous old ladies who brought in the customers, the small teahouses where you did nothing but simply looked and enjoyed.

In the next room we admired a series of painted panels done in the style of the Kano school, iris and cranes in that bold and decorative hard-lined style that makes one think of cloisonné. Then we walked out into the afternoon sun and sat on a bench.

"I've gone to the Turkish baths though—once."

The Turkish baths. How low the sexual life of the Japanese male has fallen. Before it was the Yoshiwara, songs, laughter, a kind of elegance. Now you enter these special bathing establishments—hundreds of them, all over Japan—go into a wet and disinfected cubicle with some short girl, receive a mediocre washing-down and massage, and then she holds up a jar of Papilio face cream.

"Want me to use some of this?" she drawls.

"Why?" I asked the first time.

"It costs two thousand yen for this much," she said, dipping out a fingerful.

"But the whole jar only costs fifty yen," I said.

"You want me to use or not?" she pursued.

Eventually I caught on. It is very Japanese, this way of asking, and it always catches the foreigner off guard. Just as in the Japanese house he feels big and clumsy, more bull than man, so, in this kind of situation he feels dense, unsubtle.

Saburo was telling me about his experience, hunched toward me, smelling of pomade. "And she put this cream right down there when I told her to go ahead and then she sort of worked her fingers. It felt good. I was very surprised. I hadn't known what special service meant."

That is what it is called. Special service. Usually it is two thousand yen. Then there is extra special service where you are allowed to perform the same manipulations on the girl, but that costs three thousand yen, nearly ten dollars. Finally, there is the near-mythical extra-special service deluxe, which is what we call making love. It can cost up to five thousand yen and is granted only to regular customers. Which is why Saburo is still a virgin at nineteen.

"Did you like it all that much?" I asked.

"Oh, yes. It was fine."

The Turkish-bath girls are, it is true, very popular. They handle dozens of customers a night and presumably make a good living. I at one time attempted to read into this something about the Japanese male, his need to debase the female, etc. But no one appears to think that such manipulation is debasing to either party. No one, apparently, except myself. It is popular only because it is what is available.

"Do you go often?"

"No, I only went once."

"But if you liked it so well?"

"I can do that good myself," said Saburo candidly. "Besides, it may be wrong of me, but I don't like to pay money for that. I think it should be free."

I agreed and we walked through trimmed bushes, over a small rustic bridge, into another section of the park where the pleasure-loving daimyo had been pleased to construct a miniature wilderness

74

with a purling brook, a tiny waterfall, and a baby mountain surmounted by a rustic pavilion. Here we sat down again. We had a lot
to talk about with each other.

"Then women are slower?" he was asking in something like dis-
may.

"Yes, much slower. A man must be careful."

"But I can't be that careful. I'm always fast." He thought about
this, hands folded, brow wrinkled. "But, on the other hand, I can do
it many times."

"Well, there. That's the answer to your problem." After this the
talk became clinical. The nature of the orgasm in women, how it
differed from that of the man. The labia majora, the labia minora,
the hymen, the clitoris. Did Miss Fonda have one of those? Yes,
probably. There we sat huddled in the pavilion, heads together, the
beautiful sunshine, the outspreading park, all unobserved. Saburo
was red, intent. He kept clasping one wet palm against the other.

Carried away by my new role, I launched into the cycle of reproduction. He straightened up. He was not interested in babies, it
appeared. "Tell me more about that, down there," he insisted.

But I had told him everything I knew. Already I had told him
enough that he would never again look at Elizabeth Taylor in the
same way. I had come to feel like Doctor Schweitzer among benight-
ed natives, and my first-aid chest had run empty.

He sat back, exhausted. Then he shook his head and smiled at the
ways of the world. A certain atmosphere, a kind of oppression had
gathered, called up by our excessively specialized conversation. To
disperse it, I turned to the garden, observed that he seemed to know
it well.

"This is my first time here," he said, smiling. "I never thought I'd
like it, but I do. Some Sunday, you know what I'm going to do? I'm
going to bring this girl I know. She works in the cloth store next door
to my father's. I'm going to ask her out on a date. And we're going to
come right here. Right here where we're sitting—just for luck—and
then I'm going to finally have an experience."

I observed that the spot was rather open.

That made no difference. He was going to tell her all about the
labia majora, the labia minora, and—finally—the clitoris!

Well, I decided, as we walked back back to the main gate, the now

75

cheerful and animated Saburo by my side, there were worse ways to have seen a famous and classical garden.

*   *   *

I WAS LATE for the boat the next morning. After the garden viewing, Saburo and I had gone eating and drinking. He had suggested the coffee shop, and there we sat discussing what few details had been neglected during the conversation in the park. Delighted to have discovered a fund of information otherwise difficult to locate, he had walked me back to my inn, had come in for a cup of tea, had asked more questions, had finally spent the night.

As I lay awake in the shuttered room, Saburo soundly sleeping, deeply breathing, I thought of the young man back at Iejima, of the girl on the boat, thought of Saburo, of all the people I had so far seen. Their differences from each other were apparent, but so was a subtle difference from the mainland Japanese.

I feel it is connected with the sea. The Japanese are really a sea people; they are all really islanders. To see them hedged in their enormous cities is to see them unnatural. The people of Himeji were a sea people, though now long domesticated to land. But even there their gaze still carries something of that look of people who gaze at horizons. The sea, flat, a line between air and water—this is the true heritage of the Japanese, not the ancient castle, not the modern city.

Long ago, the earliest travel journals imply, the Japanese were a rough and lively, lusty, impatient, enthusiastic, open, loving and hating people. So, to an extent, they still are. But history changed them. The longest-lasting totalitarian state in history turned the land people into something more circumspect, something sometimes suspicious. It inculcated in them perhaps more civilized but certainly more stultifying virtues.

I recognize in my city friends both that earlier and this later people. Flashes of enthusiasm, bursts of generosity. There is a quality that I seek and, when I find it, admire. It is more a Mediterranean than an Asian characteristic, but it exists in places in Japan and must once have existed everywhere on these islands. It is that quality which the early journals would have called Elizabethan. And it is this that I have found and hope to find again. In southern Kyushu, in the remoter parts of the Boso Peninsula, in those sections too far or too unimportant for the long arm of the Tokugawa government to

76

have reached. The young man at Iejima, the girl on the boat to Shodoshima, now Saburo, flat on his back and beginning to snore—they are from a different, older race.

So musing, I put myself to sleep.

We awoke late the next morning. Though overdue at work, Saburo was cheerful and dawdled over morning tea, already enthusiastic about Sunday with his doubtless somewhat startled girl friend. I was sleepy, had drunk too much. Consequently, I missed the boat I had wanted to take, and barely made the one I did not want and unwittingly took. It was going to Oshima.

*   *   *

IN THE WATERS surrounding Japan there are thirty-eight islands named Oshima. The man who counted them was a priest with apparently nothing better to do. He had only had a small map, he wrote; if he had had a larger one, he would have found more.

Oshima means "big island," though most of them are quite small. The one toward which my boat was carrying me was one of the smallest, about an hour's sail from Takamatsu. It was a low, flat island, rising at either end, a saddle between, in which I saw low, whitewashed buildings, too many for a village, too few for a town. The trees, mostly pines, were low, and the shores were long, white-sand beaches. It was a beautiful island—the kind that Stevenson would have liked, or Gauguin.

Then I heard the bells. They sounded like wind bells, the high thin sound carrying on the still air of midmorning, audible over the noise of our motors. As we neared the single pier I saw a group of people walking along the shore. The sound seemed to come from behind them, in the pine groves. When the motor had coughed its last, the chiming of the bells was clear. The people walked nearer, a dozen of them, black against the brilliant white-sand beach. The chiming sounds hung in the air about them.

When they came nearer I saw that they were very old, and that they were all blind. They carried bells in their hands or attached to their staves. They stopped by the pier, and as the few passengers stepped from the boat, they turned their heads, eyes white as marble, to follow the sound of our steps.

Many of the women had lost their hair except, occasionally, for a long white or gray lock hanging beside their faces. Some of the men

77

had ears that were blackened at the edges, crinkled like leaves, as though charred. Several of the old people had no noses, just two holes in their faces. Their hands were like birds' feet, the fingers drawn clawlike to the palm.

They were lepers, the first I had ever seen. Old men and women standing together, looking very much alike, heads slowly turning, eyes like those of statues. They carried bells so that they could be found if they strayed away. They stood in the brilliant sun, which they could not see, like nomads, like a band of survivors—surrounded by unseen beauty. This was the Oshima National Leprosarium.

It was a beautiful island, very beautiful. Rows of old pines like pillars in the white sand; rolling grass-covered hills set against the deep summer sky. On the height at one end was a cemetery, the stones shining. At the other end the island broke into inlets, rocks scattered toward the land. The island held the bay in its arms and the water was so clear that one could see squid lazily puffing themselves along the sandy bottom.

Lepers are often sent to beautiful places, as if in compensation for the ugliness of their disease. Or, perhaps, it is just that, being sent to places far away, they naturally live where the hand of man has not as yet completely destroyed natural beauty.

Later, the doctor at the hospital told me about leprosy in Japan. The majority of lepers come from Shikoku. They suffer what the Japanese call "heavy" leprosy. The light variety, found in India and the rest of Asia, means more noticeable mutilation—fingers missing, toes gone, the terrifying "lion face." Heavy leprosy takes a more interior route and only near the end does it surface and eat into nose and ears. Much earlier, however, lesions appear on the skin, the hands contract like claws, hair disappears, testicles wither and decay, the optic nerve is attacked.

In Japan there are more men than women lepers. Here on Oshima there are 463 men and only 289 women as of this writing. A total of 702 in a hospital compound with a capacity of 860. Originally, it was thought that there were more men because they do more outside work than women. In the Ryukyus, however, the population of which is also prone to this disease, it is the women who work outside, yet the proportion is the same. Men catch leprosy more easily than women do.

If one can say that leprosy is caught. The chief doctor, a gentle, kindly, fussy old man, told me that the only case he had ever known where the disease was actually transmitted directly was the celebrated infection of Father Damien. The doctor's theory was that leprosy, like tuberculosis, is always present, and that only particular constitutions succumb to it. I, he said, was harboring the leprosy bacillus just as, doubtless, I was already full of the tubercle bacillus. That I did not fall ill simply proved that I was not ready to. Those who have leprosy actually die of tuberculosis. Leprosy weakens but takes too long to kill. Its cousin, tuberculosis, gets there first.

Since the disease is not actually contagious it is difficult to understand why lepers are treated as they are. But this lack of danger is something people cannot understand, do not want to understand. This horrible thing must also, somehow, be dangerous. As a consequence lepers are sent to beautiful but inaccessible places such as this island, while sufferers from the much more contagious tuberculosis are allowed nearer civilization.

In Japan the idea of leprosy does not cause the horror that it does in Christian countries, brought up as their inhabitants are on the Bible and *Ben-Hur*, but it is no more widely understood. In addition, the Japanese have a thing about cleanliness and are pleased to find leprosy unclean. At the same time there is more of the disease here than in the West. Consequently, even though a kind of cure has now been discovered—effective, it is said, if the treatment is begun early enough—lepers are forced to live apart in places like this.

It is assumed that I want to see and talk with some of the people on the island or else I would not have come, that I have some kind of authority for being here or else I would not have taken the boat. The doctor makes arrangements for me to be introduced to some of the lepers.

A young man is called from one of the buildings. It is the dormitory where the single men live together. There is another dormitory for unmarried women. Married couples live in apartments. Some of these couples have healthy children. These are allowed to return to the mainland, though the parents must remain behind.

The young man is tall, athletic, about twenty-five. He is the leader of the young people and he looks it. He has that look of sober responsibility that, in Japan as elsewhere, indicates an ability to assume authority. Signs of the disease are already visible. The tips of his ears are brownish, as though tarnished, the flesh in their curves is sunken.

79

His hands are large and strong, but the fingers have begun to curve inward toward the palms. There is also a widening of the jaw. The doctor had told me about these symptoms.

In this young man's case, the disease is taking a rare form. The hairline will recede; the eyebrows will disappear; the nose will collapse, flatten, leaving the nostrils staring; the lips will retract and at the same time the face will widen, furrows growing until the skin is a folded mass around the mouth of a snarling animal—the dread lion face. All of this is twenty or thirty years away. The change will be very gradual. But the young man knows it will happen. He knows what he will look like.

Now he sits beneath the pines with the other young people called out to talk with me. They sit in an attentive semicircle, friendly, smiling. A man near thirty from Shikoku has hands like bird claws yet manages to light his cigarette. Near him are: a girl from Ehime in her twenties, eyebrows gone and now drawn straight with grease-pencil, giving her an impudent expression; a beautiful girl from Kyoto, just nineteen, not a sign of the disease; a man, twenty-two, from Kochi, suffering a swift form of leprosy, one eye already clouded over, hair gone, feet turned in; a boy from Okinawa, fourteen, dark skin, dark eyes, no visible sign as yet of the disease.

They all sit in front of me, silent, expectant. It is understood that I am to talk to them. I tell them about myself, tell them about Tokyo, talk about the traffic jams. They laugh politely but with pleasure, the easy laughter of those who have little to amuse them.

Then I ask them questions about themselves. The boys all like sports and continue to play for as long as they are able. The two leprosaria off the coast of Okayama send their ball teams over and they hold baseball competitions. Everyone likes music, and some of them still play the guitar or the piano. There are two bands, the Stars and the Olives—the latter consisting, mainly, of harmonicas. When I ask which is the better, everyone laughs. The leader explains that the Stars are the better, of course, because everyone in the Olives is blind.

With the bands, is there any dancing? I ask. Well, there was but not so much now. The disease progresses, hands curve, feet curl. There used to be amateur theater too. They still have the sets and props—supplied by the government, as is everything else on the island. But now there is no more theater. The older people were the only ones who knew the parts. But as time went on they could no longer handle the properties, the wigs would no longer fit, the make-up became too painful.

Also, people die off and occasionally one of the younger patients is cured and allowed to leave. In either event the number dwindles. In fifty years, the young people tell me, there will be no leprosarium here. All the old ones, including themselves, will have died—all the young ones will have been cured.

They speak of a cure and they smile as though they know something that I cannot. I have seen this expression on people's faces when they speak of their religion or of a deep and private emotion, such as love. The leader too talks about cures, though he knows that for him there is none.

The beautiful girl from Kyoto turns and looks at the sea. There is no hope for her either, and she is cured. The doctor told me about her. The last of her lesions, just there, along her side, under the light, freshly starched summer kimono she is wearing, will soon vanish. But she cannot return. Her family has disowned her. She has no place else to go. They did this because disease is a disgrace. If it became known that she was a leper, her sisters could not make proper marriages, her brothers could not find proper employment. Her name has been removed from the family register. To the outside world it is as though she never was. And the law is strict. If you have no place to go, no one to take you, then, even though you are cured, you cannot leave. So, for the rest of her life, this healthy and beautiful girl will remain on this island, looking, as now, toward the distant land.

After we have talked we take a walk to the graveyard—the most beautiful spot on the island. Here, with death so near all of them, they treat their dead with care, put them where they can enjoy what they thought beautiful in life.

It is a large cemetery filled with graves and markers, surmounted by a rise on which is a large stone inscribed with the name Amida Buddha. The little boy from Okinawa runs ahead, looking under the bushes, in the lower branches of the pines. A great insect-catcher, like most Japanese boys, he knows where to find the fattest and noisiest cicadas. They always come here, he tells me. There is a buzz in the bushes. He has caught another. He will be saved, I learn. His parents want him back. He has been here one year. Another half-year will see his complete cure.

After we have seen the graveyard, the others drift off. They thank me, they enjoyed the talk, they shake hands or bow. But they have their duties. The boys go back to their fishing or to the carpenter shop to make tables or bird cages, the girls to their sewing, knitting, weaving. Tonight there is a movie. They have a movie once a week. They look forward to it.

I look at them. There is no discontent on any of their faces. Only reserve, friendliness, shyness. They are not despairing but neither are they cheerful. They are dignified.

The leader walks part of the way to the wharf with me, then bows and goes. From the back he looks like any other strong island man, his shoulders square, his neck hiding, from the rear, the widening of his jaws. He is brown, deep brown, from the sun and the boats. But not from swimming. No one swims. The salt water hurts the lesions.

I wait on the pier with the surgeon who comes twice a month to operate. All morning he has been operating. It is useless, he says. He operates on hands, severing tendons. The hand can no longer be used but it looks usable and this to some is preferable to the clenched claw. The nerves are usually so atrophied, he tells me, that he performs even extensive operations under only a local anesthetic.

I hear the bells again and turn. The old blind people are under a stand of pines, their faces in the shade, shadowed from the summer heat. Their heads turn toward our voices as we wait for the boat to leave. Old men, old women, herded closely together, standing there as though waiting for someone.

*   *   *

THE BOAT RETURNED ME to Takamatsu, where, wishing to prolong the beauty, the horror, of Oshima, I stopped at a small stand on the pier and drank a Coca-Cola and thought about what I had seen. But what can I think of something like this? I can only remember, imagine. And then comes the natural celebration—ignoble, we are taught, but natural nonetheless—that I have ten fingers that work, that I can see, that I will live a long time. Invariable as a boomerang, thoughts of disease, of death, turn to thoughts of self.

I live in this country as the water-insect lives in the pond, skating across the surface, not so much unmindful as incapable of seeing the depths. This is because I am not Japanese and can barely imagine what it must be like to be so. I can observe, I can speak the language fairly well and if I cannot read I can at least have things read to me, but Japan is a land that repels empathy. I cannot know what it feels like to be Japanese, but I should guess that the feeling is very special.

The white man who goes native in Samoa or Marrakech, the Japanese who goes native in New York or Paris—this is possible, but it is, I think, impossible for anyone but a Japanese to go Japanese. Perhaps I am too impressed by this people's ideas about themselves, by their real need to find themselves enigmatic. I don't think it is a question of enigma, however. It is simpler. In Marrakech foreigners quite naturally wear native clothes. In Japan no one does and the idea is embarrassing. This is not because the Japanese no longer wear kimono—they do often enough in the country or, on holidays, in the city as well. It is because that acceptance which makes possible the wearing of native costume when one is not a native is missing. It is presumptuous to do so, it is indecorous.

This is very strange. Just as strange is the fact that here expatriates do not become citizens. To be sure, a foreigner's taking out citizenship in Japan is officially all but discouraged. Even leaving aside this and the expatriate's reluctance to belong to anything, his cherishing his own inability to be a part of anything larger than himself, even so, one would think that . . . no, not at all. I only know of two foreigners, there may be more, who have in the past twenty-five years taken out Japanese citizenship.

It is particularly strange when one considers the basic pattern of the expatriate in this land. It begins, like most love affairs, with a great infatuation. Japan is wonderful, the people are marvelous; it is the epitome of nations, the flower of mankind. Since this is no more true of the Japanese than it is of any other people, in time enthusiasm often gives way to disillusion, resulting in an equal swing in the opposite direction. Japan is a prison, the people are guards; it is a straitjacket of a land, home of hypocrisy. But, since this latter stage is as false as the former, it must naturally be succeeded, finally, by something more realistic. If the expatriate persists, refraining from returning to whatever better place he once came from, he will eventually realize that, in some ways, Japan is a nation like many others; that one cannot love or hate an entire country; that one's experience is not large enough for this. Both honeymoon and divorce over, he would be in the mood, finally, to get married.

But he does not. He merely continues to live with his mistress. Perhaps it is because she doesn't want to get married. Perhaps it is that he doesn't want to. Japan is different. It is not better, mind you, not for everyone, but it is different.

I think of those people I know, foreigners, Japanese, who have actually married each other. And I don't remember a single happy couple—though there may be many I don't know of. If he is foreign and she is not, she finds herself transplanted in her own country, and she fades, withers. If she is foreign and he is not, she is suddenly plunged into the reality of being Japanese—water-bug gulped by fish—and the experience either kills her or sends her home.

Of course, I, being married, have a rather poor opinion of the institution and find that one of the parties—me—usually suffers from the union. Still, turn the object as I will, there is something about Japan that does not accommodate itself to my hands, my head, my heart.

*   *   *

COCA-COLA LONG FINISHED, its remains attracting bluebottles, I walk slowly back through the pleasant city and continue my ruminations.

The Japanese always think us younger than we are. That is because they are all so young. The reason they are so young is that they have no conscience, maybe, certainly that there is no cynicism and no corollary of disillusion. No one ever taught them to expect more of life than life can in fact offer. Appearances are reality, the mask is literally the face, and the cynic can find no telltale gap because none exists. The result is a kind of innocence, in our eyes at any rate.

And we know all about this. We moaned its lack all during the nineteenth century and now the new romanticism in manners and clothes, in novels and movies, continues to indicate the extent of the loss we still feel. Since we can still find this quality in children, we call it childlike.

Actually children are destructive and amoral little savages, rendered safe only by their small size. A six-foot two-year-old would be very dangerous. Such observations, however, do not occur to those who moan most loudly over lost innocence. They always like children.

What one finds in Japan is something different. It is a grown-up, very civilized nation that has, somehow, managed to retain this

84

quality that we so prize and that they never think about. To be sure, not all of us like it. Then we find the country vacuous, filled at most with a frenetic gaiety and a morose bathos that all but mock our own earnest and adult endeavors. (Such a feeling was certainly behind General MacArthur's patronizing and ill-judged remark that the Japanese are a nation of twelve-year-olds. Actually, of course, they are a nation of eighteen-year-olds, that excellent age when innocence and experience are as nicely balanced as they ever will be.) But those of us who prize the quality gratefully discover a land where one may be serious but seldom earnest—except when writing books about it —where one can be sad but never tragic.

The Japanese may occasionally be childlike. He is never childish. He knows who he is (alienation is a very recent urban phenomenon in Japan) and what he can do. Perhaps that is why he is so stand-offish when alienated expatriates come moping to his shores. He welcomes them for what they bring—money, English, a breath of fresh air, reflections of foreign lands in those strange blue eyes—but he doesn't bring them home. He puts them up in a hotel.

So considering, I saw that I had reached my own—a perfectly adequate city-type inn with a tiled roof, a dwarf pine or two, and new tatami—smelling like freshly cut grass—on which I lay down and took a nap.

*　　　*　　　*

THIS MORNING I catch the proper boat. Saburo woke me in time, the meatshop having chided him for his lateness yesterday morning. We agreed that he would write me in care of general delivery at Hiroshima telling me the result of the Sunday meeting and anatomy lesson, and that when he came to Tokyo he would stay with me and I would perhaps introduce him to young ladies of easy virtue. He rode off on his bicycle wearing his touring cap, and I walked from the inn to the pier and was first on the boat.

It is going to fabled Onigashima—the island of the ogre-like *oni*. At least that is the name the tourists give it. The natives do not, to them it is plain Megishima, a tall, humped island, covered with trees, and only an hour's boat ride from Takamatsu. Its distinction, however, and the only reason anyone ever goes there, is that it was here that the brave Momotaro—little peach-boy, a version of whose saga

85

I had heard from the fisherman on Iejima—is said to have come with his animal cohorts and chastised the bad *oni*.

It is a typical Japanese story. The Japanese worship success, and it is not surprising that this most famous of fairy tales is about this quality. Momotaro comes and takes away the collected wealth of the *oni*—an admittedly unprepossessing race with fangs and horns—and this he is able to do because he is strong, brave, and has good connections—a dog, a monkey, a pheasant. Also, Momotaro is good and the *oni* are bad. This is important; otherwise the hero's exploits might be interpreted as imperialistic. Not that such a notion ever occurs to any Japanese schoolboy. To be strong is to be good. To be successful is to be even better.

The underdog finds no friend in Japan. Rather, it takes a sentimental culture, such as ours, to find some virtue in being weak. In Japan failure is punished as rigorously as sin is punished elsewhere. The *oni* are wicked mainly because they let Momotaro be victorious. If they had not, there would have been no fairy tale. Fallen heroes are given no apotheoses in this country, unless, as occasionally happens, they fall in recognized attitudes. General Custer would be no hero, though the Apaches might prove popular. If it were not for the stature of such beloved losers as Saigo Takamori, a single Waterloo —one might think—would wash a local Napoleon off the pages of history.

The caves of the *oni* are at the very top of the mountain and are advertised by an enormous full-color plyboard cutout of Momotaro holding a peach in one hand and a sword in the other. Shown as about five years old, the resolute hero, small but powerful, which is how the Japanese think of themselves, is known and beloved by all children and most adults. There are no huge plywood cutouts of the *oni*, I notice.

The young girl guide to the caves appeared to believe in neither Momotaro nor the *oni*. But her actual opinions and those of her memorized tour lecture were difficult to distinguish, and she herself gave little indication as to which was which.

I was the sole visitor. Outside the entrance we had been chatting of Tokyo and the fact that the caverns gave her endless colds. Once inside, however, quite suddenly, looking straight at me, with no self-consciousness whatever, she began her speech. It was for me alone and was apparently, word for word, the same she had been giving, season in and out, to boatload after boatload of awed schoolchildren and their equally impressed elders:

"This cave or, better perhaps, this series of caverns, was initially discovered in the sixth year of the present Showa era. Its origins, however, are veiled in antiquity, and the combined efforts of the anthropological and social-history teams of both Tokyo and Osaka universities have been unable to disentangle the many theories that would account for the existence of these remarkable caves. Now, if all of you will just step to the left—being careful of your heads, please —we will enter the first of the caverns, one which has become known as the entering-room."

All of us—she and I—entered the entering-room, she solicitously holding the flashlight behind her to illuminate my path. Then, standing in the middle of the chamber, she continued, speaking in the rapid, breathless manner of the bus girl, using the high-pitched and hopefully genteel tones of the female radio announcer—both quite different from her ordinary pleasant voice:

"You will be so kind as to observe the central pillar of this chamber. Hewn from solid granite, it is thirty-six meters in circumference. I repeat, thirty-six meters round—and, in either direction, from the corridors you see leading from left and right, you will be enabled to view the presumed assembly hall of the so-called *oni*." She stopped, then said, quite naturally: "You see? You can go this way or that way but either way ends up in that big room. If this pillar ever fell down, I don't know what would happen."

"Is that likely?"

"No, I don't think so." Then, again, professionally: "We will all proceed. Please to be careful of feet and heads." She stopped, looked at me, and said: "On account of the ceiling's being so low here."

And so we went from cavern to cavern. Nothing was left out. She included even the jokes that must have made apprehensive country people chuckle and nervous children titter. At a large, drawer-like recess, she said: "And here is where the so-called *oni* kept their presumed treasure, the fabled hoard of which you have all heard so much. By stepping closer—and please to be careful of that slippery rock—you will observe where this fabulous treasure is said to have once lain. (Pause.) But, alas, there is none there now. (Pause.) Alas." I laughed. She laughed. Then: "And watch out for your head now, one man banged his terribly last year."

87

The lecture continued, room after room. Finally, to dispel the gathered gravity, I asked, lightly: "Do you believe in *oni*?"

I was answered with: "Just who or what the *oni* were is a matter of some scholarly conjecture, but it has become clear beyond reasonable doubt that the folk hero now known as Momotaro was in actuality the son of the then-reigning emperor and that, likewise, his followers in the tale are mere animal personifications of various clans which may, indeed, have used totemic symbols equivalent to dog, pheasant, and monkey. These clans, then, he gathered together for a prolonged attack against this island and against those inhabitants whom we know only as *oni*. Perhaps, then, the *oni* were merely pirates who at that time ravaged these shores."

"Well, then, do you believe in pirates?"

"Not at all. Look, no pirate could ever dig holes like these. All pirates ever did was to sail. Whoever made these caves knew a lot about stone. My father's a stonecutter and he says that in all the time between those people who made these caves and him no one ever found out anything new about how to cut stone. He says these caves are perfect, that they'll never fall down and they'll never need supports. I think slaves made them. Lots of slaves working for a long time under someone who knew something about stone. Slaves always make big and impossible things like this."

"Are you from this island?"

"Yes, I was born here. Why, I've never even been to Osaka. And now, if you will all please to come this way, being particularly careful of this large and overhanging boulder, which some say was so constructed as to fall and block the passage, we will explore the inner chambers."

After more chambers and more explanation, we returned to the entrance. Since I was the last, and perhaps the only, visitor that day, she closed the caves after us. They were secured with only a little latticework bamboo gate, the kind one sees in country gardens. Then we walked down the steep and winding path to the pier.

I wanted to know more about the caves and, in particular, the *oni*. What did they look like? Were they really red, or blue? Did they have fangs and horns? But I was afraid such questions might begin the lecture again. It apparently revolved continuously in her head and any stray remark might set off a segment. So, instead, I told her I had liked the caves.

She smiled. "Did you?"

A silence fell, she kicked at the dust as she walked, then said: "No one ever comes back. You see the caves once. Then you've seen them. Me, I have to look at them every day. All day long I'm up there." She stopped and smiled again. "And I remember when I was little how afraid of them I used to be. All the children were. Maybe they still are. They think the *oni* are still in the back in there some place, all ready to come out and get you. I used to think so too."

"I've always rather liked the *oni*," I confessed. "At least better than I've liked Momotaro."

She looked up, thought, then said: "Oh, they weren't really very nice, I suppose. But, you know, this isn't even the island Momotaro went to, if he ever went to an island. It would be way on the other side of Japan. We started this up on the island here only ten or twenty years ago. No one even thought of Momotaro until the man who had bought the caves came down from Osaka and told us that Momotaro had been here. Of course, the *oni* we had already thought about. Something must have lived in these caves, we thought, and so we decided it was probably the *oni*."

There was another silence. We were waiting by the boat. It showed no sign of leaving.

Such moments always embarrass a Westerner. He is in between: something has ended, something else is beginning, but neither is yet accomplished. He grows gruff, blows his nose, looks in the direction in which he hopes shortly to be moving. Not the Japanese. This is one of the great moments, one of those when the eternal flow is nearest the surface. Hence, I supposed, those painfully prolonged scenes of departure in railway stations all over the country. Hence the good-bye songs over loudspeakers at piers and wharfs. Hence all the colored streamers on a boat that, after all, is only going to the next island. Such a moment is relished, prolonged, and—to the Westerner— stretched out until embarrassment becomes its own anesthetic.

She was silent. The boat was silent. I was silent.

"No one ever comes back," she said, "but you ought to—there aren't enough men on the island. It's two-thirds women."

Not having expected an observation this personal, I, as is my way, backed off and diverted her with: "What about him?" and indicated a boy in a pink shirt, lounging by the railing with a friend in a green shirt. "And him?"

89

"Oh, the first one is spoken for, for years now. And the other one nobody much wants. He's sort of silly."

"And you—will you stay here?"

She looked up and smiled, a plain girl with fine eyes. "Yes, I am to stay here. I'll always be either here at the pier or else up in the caves."

I wanted to say something encouraging, wanted to say that I at least would be back, but the small boat suddenly hooted and instantly began industriously moving away from the pier. I jumped on board. She waved once, then stood there, looking to sea.

*   *   *

ON THE BOAT to Naoshima I pass nearer that perfect cone of an island I saw earlier from a great distance. It is a volcanic-looking peak that makes me think of natives and coral and birds of paradise. Like Fuji, which it somewhat resembles, it compels interest and attention. It is called Ozuchijima and, like all perfectly formed things, has a great power of attraction.

If the Great Pyramid were stripped of all of its human and historical interest, people would still continue to visit it because it is perfect. This searching after geometric beauty, this remembering, as it were, of perfection, is to be observed almost every place in the world. Not, however, in Japan. To the Japanese the perfect is unnerving, suspicious. This wooded triangle reaching toward the sky moves me but not my fellow passengers. They look at it, but they do not approve. It is too big for one thing, too regular for another.

I ask, but no one on board knows a thing about it, except one man who has heard that it has no water and is therefore uninhabited. Finally, however, an old lady, sitting some distance away on the matted deck, says that once there was a snake there, a big snake, an enormous snake. Then a goddess came down and killed it and that is all that she knows. What was the goddess's name? Doesn't know. What was the snake's name? Doesn't know. Probably one of those old-time deities, goodness knows which one, it was all so long ago.

The other passengers are staring at this perfect island with something approaching resentment. Suddenly, there is a pleased cry from the other side of the cabin.

On the other side we are passing another island, all rocks and sands

90

and pines, terribly Japanese. With relief, all the passengers crawl across the mats to look at an island they like. I am left alone with this mysterious, pointed, wooded, waterless island that looks so very alien in this Japanese sea.

*　　　*　　　*

NAOSHIMA IS a small, beautiful, somehow sad little island. A tiny town in squares and patches. On one side, beginning several feet back from the sea, a ruined shrine, a general store, a shaved-ice shop. The sadness comes perhaps from the loneliness—in the early afternoons there never seems to be anyone on these islands.

One old man, however, is sitting in front of a weathered store front. He is sorting dried squid into various sizes. He clears his mouth with a dipper of water, spits it out, takes another mouthful, sprays it over the squid he is holding, then lays it aside, takes another dipperful, spits it out, takes another mouthful, sprays it over the next squid, lays it aside. When he sees me he stops and courteously answers my questions.

This small island, he says, used to belong to the mainland clans, and they were so loyal here that even after the Meiji Restoration they insisted upon continuing to give their rice to the lord of the clan instead of to the emperor, but that nevertheless the emperor once came here and, if I didn't believe it, I had only to go over to the other side of the island, a short walk, and look at the big monument commemorating the event.

Typical island, typical legend. Many of these places I am finding have stories like this—dull, pointless, indicative only of loyalty. All have happy endings—it wasn't really disloyalty to the emperor after all because someone big comes along and says it is all right, that they can give their rice to the emperor's tax-collectors but in the name of the former lord, and so no one loses face.

Japanese loyalty. I cannot approve of it, and I certainly do not like it. Mindless devotion—whether of samurai or kamikaze—leaves me as unmoved as does the less spectacular variety back where I come from. It is actually a kind of laziness. You let something or someone else—country, flag, government—make up your mind. You also, of course, make them responsible. Perhaps this is the true attraction

91

of devotion. If you can make someone else responsible, then you don't have to be responsible for yourself. Nothing—including your own life—is your own fault.

The Japanese carry it one step further. Nothing is anyone's fault. This is because no one will take responsibility for anything. It is passed around like a plate of suspect *sushi*. No one will take a piece; everyone declines politely. The same thing occurs in the West as well, to be sure. But there, eventually, someone will step forward. In Japan no one does.

It is a mystery, therefore, how anything gets done. And things do get done, at a ferocious rate, in Japan. I used to think that behind the ostensible leaders stood others, less well known, and that behind them stood still others, each more powerful than the other until, their numbers dwindling, we eventually came to one bent old man, whom none of us had ever even heard of, who from his rustic retreat would say yes or no; and, personal responsibility bringing with it personal power, he would be instantly obeyed.

I no longer think so, not now that I know about the conference, the joint meeting—an institution so typical of Japan that I would not be surprised to learn that it is a Japanese invention. Here no one needs to take responsibility. The board takes it. A consensus emerges. A decision is made, but it is the board that makes it. And the board is no one.

While I was thinking, the old man was continuing, apparently happy for a listener. Other famous visitors included Toyotomi Hideyoshi—contemporary of Ivan the Terrible, Dianne de Poitiers, and John Calvin (my interjection, not his)—on his way to the Korean wars, and the remnants of the Heike clan, whose retreat from the battle of Yashima covered most of these islands. Also there was Keikoin. He was a very strong priest, and he was born here, a local hero. He was useful. When the great west winds came and the boats could not leave, he would go out, tell everyone to hang on, and push, right into the teeth of the wind. This single push would carry the boat safely to its destination.

There was more, but I have forgotten what it was. Finally the old man stopped. He picked up the next squid, sprayed it, laid it aside. He was a very old man. Under his open kimono his chest was brown but the skin seemed thin as rice paper. The sparse hairs were white against it, the bones showed through, the kimono rustled as he sorted the squid.

The boat that had brought me finally left. I sat on the pier and watched it grow small. I could hear the sound continue behind me, the slap of each squid as the old man went on adding to the pile at his feet.

*   *   *

THE SUN SLOWLY DISAPPEARED, hidden behind a late-summer haze. I turned away from the silent village with its single old man sorting squid, and walked along the deserted black-sand beach, following the course of the ship, looking out at it until the last trace of its smoke had disappeared from the horizon. I felt left behind, though the choice to stay here had been my own. I felt lonely.

Several schoolboys were digging away in front of me, busy with sticks and shovels. They were uncommunicative because they were digging sandworms for night fishing and this was serious business indeed.

I turned from them. Above the beach, standing in a grove of pines, looking out to sea as though they too had been following the vanished ship, was a group of girls. They stood holding the handlebars of their bicycles. They were about fifteen or sixteen years old and wore school uniforms—navy-blue, white-piped sailor collar, buttoned cuffs, ankle hose. Their hair was either in pigtails or worn long and straight and held by a ribbon.

I looked up at them, then walked slowly past.

One turned to the other and I heard her ask: "You think he can speak?"

I stopped, looked up at them, and said that I could.

Smiling at one another, they walked slowly out of the grove and down to the beach, trundling their bicycles, hands on handlebars. They looked like girls being led by animals, hands on horns. We began walking along the beach.

They were at the age where they were both children and adults. From time to time one would chase another as though they were five-year-olds; at other times, they walked as straight and solemn as if they were twenty-five. They walked beside me but apart. I would

93

turn from time to time to watch them. Sometimes they screamed with laughter and dropped their bicycles. Sometimes they walked straight, looking ahead as though deaf. The tires left long snakelike tracks in the sand ending at the now distant stand of pine and the almost invisible group of little worm-digging boys.

If all girls of this age are shy, then Japanese girls are sometimes more shy than is normal. I did not speak, not wanting to lose them. It was nice walking with them on a beach where I had never been, my footprints separate from theirs and their tire tracks.

Finally, one spoke. I must find it strange that they should be wearing their school uniforms when school had not yet begun. Well, the reason for this was that the uniforms had been in mothballs all summer long but now autumn was almost here, and they were airing them by wearing them.

"We smell very strange," said the smallest of the girls.

"We smell like mothballs," said another, giggling.

I turned to the girl walking next to me, a beautiful girl with long hair and fine eyes set wide apart, and asked what they did all during the long summer when there was no school.

Oh, they loafed, she said, using the Tokyo slang phrase *bura-bura*— they loafed around and didn't do much. They certainly didn't study. There would be enough study all winter long.

Did they help their mothers?

But this was talking down to them. For a second or two there was no answer, then the girl at my side turned—graciously, she was no child, not at this moment at any rate—and said, yes, sometimes. She must have looked much like her mother just then, she was suddenly a young lady. At the same time two of her friends ran their bikes into each other and collapsed, screaming with laughter, like little children.

Yet talking with the girls was easy. They used simple words, accommodating themselves to my grammar and vocabulary, using the standard language of Tokyo, though among themselves they occasionally murmured in the island tongue, which sounded somewhat Osaka-like but was still incomprehensible to me.

At the very end of the long sand beach we sat and rested on a group of rocks. We also stopped talking. When you sit down, you become a group, and if you do not know each other well, there is silence. There was no rushing to fill it with meaningless conversation. They waited until it was naturally over. They looked idly for shells, or spread their skirts on either side of them on the rocks. They looked at the sea or the sky or me—all with a natural grace rare in city girls.

None of them were beautiful except the girl nearest me, but they all seemed beautiful. Their silence, their calm waiting for the talk to begin again, their acceptance of things as they were—this made them beautiful.

They had the dignity of being fifteen. This natural dignity, as though they were already mature, seems to last longer in the country.

All during the latter part of our walk the girls had talked freely, had asked questions and answered them. They seemed never to have heard of that horrid ideal—the well-brought-up Japanese maiden. This creature must gaze with downcast eyes at your feet. She must answer only with faint murmur or, better, insulting giggle; must be vague in all matters, including her name and age; must appear to do everything with the greatest reluctance; and should, as often as possible, appear almost disagreeably pensive. But these country girls were natural, charming, candid.

The silence grew, stretched, then waned. When it was time, the girl next to me asked me to tell them about Tokyo. I started with stories of traffic jams and other disagreeable aspects of city life.

"No, I don't mean things like that. I mean, what is it like? Do—well, do people stay up all night?"

I supposed that a few probably did but that most were asleep by midnight. New York, now, on the other hand—

She was not interested in New York. "Midnight," she said, wonderingly. "Here, on this island, everyone is asleep by nine."

They went to bed early because they rose early, about five in the morning, when the fishermen went out, when the farmers left for the fields. Her father was a farmer and she had never in her life slept past seven in the morning except once, and that was only because there had been a funeral and the whole family had gone, but she had been sick and hadn't gone, had stayed at home alone.

She smiled at her sloth. She wanted to sleep, just once, until eight in the morning, just for the thrill of it. But she never had and she guessed she probably never would.

The other girls sighed. They felt the same way. I said that I was certain that, after they had grown up, sleeping until eight in the morning would be a common occurrence. The others smiled at this, smoothed their skirts, poked fingers at roving crabs.

The girl sitting next to me did not smile. She looked out to sea. The possibility of being in bed until eight in the morning seemed unlikely. Growing up seemed unlikely. She looked like some lady in exile, past despair; she turned her eyes to the horizon, but expected no sail.

"What will you do when you grow up?"

She turned and gently smiled. "Oh, I will get married and have children."

"Here?"

She nodded.

"But that is such a long time away."

She smiled again. "Not really. I leave school in two years." Then: "Did you see the boy at the store, the son of the owner?"

I had not.

"Well, he is seventeen now, just out of school. I will marry him."

I smiled, thinking this some last childhood dream. Perhaps not even that, perhaps it was some ambition she was confiding; perhaps he did not know of her feelings; perhaps her only assurance was that of hope. I said it sounded romantic.

"No, it isn't romantic. It was decided last year. His father came to see my father. It didn't take even fifteen minutes. Girls marry early on this island."

"But do you like him?"

She nodded, looking out at the sea. "He is a nice boy—he works hard."

The other girls seemed not to be listening, but they were very quiet. The sea lapped against the rocks. A bird called. An invisible boat hooted. The girl with long hair looked at the sea.

In another ten years she would look like her mother and would have had several children. She would no longer be what she was now.

At fifteen there is an awakening. A girl begins to know who she is. And she is not only a wife or a mother. She is more. But eventually she will be forced to forget. She will be the honored *oku-sama*, the person-inside, or the person-around-in-the-back, however you translate it. Her husband will do whatever he likes. So will her children, if they are boys. She will think that this is somehow right. And that it is also somehow right that she never gets to do anything she herself wants, and never again meets the person she is now.

"I'll marry him," she says. "I will stay on the island. I will have children here." She seems to have abdicated already. Just now she has begun to discover what kind a person she is. And just now she is turning away.

She has abdicated but she has not yet forgotten. She sits on the rock, a schoolgirl, her bicycle lying in front of her. She is still whole. She still belongs to herself. Soon she will make herself forget what it was like to be fifteen with the whole world inviting.

*   *   *

THE OTHER GIRLS had raced off down the beach like children, screaming and laughing. The conversation had not been very interesting, not to them. Now freed from the restraint of the occasion, they raced away, their hair flying behind them, their sailor collars stiff in the breeze. The beautiful girl with whom I had been talking stayed. She was returning to town and so was I.

It was late afternoon but a summer haze had settled and it seemed like dusk. The way back was long and the beach was darkened. We talked about my country and her country.

"Don't you get lonely?" she asked.

"Sometimes I do."

"But being away from your country and your people. I cannot imagine being away from mine."

"You would be if you went to Tokyo."

"Yes, I suppose so. I'd like to go. Just once, just to see it."

"Maybe on your honeymoon."

She smiled. "I know. But we don't have honeymoons here, you know. We have a big party and almost everyone drinks too much and then we all get up and go back to work the next day."

"Are you going to have children?" I asked, delicately. She was fifteen and should know about things. At the same time I felt hesitant. She was still a child.

She was not hesitant. Yes, she was going to have a number, she decided, but not too many. Besides, they would be busy working. And, besides that, the island had been electrified several years before.

I stopped, thinking I had misunderstood.

I hadn't, however. She went on to explain. Last year, she had read, a remote part of the southern island of Kyushu had finally been electrified. And this year's birth rate was just a fraction of what it had

97

been the year before. You see—if there are no lights, then people go to bed before they are ready and they can't sleep. And if you can't sleep, then there are only a few things you can do and making babies is one of them. Did I understand?

I nodded. At the same time I was surprised. No fifteen-year-old Japanese girl I had ever met had ever said anything like that. I glanced at her as she walked beside me, her profile against the pines. It was bland, unreflective, innocent.

We were nearing town. We passed the general store. I looked at her again to see if she would look in to see her future husband. She did not. We walked on.

"There's the inn," she said. "If you're going to stay, that's the only place. And you will stay, I think. There are no more boats." I thanked her. "I will help you," she said.

She did. Introduced me to the innkeeper, a fat woman, took me up to my room, inspected it, complained about the view, sat down when I asked her to, had tea with me after the woman had padded away, floor creaking.

We leaned against the low sill, looking out of the window at the sea, now dark. The light was gray, pearly, the cloudless haze-covered sky was like half an oyster shell lowered over us. I looked at her arm, lying next to mine on the unpainted wood of the sill.

Her skin was beautiful. Perhaps nowhere on earth is there more beautiful skin than in Japan. Usually hairless, it is not like a mere covering. It is as though the entire body, all the way through, were composed of this soft, smooth lustrousness. I touched her arm. She looked at me, her eyes dark under the darkened sky.

*   *   *

I HAD MADE a mistake. To me it had seemed natural. Our being together. My loneliness. And then—for this is the way we think—the frankness about Kyushu when it was still dark. And then her not looking for her boy-husband, nor being ashamed of being seen with me, even though engaged. Then this extraordinary business with the inn and her sitting close to me and the fat woman regarding this all impartially as if it were usual. Perhaps, I had been thinking, this was some lovely island custom of which I had been aware. All of this led me to my mistake.

She did not understand. She allowed me to stroke her arm—soft, full, with that translucent skin; let me turn her hand over as though it were some marine animal we were both examining, and hold it; did not object to my putting a hesitant arm around her waist; and was completely and genuinely surprised when I tried to kiss, touch cheeks, rub noses—whatever it was I had on my lonely mind.

How often does this happen in Japan, I wonder—daily, hundreds of times, I should guess. A Japanese would have known that it was impossible; a Westerner always hopes that it won't be.

The foreigner who gets excited in the mixed bath, that classic comic character. I often enough make fun of him; I often enough become him. This is because of what we feel in Japan—the promise, the lure of the place, the mirage of pleasure, the distant vista of—uh —happiness.

It is never quite where you are but it is always just around the corner. The people are so agreeable, so permissive. They are, after all, very different, and you are, after all, very different from them. Why not?—since it seems to be offered, why not just take what you want, what you need?

You can, I suppose. Certainly a part of my quest is devoted to seducing the natives—a travel adjunct observed by traveling foreigner and traveling native alike. But in the case of fifteen-year-old girls you would be wise not to. If you are like me, you want to seduce rather than corrupt, and you attempt to maintain the fuzzy line separating the two. I want to take without hurting, I tell myself. This is not, however, true. I don't want to take. I want to be given. And this is what the friendly Japanese always seem on the verge of doing —giving. And sometimes they do, though I should add that it is easier to make friends with boys than with girls.

And I, innocent despite experience, go around hoping to be seduced and consequently read such unlikely intentions into the thoughts of this little girl who has kindly helped me find a room, into even those of the fat woman who has, of course, seen nothing unusual. They must have many such helpful children on the island.

I did not, I was happy to observe, feel guilty. My years here have taught me at least this much. But I did feel—Japanese feeling— ashamed, and—universal feeling—put out.

Nor did I share any of this wisdom with the suddenly sober little fifteen-year-old who, I had managed to convince myself, had been making advances to me. Instead, I sat back, smiled, and looked out of the window again. So did she. Then she giggled and began prattling again, smelling of moth balls and, under this pervading odor, of her own soft skin, that delicious rice-powder smell that makes one think hungrily of bread freshly baked.

I sat there, at least enjoying some of the feeling of the shame upon which I insisted. Ashamed of being big and lumbering and stupid. This is how the foreigner traditionally feels in the small, fragile Japanese house. There he sits all hands and feet, afraid of sticking an elbow through a *shoji* pane.

He never gets over it, even after many years. He may, however, refine the feeling, as I have done: I no longer feel clumsy around their houses; I feel clumsy around their feelings.

My major feeling, however—I have no idea what hers was, if she had any—was petulance. I had been, somewhat obscurely it must have seemed, offended. Now cross, querulous, I sat glumly, and she finally, perhaps sensing a lessening of welcome, stood up to take her leave.

She had short legs; she looked dumpy in her school uniform; her eyes were too far apart, making her look bovine.

Could she and her little friends come and call in the evening and talk some more?

No, they could not, I answered, adding churlishness to my other faults.

I went to bed early. It is perhaps true that the best way to get to know a people is to sleep with them, but this is complicated in Japan. Innocence always gets in the way, just the kind of innocence that I—like everyone else—want to go to bed with. I occupied an indulgent half-hour or so with thoughts of what I should have done, what I now decided (safely alone in bed) I had really wanted to do: torn schoolgirl uniform, thighs immodestly up in the air, cries for mercy, etc. Eventually, however, I grew bored and fell into a deep and satisfactory sleep.

*   *   *

THE NEXT MORNING the boat waited at the pier, smoking, the sea hidden by the mist. The sun was still behind a mountain. The sky was gray. The mist rose from the sand in the growing warmth. Still

100

sleepy, wanting coffee—apparently unheard of on this island—ill content with a cup of green tea, I was walking up the plank gangway to the ship when I heard myself called.

Gaijin-san—Mr. Foreigner. I turned and there in the mist was the girl. Slightly behind her, dimmer in the morning fog, two of her friends were standing. They had come to see me off.

"Did you sleep well?" asked the girl, gravely.

"Not very well. Did you?"

She smiled. "Oh, yes. I always sleep well."

All three stood there silent in the rising mist. She was beautiful, brown eyes wide apart, long hair at her shoulders. Her hands behind her. Then I saw that they all had something in their hands. They were hiding something. They showed me. Three spools of paper ribbon—green, blue, red. They held them out. She took the loose ends in her hand and gave them to me to hold.

"Are you going to Tokyo?" she asked, the mist rising between us.

"Yes, eventually." The first morning breeze.

"Will you ever come back here?"

"Probably not."

The air was stirring, the mist was thinning. It was growing lighter. She turned to hear what the other two were saying. They had discovered a butterfly, a brilliant yellow in the morning mist. They gave her their paper ribbons and went chasing after it, disappearing into the mist.

"It would be nice if you could stay," she said, looking straight at me. She meant live on the island, talk to her and her friends occasionally. That was all she meant.

The boat whistle sounded, high, thin. Her friends raced back, the last of the mist swirling about them. Each took a spool of paper ribbon.

Now the mist was rising fast. The sky behind the mountain was red. The yellow butterfly danced over the water. The girl pushed back her hair, stirred by the breeze. I stood on the deck, the paper-ribbon ends in my hand. The boat shuddered, whinnied, began wallowing. I smiled.

"Come back sometime," said the beautiful fifteen-year-old girl with the long hair.

The boat pulled away, the paper ribbons unrolled, the spools turned in their hands, three slender strands of colored paper looped

101

between pier and boat, the sun rising behind the emerging mountain.

The paper unrolled. The girls smiled and waved. Then the free ends floated from their hands, floating on the sea breeze like pennants. I held the three strands, which floated high in the air and then sank to the widening sea between us.

The mist rose like a curtain, obscured the mountain, revealed the beach, the pier, the three girls. They looked like small children, small on the black pier, the black mountains behind them.

The sun lifted itself above the mountains, flying. The rising mist turned gold. The entire island floated large on the sea like a mirror. The girls were gone, swallowed into the morning.

*   *   *

AT THE PORT of Uno—now a part of Tamano City—you know at once that you are not on an island. Not only are there factories and smokestacks, but the back of the city is turned on the sea.

Except on large, mainland-like islands such as Shodoshima, islands welcome the sea: it is their road, their kitchen. The mainland, however, uses the sea as a garbage can and resents the timeless presence of an ocean observing the ephemeral activities of town and city. Quite obviously, Uno's interests are not marine. It barely tolerates its own port.

Civilization always makes a mess at its boundaries. This is why suburbs are so untidy, why port towns look disreputable. Islands are clean, spare. Countries are dirty, wasteful.

Waiting for the bus, I spend the time watching the crabs on the rocks stalking back and forth, menacing each other.

*   *   *

THE BUS IS CROWDED, and in the press opposite me there is a country man in a gray felt hat making what I guess is a trip from the town to the city. He wears rubber boots and Western clothes of the kind always worn by country people on trips: brown, gray, tan, the colors of the earth itself. His white shirt is buttoned at the neck but he wears no tie. He carries an umbrella with a mottled celluloid handle and around one wrist hangs his purse, big, black, imitation-leather, large as a lady's handbag. It probably contains his money—though it is

102

also probably much too large for the amount carried. People from the country, more than most, are terrified at the thought of losing their money.

His nose is flat, a farmer's nose, and his teeth are all gold. He is unshaved but has put on his hair a pomade that I can smell from where I sit. His hands are twice as large as mine, with cracked nails and skin red with years of wind and sun. His eyes are the eyes of country people all over the world. Set in wrinkles, they seem blurred, as though he cannot focus them, as though he, who has spent his whole life standing in a field, cannot see the swiftly passing forest, mountain, village, as though he can see only that which is still: the wide field, the distant sea, the open sky.

*   *   *

AFTER A FEW HOURS of the long, dirty bus ride from Uno to Shimotsui, after the identical coastal cities, the depressing stretches of mountains, I do not feel like another trip to the celebrated heights of Washu-zan. This is a sea trip, not a mountain trip. Besides, I have already been there.

Washu-zan is impressive. From its heights one gazes out over this middle section of the Inland Sea, and on clear days the peaked mountains of Shikoku stand faintly sketched on the horizon. If I stood there now, I could look back over my travels. Naoshima, Oshima, Onigashima—the islands would stretch like steppingstones back to my journey's beginning.

The heights of Washu-zan seem to have been named after the eagles that congregate there. Big sleek eagles, like enormous crows, with wild staring eyes holding that half-demented look that all eagles have. They glide above, staring, while the tourists gape below.

The view is celebrated, and how the Japanese love a view. Vistas are to them what forests are to the Germans—occasions for more than pleasure, opportunities for an almost mystical union with something deep and solid in the national character. And if no mountains are available from which to view, the Japanese will troop to the top of anything else at hand.

Every department store roof is jammed with admiring people. Tokyo Tower, that orange four-legged monster, taller than anything except some obscure television antenna in Arizona, was put up,

103

apparently, so that thousands could scramble to its top and look off. Children press their noses to the glass, old people gaze, stern and sad, boys and girls talk of flying, jumping. There is a continual commotion about the high-fenced edges.

High places excite the Japanese. Jumping from a height remains a favorite form of suicide. There is no question of jumping at Washu-zan, however. The slope is too gradual. It is covered with rocks, azalea, and the debris of the sightseers. Every day, hundreds come, pulled up the slopes by smoking diesel buses. Monthly, thousands stand transfixed, not by beauty but by height.

There is something in the Japanese that responds inordinately to height. The love of ropeways, cable cars, lifts. No respectable mountain now comes unequipped. The Vesuvius funicular may go into receivership, but little Tsukuba in Ibaragi, a hill one can walk up, has a cable car that makes so much money that both a restaurant and a hotel on its modest summit have proved possible. Plans are afoot for a lift up Fuji, that last bastion of popular mountain-climbing. There is none as yet, however, at Washu-zan.

There is really no need. The slope is very gradual and a highway reaches the top. The bus company makes all the money. It has opened up the small restaurant, the ice-cream stands, the kiddy rides for uninterested youngsters, the photo cabinets. The happy mountaineer gets an ice-cream cone, has his picture taken, eats some noodles, buys some postcards, glances at the Inland Sea spread before him like a banquet, and then, happy at having been high, gets back into the bus for the hour-long drive back to Okayama. He has seen the view.

*   *   *

VIEWED FROM A HEIGHT—from the top of Chikami-yama on Shikoku, or from this terrace of Washu-zan—the islands spread out as though on a table. They remind one of a scattered jigsaw puzzle or a mighty game of checkers. A calm sea reflecting each low shape, these convoluted and somehow decorative islands stretch into invisibility. They remind one of something man-made. One thinks of Sesshu, of Claude Lorrain, of Seison, of Poussin.

To look at a Japanese landscape is, often, to think of art. To look over the middle Inland Sea is, for me, to think of the rock garden at the Ryoan-ji in Kyoto—a rectangle of white sand from which rises a number of large stones—and to realize what this amazing piece of landscaping is about. It is not about a mother tiger and her young crossing a river, nor about geometry, nor music, nor astromony, nor mathematics—proffered explanations all. It is about islands in the sea.

Others, looking at the Inland Sea, have thought of tray landscapes, those common and artfully constructed dishes of miniature seas and mountains that have been called imaginary landscapes made for the pleasure of artists to whom reality is, perhaps, a disappointment. Not at all—tray landscapes are like photographs: no imagination needed, no fancy necessary. You take a tray, some stones, some sand; you bring them to a height, sit down, and faithfully copy.

To the Western eye a landscape this artful-appearing does not seem quite real. It is so beautiful it seems ideal. It seems, literally, too good to be true. To the Japanese eye, however, such perfection seems real enough but unwelcome. Tray landscapes are not considered a major art and, with the exception of a few celebrated heights, the beauty of the Inland Sea is little noticed. We of the West, however, are ravished by such scenes, no matter how unreal they seem. And at the same time we are intrigued with a sense of the familiar.

Then we recognize where we have seen similar views. When Gozzoli or Paolo Uccello wanted an imaginary backdrop, when Giovanni Bellini or Piero di Cosimo needed an exotic landscape in the distance, when Puvis de Chavannes or Maxfield Parrish required an ideal land—then all of these painters created a painted paradise that closely resembled the humped and humanized country of the Inland Sea.

It is not to the taste of all travelers. Perhaps the eighteenth-century wanderer, with his sense of the ordered and the ideal, would have most loved it. This is where Rasselas and Vathek should have come, where Haydn ought to have placed his uninhabited island, where Paul and Virginie belonged. Consequently, perhaps, the succeeding century would have found here little to please. The Japanese continue to regard unfinished nature with the delight early evidenced by Chateaubriand and are to this extent still nineteenth-century—or else the romantic sensibility as it is known in Europe is Japanese. In any event, Byron, with his taste for crags and tarns, would have passed through the Seto Naikai without a glance. Great ravines, gorges, waterfalls, the startled deer, Wordsworth country—this is Shikoku, not the islands of the Inland Sea.

The attitude of celebrated travelers would have varied. Charles Waterton, Kinglake, Norman Douglas—no matter their other differences—would have agreed that civilization was pressing disconcertingly close. Doughty would certainly have demanded more discomfort than these hospitable islands can afford. But Beckford would have loved them. If one expects nature and artifice, extensive woods and a distant pagoda, or the green roof of an ancient shrine seen floating above a grove centuries old—then one comes to the Inland Sea.

Borrow might best have liked this sea, these islands, because he liked his landscape peopled. The wilderness meant little to him. There always had to be a house in the middle distance; there always had to be someone to look at, someone to listen to. Late-nineteenth-century travelers delighted in the picturesque fisherman, the quaint costume, the amusing woman, the adorable child. They made them part of the genre scene, an undifferentiated grouping, family balancing both nearby grove and distant prospect. Borrow, who understood both landscape and people, would have seen through the picturesque. He would have suspected legend, myth, a people different from other peoples. And he would have been right.

*   *   *

ON THE BOAT from Shimotsui I became acquainted with one of the crewmen, a young sailor of twenty who, never having before spoken to a foreigner, had lots to say. We must see each other more. The boat was to spend the night at Honjima before returning to the mainland, so I asked him to visit me at my inn.

He comes from Shikoku, is half a year out of the Japanese Navy, doesn't drink, doesn't smoke, and lost his virginity—just once—last year. All of this comes out immediately and is followed by presents: a sailor shirt and pictures of life in the naval base at Kure.

Hundreds of young men, all identical, all doing calisthentics; famous monument to some naval hero; he and friend—friend saluting, he with cap off, head shaved, staring into camera; he and girl on rocks, he sliding on rock, one arm tentatively about her waist, she laughing in somewhat professional manner. Was this the young lady responsible for the loss of his virginity? Oh, no, not at all. She was the friend of a friend of a friend. The youth of Japan always goes around with friends of friends.

We next talk about history. He knows an extraordinary amount, all of it from the *kodan*, that collection of spoken tales about the more heroic exploits of the Tokugawa period. Do I know about Jirocho from Shimizu? Oh, I do? But do I know about the time when he almost lost an eye? I don't? That is good. He will tell me.

He knelt on the mat, just like the old-fashioned *kodan* reciter. His imitation was excellent. At the high point he would half-stand, his weight on one knee, the other foot flat on the mat, his going-to-the-bath kimono raked up, hands in the air, an impressive gesture. He also delivered the dialogue for all of the characters, sliding opposite from time to time to sketch in the adversary. How the hero almost lost an eye I have no idea. Until I became used to it, his Japanese was old fashioned, provincial, and of great difficulty.

And did I know about left-handed someone-or-other, the famous sculptor, who was left-handed because they had cut off his right arm at the shoulder with a sword from some reason or other, but he went right on with his left anyway? No? Then I couldn't have heard about the cat, could I? No, I could not have.

He began. This time I understood more:

"Well. One day a priest asked this famous sculptor to make him a mouse and to make it lifelike. So he went to work with his good left hand and soon he had carved a marvelous mouse. Hmm-hmm, said the priest. This looks good enough, but will it fool my cat, I wonder. So he put it on the floor and the cat came in and took one look and pounced directly on it. Then the priest was very satisfied and gave the sculptor a lot of money."

Pause. I began to express appreciation, but the end was not apparently yet. Why had the cat jumped like that on the mouse? came the rhetorical question. "Because...this clever, left-handed sculptor ...had carved it...from a piece of...dried fish!"

Hearing all the talk and laughter, the proprietor of the inn, an old man, appeared, bowed, blinked, came in, sat down, and at once said: "Speaking of cats..." Then he told us the story of the monster cat of Nabeshima which was really a wicked woman in disguise who sat on samurai in their sleep and smothered them.

The young man, impatient during this recitation, waited until it was over and then told me about the great toad that swallowed whole armies and then belched them up again and wasn't even hurt by all the swords and lances and spurs.

The old man nodded gently, waited, and then, with the air of disclosing a fact of vital importance, began by observing that he didn't suppose that I had ever heard of the land of Nambu, had I? No, I was sorry, but I had never heard of Nambu.

Oh, that was all right. No need to apologize. Almost no one knew where it was. In the north somewhere. At any rate, that was the land whence came the *bakemono*. He hesitated, repeated the word, impressing it upon me. It means something supernatural but more than a ghost. A generic term, it includes all kinds of monsters, some, indeed, so monstrous that they have no proper names at all.

In Nambu, among the mists and clouds, the *bakemono* congregated in surprising numbers. Then they would descend upon this very island. Indeed, Keikoin— Did I know who he was? He was a strong priest. Yes, I had heard about him on another island where he pushed boats into the sea. Oh, he did? Well, the old man who ran the hotel didn't know anything about that, but this Keikoin once fell into the clutches of one of the fiercest of all the *bakemono*. He slashed at it, and it changed its shape. He slashed again, and it turned into four one-footed monsters, who tried to step on him. But then, naturally, he killed them all, and since that time they have ceased to bother the villagers. Now hadn't that just been a scare though?

The sailor, who had been listening with narrowed eyes, said, slowly: "Well, in my home town—and it was just a little before I was born, so it wasn't so long ago like your story about one-footed monsters and things—there was this boy who was bringing his little brother back home from fishing, and the little boy wouldn't come along properly, and so he left him, thinking he would come home by himself. But he didn't, and soon his parents and everyone else were out looking, and they looked for weeks and weeks. So, finally, they gave up, and then a year or two later some hunter saw something small and naked, and he caught it, and it was some strange little animal...."

The young man paused, looked meaningfully first at the old man, then at me. The old man was looking out of the window, his fingers absently drumming the top of the table.

"Well," said the sailor, finally, "it was him all right. And he kicked and bit and scratched, but they put clothes on him because he was all

108

naked, and then they asked what had happened. He tamed down after a while and said that something had taken care of him, but they never found out what that something was. Sometimes it seems as though it was like a man, a very tall, black man, only it wasn't a man...."

"And then?" I asked, leaning forward.

He looked pained. "That's all I ever found out."

At once the old man turned to me with: "Now, when I was a boy, and that was in the Meiji period, I personally knew an old man on Megishima, and one dark night as he was going through the grave-yard..."

The stories went on for some time until the sailor became so cross and the old man so loquacious that I began looking at my watch and yawning. After I had done this some dozen times without success, I finally took a more direct approach, saying it was so late the sailor had better spend the night at the inn. Still the old man prattled on until at last I asked if he could call a maid to spread another bed while we bathed. Finally the old man stood up, professed surprise at the time, bade us a pleasant good-night, and went off calling the maid.

In the bath, the young sailor, squatting on his heels as he dashed water over himself, observed that in his opinion old people tended to forget a lot and that that was why they made up so much.

Upstairs, back in bed in our cotton kimono, he was in better humor and began to talk about samurai and chivalry, subjects in which he had a complete interest. For him, *bushido*, the code of the samurai; *giri*, obligation to the death, and beyond; *ninjo*, for which "human feeling" is no adequate translation—all these were very real. They now play little part in modern Japanese thought, though they are much spoken of. Perhaps they never did—maybe they were always like our "virtue" and "goodness," desirable qualities but so difficult to attain that the attempt is rarely made. But this young sailor believed in them, as perhaps had the real samurai. Certainly, he seemed a rare and misplaced spiritual descendant of those who had once believed in such chivalric concepts.

For him the navy was ideal. He had left it, reluctantly, only because, an eldest and filial son, he had to have work that would provide for the expensive old age of his parents. For him the navy had provided glorious tradition; lots of virtuously doing without and putting up with; lots of rigor; some beatings and slaps in the face; more standing at full attention until fainting. He had loved it.

"If that's your attitude," I asked, "how did you ever manage to lose your virginity?"

He blushed, then said that he had thought he needed the experience. He said it virtuously, safely, nodding his head in self-congratulation at the end.

A puritan, also a little prig. The permissiveness of Japan does not prepare one for these pockets of puritanism into which one slips now and again. This smiling, healthy young man was a product of the Tokugawa times. Now he was also something of a throwback, a sport. Very rigorous with himself, his head full of laudable ideals, he was sure to get into trouble in modern Japan. The sixteenth or seventeenth centuries were his times. Now, for such few boys who incarnate the pure samurai spirit, there is only the armed forces or the gangs. In the navy he had tasted the joys of discipline. If he could have become a real big-city old-fashioned gangster, he would have found similar bonds—a whole society that still believes in obligation and blood brotherhood and the most intense personal loyalty.

Perhaps even early Tokugawa would have been too lax for him. Better, the Middle Ages. Kamakura as Sparta with crumbling Kyoto as Athens. He would have made a fine samurai. I looked at his strong, young, well-cut face. The stern and senseless symmetry of his ideas also had a beauty of its own, the dead beauty of perfection.

Coupled with this was an invincible ignorance, a triumphant innocence of the world. There was surely no one, not Lancelot, not Galahad, more innocent than the samurai, living his beehive life complicated by a hundred spiritual qualifications, all of them having to do with purity, none of them having anything to do with the world in which he actually lived. He lived in his own world of abstractions, which were in turn governed not by philosophy nor even metaphysics but by a military etiquette so involved as to be almost impossible to memorize. It reached its limit only in suicide, the sacrificial slitting of the bowels, which was in itself table manners pushed to absurdity.

I suggested that the way of the samurai was doubly dangerous. If you made yourself so ready, so prepared yourself for war and killing, then they became attractive. He disagreed. War was bad. It was bad because no one wanted it, no one liked it. But, I said, if everyone really wanted it, then would it be good?

He thought, hair falling over his eyes, head on hand, elbow among the pillows, the overhead bulb shining down through the mosquito netting. No, it wouldn't be good, but it would happen. And if it happened, then no one could help it or be responsible for it, could they?

He knows nothing about war. He remembers nothing about the last one, the big one. For him it is movies and television and stories heard from naval-officer elders. For him it is history, just as the *kodan* are history. Jiro from Shimizu could have taken part in the Pearl Harbor attack for all he really knows, could have died miserably on Okinawa.

I thought of all the other stern and puritan young Japanese who thirty years ago were twenty. Dead at twenty.

I kept my ideas to myself. I changed the subject. I attempted to corrupt this chaste if once-fallen young man with stories of the flesh-pots of Tokyo, of the charms of Miss Turko and her sisters. He listened eagerly enough and kept asking if they really did that, those girls, did they really do that—my, my.

Thus encouraged, I embroidered, but, though his initial response had been encouraging, later responses were not. One such was that this was enough to disgust you with the whole human race for the rest of your life. Another was to excuse himself, find his way to the darkened mosquito-filled bathroom, dash a number of buckets of cold water over himself, and return damp, smiling, invincible.

When I mildly suggested that there were other ways of regarding the world than his, that a code of honor took many forms, he instantly agreed, adding that this was so but that this was, after all, his.

He turned out the light. We lay there. I felt very old, very late Athens, and he, perhaps sensing this, spoke. It may have been a proverb. It may have been something he made up.

"Never mind," he said, "the ocean has many tides."

*   *   *

WE WOKE EARLY. He shook me, was already dressed, singing, whistling. The world was gray and misty, the sun still far away. More asleep than awake, I followed him, brisk, lively, conversing, down to the docks.

There was a fog at sea, rolling up over the beach. The boat looked

111

as though it were on fire. It was covered with mist, and real smoke was coming from the stack.

The boat was suddenly on the verge of departure; suddenly, the way these island boats have. He vaulted aboard and waved, waved the shirt I had given him in exchange for the one he gave me. It was pink and its novelty pleased him to an almost singular degree. Pink on a samurai!

He continued to wave the shirt, smiling broadly. And, long after his face had disappeared, the dot of pink kept moving in its increasingly tiny arc, from the center of the toy ship hurrying back to the mainland.

*   *   *

IT GREW RAPIDLY WARMER. Having nothing to do until the late-afternoon boat left, I walked along the deserted beach of white sand. It was hot, dusty. I decided to go swimming and left my clothes on an upturned boat amid scuttling crabs.

The water was warm and very salty. Floating near me were several transparent jellyfish—milky round globs. They looked as though someone very large had been spitting.

I had heard that they bit, or stung. They didn't look dangerous, but standing, water to my waist, I hailed two small boys walking along the road. One of them suggested that they were dangerous only if purple. Reassured, I swam farther out.

The water was warm on the surface but cool deeper down. Salty, filled with cold currents, it also contained a number of tiny fish that nibbled at both the fronds of seaweed underfoot and my toes. I struck out, as though in a large warm bath, my waves lazily forming a wake.

The shadows of eagles passed continually over the shallow water. Against the glare of the sun I could glimpse their great shapes, like daytime bats. Farther out I found a seaweed-covered underwater reef on which I could just stand. Nearby was a boat from which a man and two boys were laying nets.

The man and I talk. He works, teaching the little boys not to put it that way, not to make so much noise, not to push each other into the water, and at the same time tells me about the fish. I stand up to my neck in the warm water, the cold seaweed coiling around my ankles.

He continues to tell me the names of the fish—a long list—and the boat drifts about my head in a large circle. At the end of the list he adds, as an afterthought: "Oh—yes. You must be careful of the poison fish."

"What poison fish?"

He thinks. "What was its name now?"

He thinks for a long time, trying various names, shaking his head, unable to remember, while the cold seaweed wraps itself about my ankles, something brushes against a toe, something else nibbles.

Finally: "There now, I've forgotten. At any rate, they are poisonous. Very poisonous. People die, you know."

"Oh?"

"Anyway, the big thing is to remember not to stand in the seaweed, because it is full of them, and if you step on them, they bite you and kill you, you see?"

He looked on, nodding approvingly as I flailed about and began paddling on the surface. "That's right, that's right," he said. "That way they won't get at you so easily."

Then, smiling, he began to row away, the little boys, busy in their importance, pulling ropes, tying things into place. After having entangled myself in their net, for the boat had circled me, I swam back, splashing as much as possible.

When I was safely on the sandy beach I heard a banging sound and looked up. The two little boys had sticks in their hands and were beating the boat. It looked as though they were trying to make it go faster. Then the boat turned and I saw what they were doing. The net was slowly closing. The boys were banging to make the fish move into the wake. The nets would close and the fish would be caught and pulled in.

The hollow sound of wood on wood echoed in the open, sunny bay. It sounded like Buddhist drums, those hollow, gourd-shaped, ball-like objects in every temple, like the empty tone they make when struck, which carries so far and makes one think of vestments, incense, and the musty smell of old temples.

*   *   *

THIS BOAT, now carrying me southward to Shikoku, is the kind you mostly see in this sea. It has a high, old-fashioned-looking passenger

113

cabin that is very straight, very precise, a big box like an early American china cupboard with its doors closed. It also looks like a floating trolley car. Hundreds of these pleasant, white-painted little boats shuttle about this small ocean as if it were a lake. They operate with the frequency of buses. If you miss one, you sit and wait for the next. The little ship glides in, lets people off, takes people on, starts off again with a short whistle. This is how the people who live here move about.

It is quite different from travel on those big steamers that stop only at Takamatsu and Matsuyama in Shikoku but bill their invariable and uninteresting route as an Inland Sea Cruise. All these little boats are blind, however. They do not have eyes to see where they are going, as some Aegean boats do. The Japanese imagination does not lie in this direction.

The boat rounds a corner of the island and there stands an enormous white building, brand new. A hotel, a school, a hospital? It has pillars, is made of concrete, carries a vast tiled roof. It stands there like a blinding mirage on the slope, right in the middle of nothing, surrounded only by the scars of its own making. I think of some Soviet monstrosity, some modern Chinese culture hall.

The people on the boat tell each other that it is one of those new hotels. An older man, however, knows better. Nothing of the sort. It is a temple belonging to Tenri-kyo, one of the new religions.

This means that it cost a lot of money and will be garish as a Chinese restaurant on the inside. There will be hundred-mat rooms filled with people singing songs that all sound like "Yes, Jesus Loves Me" and worshiping someone still alive or only recently dead. They will have made pilgrimage to this distant island and will have left substantial donations. They will stay to gaze at the recently painted ceiling, the newly sewn banners, the just-gilded altar.

As a study in economics the new religions would be fascinating. Soka Gakkai, for example, is extraordinarily wealthy, the money coming from the thousands upon thousands of converts and those whom they in turn have converted, sometimes militantly, almost forcibly. As a study in theology, however, the new religions have no meaning at all. They are not about religion. They are about power, about the herding instinct.

Which is very Japanese. I know of no people more lacking the religious sense than they. They love the rituals of religion in the same way they love the ritual of the tea ceremony, the etiquette of an intricately choreographed wedding. They admire the panoply, the art, the architecture, the ostentation that religion produces. They love belonging to an obviously successful and powerful organization. But the spirituality behind these concrete manifestations—it does not exist for them.

Not only have they never been religious, they have also never felt the need to be. Shinto shrines, Buddhist temples, Christian churches — all are attended, but the same man will sometimes attend all three —apparently just to be safe—and not find the tenets of any one antithetical to the others. The Japanese choose to believe in the surface of things and do not welcome the probing or the hopefully profound. They live on the surface of life and rarely seem to feel the need for deeper meaning. Granted that the more esoteric types of Buddhism have, or had, a vogue in Japan. Still, I do not think that it was their profundities that appealed, nor their deeper meanings that were believed. The appeal lay on the surface and the meaning was the ostensible meaning.

These new religions are really new superstitions, because the Japanese are also, and typically, superstitious. This is the land were one day is luckier than the other, the wedding halls are packed on the best days, empty on the worst; where someone is saying something good about you if your right ear itches in the morning or your left in the afternoon; where one sneeze means somebody likes you and two sneezes means somebody doesn't; where a dropped comb is left lying because its name is *kushi* (*ku* can mean "trouble," and *shi*, "death"); where Coca-Cola causes impotence and the birth-control pill is responsible for ailments so little known and consequently so mysterious that many women will not use it. All of these, and more, are not perhaps generally believed by everyone, but a day does not pass but that some superstition is to be observed. A new religion is like a charm or an amulet—of recent and therefore superior construction— designed to keep evil at bay.

Thousands are sucked into such organizations. I am sorry for this because I cannot believe that the heads of the religions are as gullible as their converts. Still, such membership—with its clappings and singing and socializing—is perhaps not too high a price to pay for being constitutionally prey to superstition but consequently, I think, immune to religion and hence to the guilty vagaries of that imagined conscience that has been so long fostered in the West.

The old man is continuing on about Tenri-kyo. "And they have a golden dragon, brand new. A statue, of course, but splendid. My boy went over to see it and got himself enrolled. It was that grand. And they serve a good meal, too, he said. They have this pretty tune they sing so that evil won't come. It was very nice, he said."

The others nodded and the boat putted on.

*   *   *

IT WAS PERHAPS somewhere around here—between Honshu and Shikoku—that the Kabuki actor Ichikawa Danzo VIII stepped off a boat, into the sea, and on into immortality. An old man in his eighties, retired from the stage, he had—as he had said—nothing more to live for. The boat set sail, plowed through the shallow sea all night; in the morning he was no longer there. This is, one might think, a bit of local folklore. Not at all, though it is fast becoming so— it occured in June, 1965. And its repercussions still sound. No one much remembers Danzo as an actor, and he was not, it is agreed, among the greatest. What everyone remembers is his death. His final moments were thought much greater than his entire life on the stage.

Everyone loves a romantic death, all countries have such favorite tragic heroes, but it is, I think, only the Japanese who would remember a man not for what he had done with his life, but solely for how he had arranged his death.

A parallel will be instructive. We have Hart Crane—another artist—who disappeared from a boat crossing the Gulf of Mexico. And, to be sure, the idea of such a death is appealing. Yet, even now, we think of suicide as a kind of illness, as a temporary derangement that got out of hand, and we think of Crane as sick, as escaping. While almost morbidly interested in the cause and manner of his death, we also think that it would have been better somehow for him to have faced up to Cleveland. And, in any event, if Hart Crane had not been one of America's greatest poets, his death would not be celebrated.

Japan celebrates Danzo's death alone. He had done, it was agreed by press and public alike, a noble thing. And, it is true, while we celebrate anonymous boys who stuck fingers in dykes and saved thousands, the Japanese celebrate equally anonymous samurai who happened to slit open their own stomachs particularly well, saved no one, and only killed themselves. Obviously we have here an attitude toward death—and toward life—that is different from our own.

Asia does not, I think, hoard and treasure life as we do. Life, to be sure, is not considered cheap, but at the same time, one does not see the tenacious clinging to it that is one of the distinguishing marks of the West. And this is, indeed, what one might expect from a culture that lives so close to nature. Death is, after all, preeminently natural. Perhaps the attraction of Danzo's death was that he—accepting this natural termination—merely decided upon the timing of the event. But certainly another reason for the public celebration that resulted was his tact in doing so. Not for him the common sleeping pill or gas-filled room, the corpse left over for others to cope with. His death was neat—it was tidy. It caused no trouble, was not unsightly because no one saw it at all, and it was discreet.

Just as the gardener decides which branch to lop off while still retaining the natural shape of bush or tree, just as the landscape architect decides which boulder to remove or place in order to retain or create the natural appearance of the view, just as the flower arranger decides which bloom or blossom to remove to make visible the natural shape of branch or twig—so Ichikawa Danzo, having lived his life as he saw it, exercised his right to remove the last straggling years. I am certain that these last moments were not spent with such aesthetic reasoning, but I am equally certain that it is with such thoughts or feelings that the manner of his death was commented upon and made much of. So much that now, as I've said, though few remember his living, his acting, everyone remembers his dying.

And as I sit in this small boat and watch the changing panorama of islands and sea, I wonder if it was not the sight of just such beauty as this that illuminated the old man's last moments. Didn't he perhaps pause in the starlight and take just one more look before stepping overboard? Yes, I tell myself, wishing I too might some day be able to choose my place. It is just here that I too should like to die.

*   *   *

IN THE SMALLEST TOWNS—here in Sakaide on Shikoku, for example—coffee-shop culture continues its influence. I sit in this stylish little

117

shop with its bleached-monk's-cloth walls, its indirect lighting, its abstract water colors, its tropical plants; listen to the stereo play music from *La Dolce Vita*; and watch two local young ladies enjoy an afternoon cup of coffee. One is in simple black. The other is in simple purple. Both have their hair ratted and teased into the messy beehive-look popular in the cities several years back. The coffee is excellent. One has a wide choice. There is a menu with Brazil and Java and Blue Mountain and other varieties listed, and each cup is made as ordered. There are also a number of wax sundaes and parfaits displayed in a glass case to stimulate the appetite, and a large and shining ice-cream machine. Yet this is a tiny, idle seaport that closes its shutters at nine in the evening.

The coffee shop is to Japan what the promenade or the open café is to Italy or Greece. It is where people meet, by design or otherwise, where news is discussed, where you relax and enjoy yourself. That it is also surrounded by four walls and covered with a roof makes it Japanese. These people are mole-people. They like to feel snug, were until recently rarely seen sitting eating in public for all the world to watch. Coffee shops are ideal Japanese habitats: small, cozy, dark.

At the same time, the coffee shops are also windows onto the world. Japan, it is too seldom remembered, lived in the dark for hundreds of years. The doors as well as the windows were shut. Like little Kaspar Hauser, Japan went right on growing in the dark and when the shutters were wrenched off was at first blinded, then dazzled. One does not like to leave the only security one knows; hence the cave with the picture window, a fitting architectural symbol for the country.

Before long, however, Japan began hauling the world in through the window. Everything, anything—all the knowledge on earth is eventually pulled in. The man on the street knows a little bit about plane geometry; knows the names of Galbraith and Faulkner, though he has perhaps not read a word of either; follows transplants and Yves Saint-Laurent with equal attention. Though he himself only travels for business—at least until recently—he encourages all of those outside to travel for pleasure. The Olympics, Expo, lovely Kyoto, *son et lumière* at Osaka Castle—and an endless train of distinguished visitors: Sartre, Shirley MacLaine, Joe DiMaggio, Genet, Leonard Bernstein, to say nothing of crowned heads and all of the major symphony orchestras in the world as well as most of the rock groups. Japan entices one and all into the cave, where they are wined and dined and sent home, heads reeling.

No longer is it necessary to march far away and liberate various helpless peoples—now the helpless peoples are invited in and shown around. There is such a scramble around the sill at present, however, that Japan seems just on the point of falling out the window. Beginning with just a trickle only a few years ago, already such hordes of Japanese sightseers are traveling abroad, though almost always in carefully insulated flocks, that Waikiki seems almost to belong to them and they are setting up enclaves in such cities as San Francisco, New York, Paris, Rome. In a few decades the astonishing cavern will be dismantled because all the people inside will be on the outside, out in the world. When this occurs, Japan will disappear because Japan is the cavern. And there will no longer be any Japanese, though the name will be retained, along with a few well-tempered customs. The new world simply cannot tolerate differences as extreme as those Japan still represents. Soon—happy state—everyone will be like everyone else, all will be wandering about, promiscuous, on hot concrete under a blazing sun.

My reveries are interrupted by a raised voice. The girl in purple is talking about her troubles at the hairdresser's in Matsuyama. The girl in black is nodding in mute commiseration. One has red fingernails. The other favors pearly gray. Where could such exotic creatures have come from, I wonder. Outside in the sunny streets children run naked, and bare-breasted old fisherwomen pass with baskets on their heads.

Another exotic creature is the waitress. I doubt she has been to Tokyo, but she is certainly familiar with its pattern. She wears a modish frock, has her hair up in a beehive, and dispenses coffee, parfaits, glasses of ice water in which float thin lemon slices. She accomplishes this with the pinched and sallow look of fashion that comes only from leafing through back copies of *Vogue*.

Here she comes to fill my water glass. Without a glance at me, all eyes, in the formula customary when a Japanese is doing anything particularly nice for one, she inclines her head gracefully instead of saying excuse me, holds one little finger in the air—where could she have learned this particular grace?—puts down the carefully full

119

glass, wheels with the poise of a mannequin, and goes to stand beside the monstrous and novel potted elephant's-ear, where she poses with one foot slightly out, the other slightly turned.

I doubt that, when old, she will wander the streets breasts out, basket on head. But I do not at all doubt that she used to run naked and screaming in these very streets, howling with joyful and simulated terror at the sight of the foreigner.

The two lady customers have ordered further refreshments. One is struggling with a parfait made of ice cream, red syrup, nuts, whipped cream, preserved cherries. The other is sipping beer and masticating tough strips of dried squid.

I suddenly remember Saburo from Takamatsu and wonder about his Sunday outing and anatomy lesson. These young ladies might, at first glance, prove more amenable to his efforts. I doubt it though. They are virtuous. It is just that fashion has decreed the international whore-look.

A young girl comes in, plain in a cotton frock. She stands by the counter and asks for ice cream. The man who has been making the coffee goes to the machine—an electrical affair that dispenses frozen custard from its snout, a confection the Japanese call "soft"—and twirls full a cone. She takes it, disappears somewhere in back of me, then returns at once and asks for ice cream.

Where did it go, I wonder, and turn to look. She is gazing placidly at the ice-cream machine. She takes her cone, disappears, and is then back again. Ice cream, please.

Now much interested, I turn to stare, looking for a full mouth with the tip of the third cone still protruding. Nothing of the sort. Empty-mouthed, she is gazing at the ice-cream machine. Then she takes her cone, disappears somewhere behind me, and is then back again. More ice cream? No, water please. One? asks the man. No, three, she says. Balancing the water glasses, she turns. This time, much intrigued, I also turn and lean out to peer. She and two friends are sitting behind the potted elephant's-ear, nearly invisible. Each now has an ice-cream cone and a glass of water.

Why didn't she order the three cones at the same time? That I will never know. I do know, however, that such piecemeal purchasing is the rule. The housewives of a neighborhood clog the stores at five in the evening, buying for the six o'clock meal. That one could also buy

120

for several days does not occur. Perhaps it is because iceboxes are too small or few. Perhaps.

But how then account for these same housewives who do the laundry every day? Even if it is only a pair of stockings and a few handkerchiefs, the entire paraphernalia of washday is gotten out and the laundry done daily. I think this has something to do with the way that the Japanese think. But what it is I have no idea.

*   *   *

AT THE PORT two little boys regard me closely, stare suspiciously. One turns to the other and instead of the expected—his informing the younger that this is a foreigner—I hear the word *bakemono*. The smaller looks at me, slightly afraid but ready to defend himself from the supernatural monster—two little savages from this hinterland, this Wales of Japan, this Arkansas.

The little one wants to know what kind of *bakemono*.

I smile and volunteer that I am an American *bakemono*. Oh.

My smile has not reassured them. My teeth are apparently rather long. Well, where am I from then? I am from Tokyo. This is even less assuring. The little one backs away. The older, standing his ground, stares defiantly—Momotaro, brave against the *oni*.

Well, then, where did I come from today?

I say that I have recently come from Naoshima.

Instantly they are all smiles. At first I think that this is because the place I have named is relatively near and hence familiar. But, no, I hear the older reassuring the younger that it is all right now—all *bakemono* come from Naoshima.

Having thus ascertained that I am a proper monster and not some suspicious interloper, they wave good-bye in the friendliest fashion, and run down the street.

*   *   *

GETTING TO SAMEJIMA, where I am determined to go, is a problem. There is only one boat a day and that left hours ago. I must hire a small boat. The woman at the wharf is neither hopeful nor encouraging, but, as a matter of fact, they have a boat. It lies there before me,

125

long, open, bleached, gasoline-engined. She might just persuade her husband, at present asleep, to take me. She names a modest price.

All prices are modest in the country. One's bills are padded and open cheating is resorted to only in the cities and the big resort hotels —rarely, it is true, and none too skillfully, but sometimes these things do happen. In the country, however, one is never cheated, despite the fact that all foreigners notoriously reek of money. One reason for this is that it takes a kind of bravery, or at least a sort of affrontery, to cheat successfully, and the country people are too shy for this. Another, however, is that the Japanese have learned from experience that honesty is the most economical of policies. It saves so much time. Graft on a grand scale—governmental, big-business—this is expected and well worth the trouble. But the simple matter of buying a night's lodging or renting a boat is scarcely worth it.

There is no bargaining. This is no Mediterranean country, though it looks like one. The price is stated and that is the only price. I have seen American tourists trying to bargain in Tokyo's largest department stores: they might as well haggle at Macy's. So the lady's price for the boat and the now-awakened old man is modest indeed and I, as is expected, accept.

On the way, the old man, between yawns, gives me information. We are between the islands of Samejima and Seijima, where the sea is so shallow that at low tide one may walk the considerable distance from one island to the other and the water will come no further than here—the breastbone of this short, gnarled, wrinkled, smiling old man whose black eyes, sunk deep into his face, sparkle like coal.

Also when he was a boy, back in the Meiji period, they used to have great sport out here with the octopus, which grows to great size in these shallow seas. They would catch a large one and bring it into the boat. Then they would put it on the back of one of the boys, like a knapsack, the large, snakelike tentacles wrapped around his chest, the monster first struggling, then holding like a python. With it on his back, the boy would dive into the sea.

Though the octopus was free to escape, it never did. It was too used to holding onto things; once onto something, it would never let go. Since it was back in the sea, however, it swam in its own fashion, shooting water out behind while firmly attached to the boy's back, and he could half-guide it, much as one directs a stubborn donkey.

In this way the youngster could enjoy an exhilarating ride, held up by the half-submerged octopus, propelled at a great rate, diving, gradually turning around and being propelled back to the boat, where the other boys were waiting to take their turns.

But what about the beak, I wanted to know, that awful beak I had read about, right in the middle of the body where the eight legs meet, that parrot-beak which can break a thighbone as a sparrow breaks a twig.

Oh, they never use it, not unless they are really frightened. And then, it is so brittle that, though it can make a nasty cut, there is more danger of it itself breaking than of its breaking anything. The most that can happen is that the octopus gets so frightened that he releases his ink and then—and the old man laughed to remember—you come up black as a man from Africa, covered with the not-unpleasant but strong-smelling india-black ink of the octopus.

But, wasn't anyone afraid of the monster? Of course not.

And it is true. Japan, unlike the West, has no horror legend about the gentle octopus. In Japanese folklore the octopus is always playful, no matter how large. He often wears a towel around his head and a roguish look. He is also eaten in various ways and is delicious. Japan has no more need of horrid stories about the octopus than we do of frightful legends about the cow.

But when it came time to get out of the water, what then?

Well, alone it would have been hard to take him off, that's true. One would have had to wear him home. But friends always managed to tear off those great suction-cupped arms, though they left marks. Oh, after a day of play out in the boat they would all go back home all spotted up, as though they had smallpox.

And what would happen to the friendly octopus after they had tired of their playmate?

Oh, they would cut him up and eat him.

This old man had traveled more widely or kept his ears more widely opened than most people of the Inland Sea. He could tell me me about other islands than his own. If I wanted to see a proper sight I must go to distant Kitagijima and look for the Neko Suteru Basho, the "Cat-Throwing-Away Place." There was a great stone cat, a rock cat with eyes angrily looking out to sea, apparently remembering the indignity of having been thrown away. Oh, those eyes. They look at you like as to chill the blood, particularly if you happen to pass that way in a small boat of an evening.

Why did they throw the cat away? Well, now that he doesn't know, but someone once, long ago, did do just such a thing, and that the cat remembers. Go look, you won't be sorry if you do. Oh, those eyes, enough to chill the blood!

At once I am wild to see the chilling eyes of the stone cat, but I must wait since the island is so far away—it would take all day and all night in such a small boat as this. And in the meantime, here is Samejima.

*   *   *

I WANTED TO COME to Samejima because here, well over a thousand years ago, was written the only poem about the Inland Sea to find its way into the four thousand poems of the *Manyoshu*, that ancient anthology made in Japan a century before Alfred the Great ruled in Britain. I wanted to see the place.

It is a small island, flat on the sea. A grove of oak trees at one end extends to the saddle of houses in the middle. Here is the tiny harbor, shallow, guarded by enormous, tusklike stones. In the port are children, old people, one man sitting, mending his nets on a bamboo terrace as though this were the South Seas.

Around here somewhere the poem was written, here among the rustling reeds, the sighing winds from home and Kyoto, the happy birds, free to fly swiftly over the intervening sea. Here the soldier-poet buried his dead, wrote his song, perhaps sang it, and waited to go home.

I am eventually directed to the clump of oak. Here stands the house of the teacher, and he is the man who will know all about this. His surprised wife ushers me into the parlor.

It is a Meiji-period house and so it has a parlor—a real Western parlor: sleek upright piano, doll in glass case, plate with a picture of Beethoven on it, imitation Delft scene all blue and white, a wind-up record-player with a big horn, Paul Peel's "Nach dem Bade" in reproduction—two rosy naked children warming their privates at the fireplace—a violin in the corner covered with dust, furniture covered in plum-colored velour resting on a dusty Turkish rug—all of this squeezed into a tiny room, while just out the window is the well, the family shrine, the single pine. A little corner of the West made with loving care on this far Eastern island.

The teacher, a small man with a high, worried forehead, surmises at once that it is about the poem that I have come. First off, he gives me the name and address of a man—only five minutes from where I live in Tokyo—who knows all about the poem and the island, having written a whole book on it, and isn't it a shame that I came all this way when, had I but known, there he was, just around the corner from me. Having said this, he finds an annotated edition of the *Manyoshu* and we look up the poem.

It was written by a soldier who, after a great defeat, was shipwrecked on this island. One of his comrades died here, was buried here, and here the poem was written. We attempt a translation:

> If his wife were here,
> She would gather for him
> Fresh wild herbs....
> But upon the hills of Samine,
> Have they not already faded?

We are not too pleased with our attempt but it is close enough. It is, at any rate, very Japanese—the old name for Samejima, the references to the wife (did she but know that her lord lay dead), the rustic simplicity of the wild things she would have collected (the dictionary gave the Latin *uvagi*, not nearly poetical enough, and besides, I do not know what *uvagi* is), and then the tender reference to the fading of the *uvagi* and the parallel suggestion of the fading of all earthly concerns...autumn, transience, evanescence—very Japanese qualities all.

Afterwards I go and look at the reed plains, or what is left of them. Not much. The island has been eaten away by the shallow sea. Some of the land is farmed. Now only a square patch of reeds is left near the tip of the island under the oak stand. Here, says tradition, is the site of both song and burial.

I stand there, far from Heian times, listening to the sound of the wind in the reeds, hearing the cry of the *chidori* overhead. Happy plover, free to go whenever it pleases. I feel the winds racing toward the distant capital.

I also hear the radio in the nearest house—acid rock. The big boats hoot as they pass the far side of the island. Somewhere someone is playing the harmonium—"Annie Laurie"—here, far, far away on Samejima, a place where people do not come.

* * *

"Dirty clothes," Norman Douglas says Saint Jerome says, "are a sign of a clean mind."

The Japanese have very clean minds. They wash daily in an intricate ritual of scalding water and mountains of suds—then back into the same underwear, the same singlet, the same socks. If the body is clean, the body's coverings can take care of themselves. In the same way, one's own garden is immaculate, while the street just outside is almost medieval in its ordure. Again, to a personal friend one is lavishly polite; to the stray stranger, affrontingly rude.

The public bath, here at Sakaide as elsewhere, is only incidentally a place to get the body clean. The Japanese bath is more than a bath. It is a lustration, a ceremony of cleanliness. Afterwards I watch the dirty clothes going back on. This is very Japanese. The form has been observed. Officially everyone is clean.

The bath is also a place for seeing your friends, for talking things over, for gossiping. It is what the church or the barbershop or the beauty parlor used to be in the West.

Indeed, there is something churchlike about the Japanese public bath. First there is the ritual. Shoes off at the door, you enter and put all your clothes in the basket provided. Then, naked as though newly born, you enter the bathing room with its mysterious steam and dimly seen forms. Inside, you crouch and douche with buckets full of hot water, washing armpits and crotch, rinsing the mouth over and over, blowing the nose, cleansing the dirty body. Then you enter the great communal bath, a large, square, tile tub in which sometimes dozens of others sit in the near-scalding water, faces bright red, like sinners in purgatory. Faint, one emerges, sits in the line and soaps. Over and over one washes. Nothing is missed. Everything is doubly washed. The soles of the feet are scrubbed with a cake of pumice stone. Finally, thoroughly clean, one reenters the steaming tub, now one of the blessed, to sit and enjoy the heat. Purified, one emerges, dresses, goes off with a lighter heart and a purer soul.

This is the form. This is how the Japanese tell you they bathe, warning you to be careful and never get a spot of soap in the big hot

130

tub, being equally careful to hold the towel over your privates. I have, however, been in enough Japanese public baths to know what actually happens.

You rush in naked, towel flying, make for the big hot pool, and squat at the edge for a token second to dash a handful of water on your genitals. Then into the pool; but since you have not properly douched with hot water, it is too hot to enter. Consequently you turn on the cold tap and wait until the water is properly tepid. This occasions an amount of grumbling among those inside who, already accustomed, are enjoying the heat. Then, still unwashed, still completely dirty, you enter the water and stay there until tired of it. Next you sit down and wash yourself, particularly the neck for some reason. The order is, first feet, then thighs, then chest, then face. The privates are neglected since it is not seemly to touch yourself in public. Then a quick rinse that leaves large patches of soap on the body, and back into the big tub, where the soap floats on the surface of the hot water and eventually dissolves. Convinced that one is now clean, one rubs off some of the rest of the dirt on the towel and puts back on one's dirty clothes.

Even more churchlike is the community atmosphere, the talk, the gossip. In Tokyo I have discovered the most intimate details of my neighbors' lives while at the public bath:

"Mr. Richie, you live next door to the Suzukis, don't you?"

"Yes, I do."

"Well, she did it again last night. Did you happen to notice?"

"Did I notice what?"

"She did it with that man again."

"What man?"

"How do I know—deliveryman, garbage man, iceman?"

"How do you know?"

"You know the Watanabes who live on the other side? Well, Mrs. Watanabe saw it and told her husband, who told me. But your windows are in a much better position than theirs. Look, when you go home now after the bath, you just creep into your house and don't turn the lights on, and then you can look right over into the Suzukis'. You let me know what you see next time, all right?"

I, of course, rush home, don't turn on the lights, and am rewarded with a full view of Mrs. Suzuki in her anonymous transports. These old men in the bath are never wrong. One hears about gossiping old

131

ladies, but old men are much better at it. In the old days of mixed bathing—now there are men on one side of the partitioned bathhouse, women on the other—I imagine the old men easily out-gossiped the old women.

Here in the Sakaide bathhouse there was the same kind of talk. At first, when I entered, there was dead silence. It was as though the devil himself had entered church. The Japanese think of the bath as being, properly, something peculiarly their own. There is a sense of profanation when the foreigner enters. Soon, however, curiosity overcomes scruples, he is talked to, asked questions of. His skin is examined from a distance and discussed, his privates are covertly viewed. The attitude is that once expressed by a very small boy, accompanied by his father, who caught first sight of me in my local Tokyo bathhouse:

"Father, Father, come look. A foreigner!"

"Yes, yes, I know. Come on, get dressed now."

"But, Father, look. He's all white!"

"You get dressed now, we're going home."

"But, look, just look. He's—ugh—all hairy."

"Look here now! You get dressed properly and be quiet."

"But look. Just look, Father"—pointing—"even though he's a foreigner, he's got one too."

In the Sakaide bath there was a minute or two of silence, then the conversation started again. Since I was in, I was in; nothing could be done about it. They might as well act natural. Once having decided to, they were soon acting naturally and forgot all about me.

They are discussing the bridge from the mainland to their island of Shikoku. I hear it being vehemently argued as I scrub. One old man next to me is very much against it.

I agree with him. A bridge to Shikoku would be the end. I feel for him. Then, gradually, it becomes clear that his disagreement is not with the bridge but with the fact that it is likely to come to Naruto and he wants it to come to little Sakaide. The bridge, it turns out, is a very good thing. It will bring people, prosperity, money, popularity. And here uninteresting Naruto, in the next prefecture, will be getting all the business and fascinating Sakaide will be left out.

One somehow expects old men to be conservative, but this is not so in the country where the old men are often firebrands of the most innovative variety. True conservatism is found in middle-aged people, or in the young who are just beginning to find their responsibilities weighing heavily upon them. Old men and children are free of this. Old people, retired, expensive and exacting wards of their grown children, spend their time with grandiose schemes for turning the sea into drinking water or extracting gold from the rays of the sun.

In the West, the very young and the very old enjoy little freedom. In Japan, however, this deprivation occurs between the ages of about fifteen and fifty-five. Before and after comes freedom. If one is old, one is consulted, made much of, catered to. This is the reward for having lived so long. It is no wonder that this second childhood is very real—that all the old men are quite radical and all for innovation.

It is their sons, those in middle years, who are doubtful and cautious; it is their grandsons, callow, just out of high school, who conform, who are afraid of their own opinions. Here is lost, temporarily, the fierce individuality that sees Shikoku as the center of the universe, little Sakaide as its hub.

The loss is only temporary. It is regained with age. Older people are surprised to hear that only the Japanese eat raw fish, are amazed at my tales of soap in the bath, show disbelief that the West does not live on the floor.

Here, among these proud, sometimes suspicious islanders, tradition lingers, but not in the cities, where it has been swallowed by comparison, insecurity, and fear.

*   *   *

ALONG THE COAST between Sakaide and Takotsu there are many salt flats. Miles of beach are set with racks of brush, high as houses, inverted like roofs, one rack just below the other. Sea water is piped over the top and filters through the brush to the bottom, the water leaving a deposit that looks like bird lime.

In the train opposite me is a young couple. She is a large and ample girl in pink, wearing blue eyeshadow at six in the morning. He, smaller as is the case with certain insects, is wearing matching socks and tie. They might almost be whore and pimp, so does the current fashion follow attractive lawlessness. She might be a prostitute, except she is not that pretty. And he is not spruce enough to be a pimp.

133

She is also extremely solicitous. Shall I go and get some cigarettes at the next stop? Aren't you sleepy? Why don't you lie down for a bit on that nice seat over there? He grunts or else, in the fashion of Japanese males, does not answer.

She looks up brightly, smiles at him. He doesn't see her, isn't looking, doesn't smile. She bends over her suitcase, humming: she has broken the clasp and now, with large fingers, is attempting, ineffectually, to mend it. Large girls always break things.

She gets up to squeeze past him, the train jerks, she falls and giggles. The giggle is full and tender. It suggests bedside lamps and Kleenex-like night-paper and sighs in the dark. He scowls, pushes her away—a rude gesture of the sated male. I now know what they are doing: they are on their honeymoon.

*   *   *

FROM TADOTSU the islands stretch like the stones of a garden path back to the mainland—unknown, forgotten, plain, lovely little islands.

A typical island of the Inland Sea, as you pass in the boat, consists of: a village clustered on the beach, one road along the shore, others —alleys—running back to the hills then stopping, sometimes a wide road going over the mountains to the other side, sometimes a sea road continuing around the island. Then, in the middle, as seen from the water, near the shore a temple in a grove, often the only grove on the island, or a stone torii, a shady walk, a shrine in the shade. Near it the largest building, the general store; on either side of it black houses, roofs of cemented gray tile—back and white, salt and pepper. Then the yellow or green iron-roofed ticket-house and, much farther away, a red torii for the fishermen, for the goddess. And then—on a spit— the graveyard, the gravestones high, rectangular, like teeth. Then seaweed racks, an overturned boat or two, and the island slides down and back into the sea it came from.

The particular island I am now looking at, all but indistinguishable from hundreds of others, is called Takamijima—or is it Sanagijima, or Manabeshima? In any case, I do not want to get off; so I go on sipping tea, the mats throbbing with the vibrations of the motor, and I continue talking with a lumber merchant from Shikoku who is going to Manabeshima to cut down trees for the day.

134

He got up at four in the morning in order to catch the train to take him to the boat. He does not actually know if he will be able to buy the trees to cut down. Timber is getting scarce, most of the standing forests are gone during this last twenty-five years, but he has heard that on this island there is a section left, which the man might sell. If he does, then during the day he can cut down ten trees while the sun is still up. He must then arrange for them to be carted down to the harbor, shipped back to Shikoku, and trucked to his home, where he will gradually cut them into lumber.

The boat churns on and from time to time we continue our desultory conversation. Despite, or because of, his having traveled this route for years, he knows next to nothing about the islands we pass. He regards my story of Onigashima as unlikely. It is the end of the world to him. It is far, far away, and he will not believe my telling him that it is a matter of a day and a half at the most.

The geographical ignorance of the people in these parts is invincible. The people on one island have only the vaguest of notions of another island an hour away. No, they don't know what kind of place it is. No, they never heard of a boat leaving their island to go there. Of course, they know all about the boats to Osaka or Kobe because these are the boats everyone takes. On Iejima they all knew about the boats to Himeji. Women shop there, men get their haircuts there, children go to movies there. But, until I learned differently for myself, there was no early-morning boat to Shodo.

Their idea of distance is equally remarkable. Osaka is thought of as not too far away. The much nearer Honjima is some distant, fabled place of which one has only heard. Even its existence is doubtful. Likewise strange is the idea of time. No one ever knows how long anything takes. My boat ride from Tadotsu, upon inquiry, took anywhere from three hours to one day. In actuality it took two hours to go to Kitagijima.

The boats are nevertheless the great timepieces of the Inland Sea. Like the railways on the mainland, they are punctual. You look out the window at four o'clock and, sure enough, there is the last boat to Shikoku leaving the pier. In between, however, if you ask the time, the sun is consulted and guessed at.

Yet there is no island that I have seen, however small, that does not have at least one clock store. Tiny hamlets that have neither hotel nor inn always have beauty parlors and clock stores. One wonders how the owners make a living since clock time has so little meaning and there are so many other ways of keeping time. There are bells at seven, a whistle at noon, another whistle at one, another at five, and often more bells in between. This would be enough. Since no one is very busy, since there are no appointments to be kept, since you always know what everyone else is doing, since everyone does the same things every day, there would seem to be no need to know the hour.

I think that the clock-store people are kept in business for the same reason that the piano people and the English-newspaper people are. The piano is a large, black, expensive box that is kept locked and dusted in the Western parlor. Its presence bespeaks advanced ways and a comfortable income. In the same way, the English newspaper lying unread on desk or table argues for an amount of culture. It is a talisman. Perhaps something will rub off and you will find yourself fluent. There it will lie until, still pristine, still smelling faintly of morning ink, it is put in the cupboard with all the rest, where it will repose until it is used to wrap up something or hold the tea leaves on the way to the garbage can.

Clocks are the same. Though no one bothers to look at it, or to wind it, there is a fine clock in every home. Always showing twenty to three, it is a large, expensive, beautiful, cultural object.

One is, then, free from both time and space in these islands, free of those two merciless masters who snatch our lives. One could stay here a year or a day and never know the difference. These islands are like the great undersea palaces visited by Urashima Taro, the fairy-tale hero who finally returned to discover that he had spent not a week but a lifetime. He found himself old and his children's children grown.

I don't know the date. I think it is Friday, but I am by no means sure. The sun seems to be saying noon. One could live forever on these sleepy islands with their round of days and years, time meaning boats, space meaning the close confines of your own shore. One could live naturally and therefore happily.

*   ·   *   *

KITAGIJIMA is a quarry island. The little town is attractive. It has a broad basin of a harbor with steps at one end, steps leading directly into the water like those of Benares or of Adriatic ports. There is a shiny stone torii and a row of stonecutters' shops. The town is covered with stone dust, as if with volcanic ash.

And everyone in it is dead. The apprentices lie covered with stone dust, looking like fallen statuary, sound asleep. In the general store a woman lies in her lair, a half-eaten watermelon in front of her; in the tiny government office, men in clean white shirts lie amid abacuses and telephones; a young boatman sprawls in the bottom of his boat.

The people are asleep. This is the Mediterranean of Japan, the only place where the siesta is observed. Inside this small town women are flat on their backs, arms and legs extended, a sheet pulled across the stomach because it makes you ill to sleep with your middle exposed. Men are on their sides or asleep in chairs, displaying that surprising ability the Japanese have for falling asleep just anywhere. Children are asleep in the grass. Babies are lying spread like starfish.

This occurs after the noon meal. It is very natural; it is undoubtedly good for you. At one time perhaps all Japanese fell soundly asleep after eating, as people do now in Greece and Italy and Yugoslavia. Now only in far off and forgotten places such as these islands do the Japanese allow themselves this pleasant custom. In Tokyo at this hour the city people have gulped down a bowl of noodles, taken an aspirin, and are on their way back to their offices. Here on the islands they sleep.

The siesta is so rare in industrious Japan that my first thought is that a pestilence, some kind of sleeping sickness, has attacked the place, felling people as they worked. But in these quiet islands, where nothing ever happens, the siesta comes naturally. Waiting, I sit on the pier.

Finally the young man in the bottom of the boat stirs, turns over, sits up, yawns, and looks at me.

"I came to see the place where the cat was thrown away," I say, to show myself not unacquainted with native customs.

"What cat?" he asks, rubbing his eyes.

"The cat that was thrown away."

"Who threw it away?"

"I don't know, but it was a long time ago I suppose."

"What?" He sat up, stared at me, his face heavy with sleep.

"They threw a cat away some place around here, you see. If you go there you can see it."

"If someone threw a cat away, it wouldn't still be there, would it? Where did they throw it away?"

"I don't know. Into the sea, I imagine."

"If you throw a cat into the sea, then it would die. It wouldn't be there now. Was it your cat?"

"No. This happened a long time ago."

"My friend's cat got lost last year," he told me, trying to help.

"No, this was perhaps hundreds of years ago."

He looked at me and finally said: "Well, if it was hundreds of years ago, you wouldn't find it around here now. Cats don't live that long, you know."

"I know, I know," I said impatiently. "It's a—it's a . . ."

I suddenly could not remember the word for "statue." So I said: "It's a stone cat."

He looked at me, no longer sleepy, eyes slightly narrowing. He got up, began tinkering with the boat, turning to say: "Why don't you ask at the town office?"

He turned his back to me, baited a line, and began to fish.

The officials were stretching, yawning, waking up. A girl was making them tea. I presented myself at the counter and asked about the cat.

"A lost cat," said one official, turning to another who was yawning and rubbing his back. He produced a form and asked my name, my age, my nationality.

"No, no," I said. "This is a cat that was thrown away."

But the word for "to throw away" is *suteru*, which sounds much like *shiteru*, an inflected form of the more common verb meaning "to know." Consequently the first official raised his eyes, looked at the second, and said: "It is a cat he says he knows."

Then, to me: "You know this cat?"

"No, no," I said. "I said it was a cat that was thrown away," pronouncing the word very distinctly.

"A thrown-away cat," said the official as though correcting me. Then they both looked at me. An abandonded cat, perhaps? A valuable animal? A lost or strayed cat of some significance to me?

"No, it was thrown away some time ago."

"How long ago?"

"Maybe hundreds of years."

They looked at each other, then at me, then said they had no records that went that far back. I thanked them and said I would look around.

Outside the office I suddenly remembered the word for stone statue —*sekizo*—but I did not want to go back to the town office; so I asked a girl sitting in front of the empty beauty parlor. Her hair was up in clips and Scotch tape.

"Where, please, is the stone statue?"

"What statue?"

"The statue of the cat."

"What cat?"

"The thrown-away cat."

"Is there a thrown-away cat?"

"There was. But that was hundreds of years ago."

"Oh, really?" she said, picking up a magazine. She looked at it intently, biting her underlip with one tooth. She did not look up again, eyes on magazine, so I thanked her and went away.

When I looked back at her she was staring at me, eyes wide under a forest of hair clips. My next glance caught her racing next door with the news.

The watermelon-lady didn't even answer. She was busy finishing her fruit. The muscled and stone-dusted boys were making such a racket with their hammers that they couldn't hear me. I sat on the pier and watched two little boys watch me.

Finally, hopelessly, I asked: "Where is the cat?"

"Out there," said one, pointing to a distant promontory.

"The stone cat?"

He nodded.

"The one that looks at you so as to make your blood chill?"

He nodded, pointed, and turned to the other little boy for corroboration. Then both turned toward me and nodded again.

"If I could walk there, how long would it take?"

There was some doubt. Well, was it far? This was a matter of such disagreement between them that no answer was given. Well, did it take a long time? This they did not even hear, being busy arguing.

I walked over to the young boatman. He was still fishing, his back to me. Across the inlet, the two officials were hanging from the window staring at me.

"I found the cat," I said.

He turned and looked at me, then said: "That's nice."

139

"It's out there." I pointed to the promontory in the distance. "Is it far?" I asked politely.

He looked, measuring it with his eyes, then equally politely agreed. "Yes, it looks far."

"I should like to go there."

"Is that where your cat is?"

"Oh, it's not my cat. It's a stone statue."

"It's a what?"

"It's a...stone cat."

"Oh, a stone-cat," he said, pronouncing the words as he might have Angora-cat, Persian-cat, Maltese-cat. Then: "Well, cats like fish." This was to serve as transition between my cat and his going back to his baited line.

We were silent for a time, his back to me.

"Will you take me in your boat?" I asked.

He turned around and looked at me. "You want to go out there and search for the cat in my boat?"

"Yes, please."

"And you think you'll find it?"

"I hope so."

He looked at his fishing line, then sighed and drew it in over the gunwale. "Very well, we'll go out and search for your cat in those rocks way over there."

"Thank you very much."

"Don't mention it."

The rocks were enormous and a great distance away. They were visible from the village because of their extreme size. It took an hour, moving slowly over the clear blue water, through the motes of the afternoon sun, the bottom of the sea lost in the blackness beneath. As we eventually neared the rocks, he shut off the motor. We floated in sudden quiet. He looked over first one side, then the other, as though he expected to find the animal struggling to the surface.

The rocks were high blocks, piled one upon another. I could not imagine what kind of storm could have balanced such enormous weights. The boat drifted among them. I looked at the rocks while the helpful boatman searched the waves.

"I think one of the men of Heike must have brought the cat here and then his leader or someone made him throw it away," I said.

"One of the men of what?"

140

"The Taira clan. You know, Heike and Genji."

"Oh, them."

"The cat is of that period."

"Oh." He stopped searching the waves and was just getting out his fishing line again when I saw the cat. It was so near and so huge that I hadn't seen it. The top block, big as a small house, was the head. The rest was the body, and a cleft was one of the ears. The hole was the eye that turned the blood of passing sailors chill.

"There it is! there it is!" I shouted.

He put away his fishing line. "I don't see it."

"It's made out of stone. There. See its head, and its ear? And that hole is its eye."

"Oh," he said, beginning to understand, "so *that's* what you wanted to see." Then, suddenly the earnest mentor, he explained that I should have asked for the *neko no katachi o shita ishi* ("stones in the form of a cat"), that *sekizo* meant a man-made statue. Not, he added, that it made much difference. He had never heard of it before, and he doubted that those little boys had either. In any event, he concluded, it didn't look much like a cat to him. Nor did it to me, though there was something vaguely animal-like about the shape.

"It looks more like a dog," he decided. Then: "Maybe it was a dog they threw away."

"Well, perhaps. But they told me it was a cat."

"And you came all the way from Tokyo to see this then?"

"Well, not only this. But I came to this island to see this."

He looked at me closely. "Do you like it?"

"It doesn't look much like a cat. But now I've seen it at any rate."

"Do you want to go closer? Do you want to climb on it or something?"

"No—no thank you. This is fine. I've—well, I've seen it now."

"Are you happy?"

"Yes, yes, very happy."

"I see. You are happy that you finally saw it. Is that it?"

"Yes, that's it."

"I see."

He sat in the boat and looked at me. I suggested that we might as well return, and as he bent over the engine, he said that, yes, one might as well, now that one had seen the cat, now that one was happy.

141

There was not much conversation on the way back.

At the pier I wanted to pay him for his time and trouble. Oh, no, that wasn't necessary—it wasn't far.

Nonetheless, he had been very kind to take me.

"No, that's all right," he said.

Several people had stopped, at a safe distance, to watch us. Now all the employees hung from the windows of the town office.

"I don't feel right about not paying," I said.

"Oh, no," he said. "Besides, it was educational. Now I'll know where the cat is next time someone asks me."

Until the next boat came, hours later, I sat on the pier. Passing schoolchildren whispered audibly about cats. The beauty-shop girl, now coiffed, clattered about on her clogs and with many looks and urgent nods spread the next chapter of her remarkable tale. The office windows remained full of white-shirted, attentive officials. Little work was done on the island that day.

*   *   *

THE NEXT BOAT carried me around the tip of the island, right past my stone cat. I could have viewed it with comfort and equanimity had I stayed on the other boat, though whether I would have recognized it is not so certain. We passed quite close, however, and then turned into a small port on the other side of the island.

Four little boys were playing by the otherwise deserted pier, casting their shadows after them in the afternoon sun. I leaned over the rail. They saw me and stopped playing, conferred among themselves, and then approached, all in a bunch, to test their English.

"Hello," said the first, to which I responded.

"Good-bye," said the second and I answered.

"I love you," called out the third.

Then, just as the boat was pulling out, the last little boy shouted: "Who are you today?" And I continued island-hopping: Shiraishijima, Takajima, Konojima, and beyond, to the Honshu mainland.

*   *   *

I STAY AT A SMALL INN at Kasaoka. It is new, traditional in style, made of good wood, clean and neat. Its only concession to modernity is the bath, which is rather self-consciously rustic, all shells and pebbles with water-spouting turtles and a tall and dangerous-looking pottery crane. The water is saturated with the pine extract that turns it a bright chartreuse, which country people for some reason or other associate with gracious living.

Back in my room, smelling faintly of pine scent and waiting for my supper, I look idly from the window. Then I notice the lintel. It is beautifully made, admirably carpentered. I follow the edge of the window down to the sill and see that the underside, a place no one will ordinarily ever observe, is equally well worked.

I look around my perfectly ordinary room. It is a small master-piece of joinery, obviously the work of a master carpenter. But, then, in Japan all traditional carpenters are masters of their art. They make perfect joints as the Zen archer makes perfect bull's-eyes—without thinking about it, as though it were impossible not to make a perfect joint. This skill, this philosophy of craft, is passing away rapidly, particularly in the cities with their mass-produced, jerry-built buildings; but, where it still exists, the perfection of Japanese crafts-manship is impressive; it is the product of the pride people take in what they do.

I am reminded of these observations again the next morning when, after an early breakfast, with the day lying before me, I am sitting on a bench outside the hotel, my few belongings packed in the bag beside me, waiting for the bus that will take me to the station and the train to Fukuyama, where I'll transfer to reach the port of Tomo.

As I wait I watch several old men listening to a young man, still almost a boy. He is apparently a sailor, is apparently telling them something about engines. The old men nod, listen on.

Henri Michaux has observed that "the Asiatic knows how to accept, to be receptive, to be a disciple." The Japanese, with his enormous admiration for learning, opens himself. I have seen successful businessmen listen respectfully to someone we would describe as humble. I watch these old men listen to this child.

Often as not the information is of no immediate use. The listener will gain nothing. He is not being told anything practical. But, nonetheless, it is knowledge. Its import may completely escape, but as sheer information it is valuable. It is unthinkable that an opportunity for learning something should be disregarded.

Watching, I recall the well-carpentered lintel. I do not know why.

But it seems I am seeing two aspects of the same thing. A connection, hidden but certain, is there. As in haiku, two observations ordinarily thought incongruous join to reveal their single unity. Perhaps this is why the Japanese invented haiku, simply to record this apprehension of similarity that I sense but cannot explain.

Sitting, waiting, that most valuable and pregnant of times, I myself attempt a haiku. One comes, almost unbidden, but it is not about anything I have been considering, except for the echoing of the word "disciple." It suddenly appears, nude of context, naked but for the cloth of my mind:

> Lord Buddha had more
> Disciples than had Jesus—
> And much less trouble.

*　　　*　　　*

THE MORNING TRAIN from Kasaoka to Fukuyama is crowded. Though this part of Japan passes for deep country, already the suburban syndrome is upon it. Fukuyama is not large, but it is already full up. Those who work there must consequently live farther and farther away. Similarly, some Tokyo commuters live a full two hours away from their work and return to wife, family, supper at eight in the evening, getting up at six again the next morning to arrive back at work in time.

Four hours a day of strap-hanging in crowded trains, many with their faces buried in newspapers or weekly magazines of the more scandalous sorts. Certainly the Japanese commuter reads more, quantitatively, than his counterpart in any other country, but the quality of his reading is another matter. I've often calculated how his commuting time could be spent. He could do Proust in a month, Tolstoi in a season. But instead, except for an occasional cramming student, he reads only trash. And then there are also those who simply gaze from the window at a view that, seen twice daily for months and years, has long ago ceased having any meaning for them. The passengers themselves have also ceased to have any meaning. They have each become a tiny, if presumably necessary, cog in the workings of a vast machine of which they have no comprehension. Japan, never strong on individuality in any eccentric sense, has succumbed to the times without a struggle.

Not quite, however. Some years ago I was occupied with thoughts similar to these on a crowded commuter train and had reached the conclusion that the black-jacketed, white-shirted crowds have no more distinguishing differences than have the endless gray-tile roofs of any Japanese city. Thus musing, I was suddenly presented with an empty seat; sliding into it, I continued my thoughts while viewing the world at waist level. Suddenly, my attention was riveted by a detail that had hitherto escaped my attention.

In the middle of each male, between the white shirt and the black trousers, the laced shoes and the conventional necktie, was a sign of individuality, a decoration of personal choice, directly over that traditional center of the soul, the navel: it was the belt buckle. I was staring at a small bas-relief showing a fierce tiger with red brilliants for eyes; and, just in case one might miss the resemblance, above the animal's head was the word T-I-G-E-R in rotund script. This was but the first of an impressive collection I proceeded to make in ensuing months.

A visit to a belt-buckle store soon convinced me that there were literally thousands of different kinds of buckles. There were those with university names on them—Chuo, Meiji, Waseda, usually in white letters on brilliant blue or red enamel. There were those with dogs running, cats climbing, elephants trumpeting, lions roaring. There were those with such mottoes as Truth, Courage, Charity, or, occasionally, Baseball. There were those with initials—T.S. for Taro Suzuki, or, for the traditionalists, S.T. for Suzuki Taro. There were those with imitation jewels—rubies, sapphires, emeralds—those made of butterfly-wing landscapes, those large ones on which a cast-metal skull held a cloisonné serpent with rhinestone eyes.

But it was not enough to make my mental collection in a store: I had to find the buckles in actual use. Here, hidden behind uniform jacket or three-button coat, was the last refuge of Schopenhauerian will. Each represented a free choice even if not consciously chosen—after all, something must hold up a man's trousers—and provided an illustration of one of Sartre's more important tenets: a choice is nevertheless made. Fascinated, I began investigations; convinced, I was soon ready to present my findings.

The animal people were, in general, a raffish and likable lot; they were also the men who wore caps and elastic bow ties. I speak in the past tense, alas, because even then the animals were fast disappearing. The rabbit, once a general favorite (though why one should be so fond of this timid beast I do not know), was but rarely glimpsed, and the more spectacular of the quadrupeds were few: I've not seen an elephant for years, though some strays may still roam stomachs in the farther reaches of Shikoku or Hokkaido. And even those dogs and tigers I now saw were worn by older men who had acquired their fanciful heraldry sometime before the added dignity of a recent promotion and were now retained only out of habit or indifference.

The mottoes were once worn by a mean-minded minority, those who often beat me to the empty seat or those who always seemed to covet my comfort. "Hope" seem confined to my getting off at the next station; "Courage" referred to the wearer's fortitude in waiting that long; and "Charity" seemed, under the circumstances, mockery.

Also in decline was the school buckle. Those I now saw were worn by men who could not have seen the inside of a school in at least a decade. Besides, the buckle with Meiji or Chuo upon it would seem all too labeling in these days when half of the company lapel buttons in Japan are worn inside-out to insure public anonymity.

Troubled by the gradual removal of old friends such as the labeled tiger and the skull-with-snake, I turned to the waists of the younger generation. Here I found no buckles at all, only the international-style clasp attached firmly to the leather, all alike, all indistinguishable, no longer a sign of choice, pride, individuality—now indeed merely something to hold up the trousers.

Here, to be sure, a slight element of choice is still present. Crocodile seems to be favored by the newly affluent and otherwise flashy; lizard is coming strong and snake is holding its own. Then there are those woven affairs, and even more unsightly, ones with some glitter cheaply entwined. Also, in Tokyo at any rate, signs of the new foreign fashions are apparent. Innocent country boys wear low-slung metal-studded belts, wide and dangerous looking, copied from the compulsive fantasies of fashion designers; or belts wide as corsets with intricate sewn-in buckles that look like bank locks. But these are not individual, they are, in advertising parlance, "individualized," and as far from the real thing as the religious spirit is from religiosity.

I remember back to the day when, glum in the subway, I found my attention riveted and my spirits lifted by a yellow-enamel tiger carrying off a partially unclothed maiden while a whole paradise of palms nodded gently with the motions of train and wearer. I looked up. Yes, it was a gangster—the last of the breed, the final samurai, the ultimate individual. He was delicately picking his teeth with a matchstick and betrayed none of the subtlety that must have gone into the almost Kierkegaardian choice that had resulted in this splendid buckle. Gazing, I felt like the man who shook hands with the last Tasmanian (circa 1878), or the last person to see the walking dodo or the final passenger pigeon.

Now, excited by these memories of happy buckle-hunting days, I begin to peer at the middles of the people crowded around me on the Fukuyama express. In vain. Most belts are of the kind you go into the department store, buy, and put on, already made. But I remember the days when you bought the belt and then went to another store to buy the buckle. What has happened to all the buckle sellers? Are they now sitting dispossessed in the street? And those thousands of happy and inventive people who used to make the buckles, what of them? A small point, perhaps, but a sign of individuality is passing, has passed, and—much worse—also presumably passed is the need for that individuality.

Occupied with these unhappy thoughts, I suddenly glimpse, in the standing bodies before me, a rabbit. He is new and shiny, cast from some aluminum-like metal. Since he is a white rabbit he has red brilliants for eyes, and written in English over his head, as in the illustration in a primer, is: R-A-B-B-I-T. Though he was once a member of a despised race (despised by me, at any rate, then surfeited with elephants and lions), he is now dear. I twist this way and that in my seat, attempting to get a glimpse of that happy individual, his owner. But try as I may, I cannot, though the rabbit peers out enticingly from time to time.

Finally, I make the supreme effort. I rise from my seat—which is instantly snatched—and move, or attempt to move, in the general direction of my animal friend. Just then the train slows down, stops, the doors open, close, and the rabbit has disappeared.

Standing the rest of the not inconsiderable distance to Fukuyama, I am strangely at peace. Somewhere out there is a man with a rabbit on his buckle. Things are not as bad as I had thought; there is yet hope.

*   *   *

147

THE PORT OF TOMO—now absorbed into the octopus-like city limits of Fukuyama—is a small town near the tip of the mainland peninsula from which a tiny islet hangs like a drop. Unhit by typhoons, unstruck by earthquakes, untouched by wars, and subject only to the erosion of time itself, Tomo has been a famous fishing village for the last twelve hundred years or so, a stopping place for travelers from those times to these.

Here the earliest of the famous travelers was the first emperor, Jimmu. A later visitor was the indefatigable Empress Jingu on her way to introduce modern methods to backward Korea at about the same time that Julian the Apostate was unsuccessfully attempting to reintroduce paganism to Christianity. In the fourteenth century the great daimyo-warrior Kusunoki Masashige came here on his way to Kyushu, and the place was mentioned still earlier, in the eighth-century poetry anthology, the *Manyoshu*.

The name of the place is equally ancient: *tomo* is the very old word for "quiver"—and the old man who has been telling me all this dips his finger into the tea to trace for me on the lacquered tabletop the character, which I cannot read. And here also, he continues, came the vanquished Heike.

Did the Genji come too?

Oh, you can always tell who came where because the Heike used red flags and the Genji used white. In any of these little ports where there is something red, you can be sure that the Heike came too. Why, right up in the mountains over the town, in Terasako Pass at the Sumiyoshi Shrine, there is a big red fan attached to the lintel. Written, black on red, is *Nitto Dai-ichi no Keisho*—"The Most Beautiful Spot in All Japan."

The civic pride, the all-but-Rotarian tone, of this fan inscription would make one suspect a later period in any country other than Japan. Here, however, people have spoken and written this way for hundreds of years. I can well imagine one of the twelfth-century warriors climbing to the height, admiring the view, and sitting down to pen the sentiment on his war fan.

And the place *is* beautiful. It has that casual look of most towns where progress has been late in arriving. It is a crosswork of little streets like those in Italian mountain villages. They climb up and down among temples and rocks and great pines.

Though the place is small, one can easily get lost here. There is a turn every few feet, the gray eaves meeting overhead, with glimpses of pines beyond the high walls. The streets are so narrow that one naturally looks in all the windows. Housewife cutting vegetables; young man flat on his back, asleep, newspaper over his face; children playing with string; a dog at a window, looking out; goldfish hanging in a jelly jar.

There is something in the place, however, that reminds me of a castle town. Perhaps because this was once a major port and for hundreds of years all major ports, even those facing this domesticated sea, were guarded and fortified, were places of domination and fear.

*   *   *

I RECALL THE CASTLE at Himeji, a fourteenth-century structure and just what a castle should be—extremely oppressive and eventually deeply depressing. Now nothing but walls, cyclopean walls raking upward to improbable heights, and at the top watchtowers with slitted windows that regard the surrounding countryside suspiciously, as though with narrowed eyes.

Life in these places must have been of a narrowness exceptional even in medieval Japan. Everything was rules, regulations, provincial etiquette. No, one could not use this corridor, because the lord himself was about to, or just had. No, one could not look from the north windows today—an interesting archery tournament was on. No, one could not see the children—the omens were bad. A gorgeously costumed colony of ants with a labyrinth of considerable ingenuity.

One has this feeling even in relatively relaxed and urban royal residences—the Nijo in Kyoto, or the old palace in Tokyo. (At the Nijo, one is first charmed by the corridors with floors that sing like nightingales at the slightest footfall, only to learn that the singing was not for joy but to reveal the creeping assassin; nor were the great moats of Tokyo built to reflect the autumn sky.) Only in the old imperial palace-residence at Kyoto does one sense freedom and feel space. But that gracious structure belongs to another age, the Hellenic-like Heian period long before the hundreds of years of police state that both scarred the country and at the same time formed its character.

Himeji is from these later times. When new it must have been a model of its kind, a credit to the military government. Meant to

149

impress, it does this by its isolation and its ostentation. Alone on its bluff, from the beginning a blinding and unnatural white, refusing to accommodate itself to the pleasantly rolling and multishaded landscape of which it forms a part, the castle stands, prim rather than stern, and frowns down at the town. Though originally surrounded by mansions, whole streets of houses—now long disappeared—I doubt that even then the effect was pleasant. None of the curious rambling of Italian hill-castles, none of the smiling domesticity of the old castle towns of Yugoslavia; just the castle, flaunting its power, showing its style.

Inside the horror begins. Not now, of course. Now it is filled with gaping tourists and kindly bus hostesses. It has souvenir stands, illustrated pamphlets, and ice-cream machines. But behind these the stone oozes and when one is left alone between two enormous walls, the sky a line overhead, one feels with cold fear the possibility of being trapped, of having to stay forever. A corner is turned hesitantly. The torture chamber is expected.

There is none, of course. The Japanese had no chamber. They tortured just anywhere. The implements, however, were not of the variety to last, being made mainly of light woods or bamoo. Such later developments as the sharp-edged board upon which the unfortunate knelt while stones were piled into his lap until his shins first ran blood, then broke—these have long been pounced upon by museums and local amateurs. A few crushing stones, which were piled on the chest until it caved in—these are all that Himeji can now boast.

Nonetheless, the feeling of relief at leaving the place is so extreme that even the happy tourists feel it. Round-faced schoolboys wipe their round faces with clean handkerchiefs; giggling girls begin again to giggle; old people in their best kimono turn for a final look, fascinated by this premature glimpse of the nature of the grave.

*   *   *

MORNING IN TOMO—a light rain, almost a mist, gradually resolves itself into vertical lines of heavy rain. Then the rain is caught by the sea wind, scattered, and once again dissolved into mist.

The eaves drip. Rain runs down the panes. Drops trickle along the spines of the potted palms outside the window or catch in the needles of the cacti. Over the sound of the rain, the putt-putt sound of distant boats, the cry of kites circling, wet and invisible, overhead.

I sit in a small, rustic teashop built out over the channel. In the front there is a display of Japanese bean-pastries, which are served in the rear along with cups of hot, steaming green tea. Not liking the sweet and sickly pastries, I order their principal ingredient, red beans, served hot in their own syrup—a dish called *shiruko*. It too is sweet and sickly but is, at least, not made in the marchpane shapes of little apples, clusters of cherry blossoms, and the like.

I sit and nibble at the stuff, sweet and insipid at the same time, and feel sorry for myself—alone and lonely, miles away from friends, eating *shiruko* on a wet, dead day, lost somewhere in the wilds of a land that preeminently knows how to make one feel alone. Reluctantly, I eat the last of the red beans—because there seems nothing else to do.

The young waitress, plain and neat in a blue skirt and a white apron, has been watching me. Now she approaches, excuses herself, deftly removes the empty bowl, bows, and moves away. Soon she reappears, fills my teacup neatly, brings a new ashtray, removes the used one. She does all of this, as do most Japanese waitresses, decorously, with discretion and with care. Then she disappears and comes back with another bowl of steaming *shiruko*. She allows herself a smile as she puts it in front of me, turns and says, charmingly, "*Okawari desu*"—another helping.

She had observed me, had perhaps misunderstood my reluctance to finish as a wish to savor. Now she was giving me, free, another helping because I had seemed to like it and because it was theirs.

The Japanese concept of service is doing something nice for someone, and doing it as though for its own sake. This girl expects nothing because one need not tip in Japan. Even my future patronage is not to be considered, for the likelihood of my ever returning is very slight, sitting as I am with my belongings, waiting for a boat. And no one obliges her to behave in such a pleasant fashion. She does it because it is the proper way of doing it. And it is. It is the only way to serve and not demean either yourself or your customer.

Mouthing my second bowl of *shiruko*, this time even sweeter-tasting, sweet enough to make the teeth ache, and trying to look as though I were enjoying it, as though it was just what I wanted, I look out the window:

151

The tiny offshore island, made of gray-brown stone, humped like a whale, slowly turning black in the rain. A stone torii and, behind it, a flight of steps cut into the rock, meandering up to yet more rocks and a grove of black pines surrounding the home of the god, wood painted a bright orange-red and surmounted by an octagonal, rounded copper roof with a green patina. Beside it, a small pagoda on this island in the middle of the channel. At the peak of the roof, an unopened lotus bud cast in bronze, dark against the gray sky.

Clouds float low between this island and a yet farther island. Clouds catch in the treetops. The wind blows them against the sharp pines, and they soundlessly rip. Rags are torn from them and fall dissolving into the dark forest below. The higher clouds pass on, tumbling. They shroud a low peak and then blow on to the next island, across an inlet, and are lost in the sky.

The farthest islands are a light and milky blue, with mist between. A few fishing boats are black and flat on the ruffled sea. A kite flaps close, against the wind, its wings spread. It flies but barely moves, is held aloft, motionless, outstretched, looking down at sand and sea.

I look back at the waitress. She too is gazing from the window, her young face blank, serene. How can she, I wonder, be so good, so peaceful, so deft, so pleasant? She will never leave this town, this shop, or, if she does, it will be to go to some place similar. Then as I watch her watching I realize she loves this view, likes this rain, that she is contented, perhaps even happy.

*   *   *

ON THE BOAT to Onomichi are seven tea merchants from Shizuoka. Though all are over fifty, they are as excited as traveling schoolboys. They point out to each other objects on the nearby shore: an oddly shaped rock, a big tree, the roof of a distant temple. They are on an excursion, all are wearing their best clothes, the dressed-up clothing of country people, white shirts open at the neck, T-shirts showing, wide-cuffed pants, big, old-fashioned, heavy shoes creased in the wrong places, the kind that cause corns.

For a time they are again in childhood—boys together. They shout at the birds, the rocks. They think they see whales. From a passing boat a man opens his shorts and urinates into the sea, looking at us

152

amiably the while. The tea merchants are in transports. You see that? You see what he did? He just stood right there and flipped out his prick and just pissed away. This is the life, oh, this is the life.

We exchange words, and then I ask them why they didn't bring their wives with them. Oh, we'd never do that. They'd get in the way. I express sympathy for the seven wives sitting at home in dull Shizuoka while their husbands are off to glamorous Onomichi.

"Oh, no," says one of them, with a friendly gold-toothed smile, "if they want to come, then they can all come together. It will be nicer for them." Do they intend to do just this? Oh, no, not at all. They have to stay home and mind their houses and their children. Oh, this is the life, though. And he turns back to exclaim at a rock that looks just exactly like a big turtle, doesn't it now?

Japan is one of the last countries to segregate the sexes. There is at times an almost Islamic insistence upon the men over here, the women over there. If you go to a party, you find that all the women are collecting in one corner, all the men in another. It is like those old-fashioned Western parties where the ladies adjourned to the drawing room, except that here the men never, after a decent interval, join the ladies.

This makes excellent sense. Men and women don't really have much to say to each other, at least not in Japan. Western women have told me that they never have anything to say to other women and prefer to talk to men. In Japan, however, women apparently have things to say only to other women. They can talk forever. With a man, the woman tends to become silent. Part of this is what the Japanese think is good breeding, fine manners. But the greater part of the reason is that the women can't think of anything to say. Talking to men—that is the role of the geisha, the bar hostess. It is not the role of the well-brought-up traditional Japanese woman. The men of both cultures, I believe, prefer the conversation of their own sex. The only difference is, perhaps, that the Japanese admit it.

The youngest of the seven merchants is chinning himself on an overhead stanchion. He makes other athletic movements as well, but the rest of the six sit in their white shirts and look on. Then one starts exclaiming again and the others follow suit until they're all shouting at the landscape again. Oh, look at that big tree. Oh, look at that funny rock.

But gradually their interest wanes. They sit there, vacant-eyed, mouths slightly open, watching the landscape slide past, turning from time to time, adults again, to talk of tea and Shizuoka.

* * *

THE COAST IS BEAUTIFUL, but the other side, the sea side, is spectacular. The islands stretch, one after the other, some near, some far. Sunny, open, fragrant, they welcome. They do not, however, smile.

In Europe these islands would be openly gracious. There would be a plaza or a piazza or a plaka; there would be something more genial about them. Japanese geniality is of a different sort. It is more private. Nothing is shown openly. The house front is closed, the face is blank. Once past this, once inside, then true friendliness begins. Only in the bar, the restaurant, the hotel, the home, and only after you are identified and committed—only then do geniality, hospitality begin.

Japan is not a place strangers easily enter—no matter the charm of the islands, the grace of the people. There is no tradition of anything but a politely hidden suspicion of the unknown wanderer. To be anonymous is, in Japan, to be nothing. Only after your name, occupation, family, history are known do you become real.

* * *

ONOMICHI IS from the sea a very Chinese-looking city, the houses emptying directly onto the water. The view is one of backdoors, windows, garbage cans, blinds, shutters, steps, ladders. This waterfront looks like a long line of untidy people all facing in the other direction, all with things hanging from their back pockets.

Just behind this facade, this row of rears like a flat of scenery, is a fishing-village-like street: ropes, old women with cloths on their heads, old men carrying fish, children holding cats, small stores selling crackers and fishing line, men with caps and bicycles making bargains with sandaled men in loincloths.

And directly beyond this is the front of the city proper, the main street. Very citified this, with stone buildings and automobiles and banks and women in clean print dresses and parasols. There is a kind of arcade that stretches the length and beyond it, as the city rises to

154

the mountains, to the nicer section: coffee shops, department stores with mannequins in Tokyo poses, little boutiques, jewelry stores. Beyond the main street is the railway line, the station, the mountains. One layer is laid over the other like scenery in a toy theater. It is a very narrow city.

And a very long one. Since there is no space between shore and mountains the city has stretched along the shore. It winds like a snake in its narrow nest. Always lengthening, always growing, it seems five miles long now and is still extending itself.

This kind of city is exhausting. Shimabara in Kyushu, though pretty enough, will kill you if you try to walk the length of its main street. After miles and miles, there is still no end to it. The main street is the town; there are no side streets.

Onomichi has the bus station at one end and the boat station at the other. Hence perhaps all the bicycles. No one would walk this length. It is wide enough to have side streets, however—and to hide its extensive night-town.

The places where you have fun after dark in Japan are always hidden. The unknowing foreigner walks along Tokyo's Ginza or along Kawaramachi in Kyoto, lonely, little knowing that just a few blocks over are lanes of bars and blocks of cabarets. Even in the smallest hot-spring towns the main street is primly closed by ten. One would think everyone asleep. In back of the main street, however, are the liquor, the gambling, the girls.

Onomichi's night-town is not hidden too well. Corners of it spill out in broad daylight. This is because the area is so large—the biggest I have ever seen for a town this size.

One of the reasons is that Onomichi is the main port for the middle reaches of the Inland Sea. Another has to do with its history. The place was traditionally the home of pirates. Here they had their fortress and made their homes. The location was right. Directly in the middle of this inland sea, the harbor sheltered by big Mukaijima just across the strait, the water lying like a narrow river between. The place was also equipped with escape routes so that beleaguered pirates could run off in either direction. Here also complacent pirates could keep homes and through their numerous lookouts remain appraised of what was coming. There were also caves in which to keep the looted treasure.

The caves were where the night-town now is. This is fitting because

I would guess that this warren of bars, cabarets, Turkish baths, pinball parlors, and, probably, whorehouses surely holds more money than the winding caverns of the pirates could have ever contained.

*   *   *

THE ENTRANCE to Onomichi's night-town is marked by a neon arch. Outside, the city is already dark. Inside, the lights begin at once— lines of bars with names such as Jun (Purity) and Midori (Green, but also a girl's name) formed from bent neon tubing or in illuminated letters on glass tinted purple (a color presumed to be erotic); big cabarets covered with blinking lights spelling out such names as Shin Sekai (New World) or Kopa (after the well-known Copacabana); large and expensive nightclubs, with hostesses lined up in the entryway because the evening is still young, named Gessuimei (Moonlight Water), Buruu Shato (Blue Chateau), or the like.

It is very hot: here in this labyrinth no breezes blow and the heat of the day lingers on. The lined-up hostesses favor evening gowns of georgette and velveteen, not the coolest of materials. Already their makeup has started to run and they keep touching their perspiring faces with handkerchiefs rolled up and held in the fist. One is having difficulty with a rhinestone-studded slipper. Another is drinking a glass of water with small birdlike gulps while keeping an eye on the passersby and smiling between sips.

Men walk up and down the streets. The only women are those standing in the doorways of bars or lined up just inside the nightclubs and cabarets. Most of the men seem to be sailors, but all of them are dressed up and, though they may wear clogs on bare feet, they also wear neckties around their tanned necks.

I wander on, peering into the side streets, where the neon and electric lights stretch into the distance. The bars become smaller and there is an occasional large red-paper lantern marking a plebeian *nomiya*, the Japanese-style drinking place, usually with counter and stools, where sake is more ordered than whisky and where such presumed delicacies as *oden* (vegetables and eggs stewed in a vinegar mixture) are served. I am in that valley which separates all night-towns, divides the "purely" Western from the purely Japanese.

Soon the first willow tree makes its appearance and I hear the

156

twang of the samisen. After a few more blocks I spot plastic cherry blossoms and see the first kimono. I also suddenly smell the sea and, between the houses, see the tall illuminated masts of cargo ships. I am now in the Japanese quarter of this Japanese night-town and soon reach the small creek with its invariable rustic bridge, its grouped willows, its pink and blue lanterns.

Here the customers are fewer, and, this early in the evening, these small streets seem almost deserted. A child rushes past me, late for supper; there is the sudden sound of women laughing together from one of the houses surrounding me; in the distance a phonograph is playing the "Gunkan March" and I smell squid being roasted.

At the crossroads, where I stand, there is a small bar on one corner, new, its unpainted wood almost white, and a small theater on the other. A sign proclaims it to be the sole home in this area of the *zen sutorippu*; The latter word is, of course, "strip," and the former certainly has no Buddhist connotations, being one of the words for "complete" or, perhaps, "utter." In this small and attractive theater one may gaze upon the stripper who strips all. This art is now but rarely practiced in the larger cities. Tokyo, for example, has completely forbidden it, though *han sutorippu* is permitted, the *han* (half) referring to the upper portions of the performer.

Two old men in kimono come out smiling; I go in.

It is a very small theater with five or six rows of seats and a tiny proscenium with pink cotton curtains. Among the other patrons is a pimpled adolescent sitting directly in the middle of the first row. He stares straight ahead, eyes glazed. He has, I guess, sat through at least several performances.

I rest in the pleasant half-darkness smelling that not unattractive odor of mildew, urine, rotting wood, and DDT that these places always exude.

Presently the scratch of a phonograph needle introduces the first strains of a samisen melody and the curtains sway in the breeze as though someone has opened a door backstage. The adolescent—in a white coat and round white cap, an errant *sushi*-boy, I suspect— leans forward, resting his chin on the stage itself, and the curtains slowly open to disclose a middle-aged Japanese lady in full kimono, sweat flecking her neck and forehead, ready to begin her dance.

It is a classical dance and she dances very well indeed. There is that firmness in her movements, that precision, just soft enough to be

157

human, which classical dance calls for and without which it becomes a series of postures. Her performance is more complicated, however, in that, in addition to the classical choreography, she must also gradually unloosen the many garments that bind her, dropping first one obi, then the other, turning to allow us to admire the back of her neck, a renowned beauty-spot in Japan; then she must let her outer kimono slide from her shoulders, then her inner kimono.

She performs extremely well and her slight overripeness, her impassive and matronly face, brings something attractively perverse with it, heightening the obvious fact that she is, after all and essentially, only performing a striptease. Her performance is extremely personal, is, in fact, artistic, and without this quality the erotic can never exist.

First one nude shoulder appears, then another, as she takes off her *hadajuban*, a half-kimono that covers the breasts. One breast appears, and then the other. Now she is standing only in her *koshimaki*, a red-silk slip wrapped around her from waist to knees. This she slowly opens, still moving to the sound of the samisen, faithfully performing a classical dance intended to be done fully clothed. Perhaps the adolescent does not, but certainly I experience a slight feeling of disappointment. Those charms imagined or hinted at are so much more potent than those—no matter how well formed—exposed.

Finally, as the last notes of the samisen fade, replaced by the scratch of the record, she fully opens the red silk and we see, as the advertisement promised, "everything." She stands perfectly still, sweat running, the local Benten, a provincial Ishtar, and the curtains rustle closed.

It was a fine performance, up to a point, but at the end she faltered because the dance she had learned did not, after all, include the opening of the *koshimaki*. Indeed, the original dance was designed so you could imagine that magical moment, perhaps, but never directly view it. All Japanese art—perhaps all art—lives only through suggestion.

Thus considering, I was startled by the strains of "Gunkan March." To its lively military beat stepped onto the now open stage three very young girls, two in kimono and one in a kind of drum-majorette costume, with a tall, furry, tasseled hat but no baton. While the others made vague hand motions—left, right, left, right—

she bounded about the stage, kicking and clapping her hands together beneath alternately upraised thighs.

She lost no time divesting herself of her uniform, flinging it about with simulated abandon, while the other two decorously bared their shoulders. Soon she had divested herself of her short skirt and was prancing about in gold-spangled panties, her epaulets hanging loose, while the other two hiked up their kimono to show thick legs, and the march pounded on.

The number reminded me in its enthusiastic artlessness of the private shows one could once see in Tokyo—and can still occasionally glimpse in places farther from the capital. There, on the bare tatami of someone's living room (for these shows were always held in someone's house), cramped between the wife's sewing machine and the childrens' toy-box, one witnessed all kinds of lovemaking going on just a few feet away.

One of the nicest, funniest, and most typical of these exhibitions that I ever witnessed featured a pleasant young country girl who came on naked, bowed, beckoned to her female friend, who entered somewhat more bashfully, sat down, pulled her friend on top of her, and at once went into visible ecstasies. They crawled all over each other, patting and licking, then a double-headed instrument was produced which they used with greatly evident enjoyment. Then the second girl stood up, bowed, left, and was succeeded by a young man, who bowed and at once fell on top of the waiting original girl. Nothing came of this, however, because the man suffered an attack of stage fright. Under her skillful administrations, however, he eventually recovered his self-possession and treated us to perhaps all of the forty-eight classical positions. Then, after the heights of ecstasy had been sufficiently simulated with cries and groans and arched backs, he stood up, bowed, and again the girl was left alone upon the mats.

She then promptly produced a number of objects: a banana, a full beer bottle, a length of string. With no more preamble than a small smile, she peeled the banana with her fingers, inserted it, and bit off great chunks. When it was consumed, she deftly removed it and put the mess daintily on a square of tissues. Then she bowed. Next she inserted the beer bottle and after some effort managed to pull off the cap (doubtless previously loosened). She put the full bottle to one side and bowed again. Then she tied one end of the string to a small

159

square of paper and inserted it. Next, she held the loose end out to one of the guests and invited him to pull. He attempted, and several others after after him, but she always won the resulting tug-of-war. Bowing, she removed the paper, squatted, and asked for small change, ten-yen coins. After receiving a number, she inserted them all and then asked the assembled guests to name certain amounts. Forty yen, ten yen—she never made a mistake, depositing the called for amount in her own hand and exhibiting her mathematical prowess. Then, like a proper housewife returning borrowed dishes, she offered to return the coins to their original owners, smiling only slightly when repayment was declined by all.

Then she made a low and formal bow, stood and with two hands hid those charms the talents of which we had so fully viewed, smiled a most charming smile and—the reason I remember this girl with such affection—said: _"Domo, shitsurei itashimashita,"_ a common polite phrase that might be translated as "I have been very rude." All of this was accomplished without the least suspicion of irony because there was no irony, and none was necessary. This is what you say when you must leave, when you have stayed perhaps a bit too long, when you wish to reassure and at the same time show an attractive degree of gentility.

It was only I who found this degree of the incongruous irresistible. None of Japanese in the audience thought it funny; they did not smile and try to hide their laughter. They were busy finding their coats and, one after the other, bumping into the sharp edge of the sewing machine on their way out. Innocent themselves, they did not appreciate a display of innocence as extreme as this, at least not as much as I did.

Try as one may—at least in my case—it is impossible to find anything sordid in Japan and, consequently, one is oneself a bit freer of this mental color, this psychological taint. The girl busy with her bananas and her small change was not dirty. She was doing her work, and doing it well.

And so was the younger girl now up on the stage. The march was thundering to a climax, the gold-spangled panties had been thrown aside and there, glimpsed between kicks, was the small and furry opening that attracts all eyes.

It particularly attracted the now bloodshot eyes of the _sushi_-boy, who, mouth hanging open, moved his chin slowly across the stage floor until the edge hit his throat and prevented further progress. The kicking stopped, though the music continued, and the girl, smiling—perhaps the boy *had* remained through several performances—and with the best will in the world, spread her thighs and knelt directly in front of him. His eyes rolled up, his head lying on the stage as though severed. Then she made a small movement and brought herself within inches of his nose. He emitted a rattling sigh that I could hear above the deafening march, and she was at once on her feet again, kicking and prancing, smiling, sweat falling like rain, her two companions, also nude, writhing in some kind of imitation snake dance, and the curtains closed. The performance—all half-hour of it—was over.

When I left I glanced back; the *sushi*-boy was still there, sitting back in his seat now but unable, apparently, to move farther.

*   *   *

OUTSIDE, THE FIRST STARS had appeared, and I was thirsty. I went into the first bar I found and excited much tongue-clucking and curiosity by ordering iced sakè, a city drink. And in this fashion I met Momoko.

She came in later, but the old lady who ran the single-counter bar with its rows of glasses, its god shelf, its geisha doll in a glass case, its Daruma image (one eye carefully drawn in, with the promise of giving it the other eye when money started rolling in), had been singing the girl's praises to me through several glasses of what she called, delighted with its novelty, *sake on za rokku*, "sakè on the rocks." Momoko (Peach Child) was the most gracious, the most beautiful, the most talented, the kindest and sweetest girl among the many of her acquaintance. Eventually I understood that this sweet and talented young lady was up for sale, such being her business, and that this kind elderly lady was, in fact, her agent.

After several mysterious telephone calls, the sending of a young boy helper out to look, and the receipt of a telephone message, during which the older woman permitted herself only guarded grunts, the celebrated Momoko actually appeared.

She was a sallow girl in her early twenties with great sad eyes and almost colorless lips, wearing a kimono far too bright for her age—such vivid colors being reserved for the very young and the very old,

161

to the point where little boys' clothing and old men's clothing much resemble each other. It did, however, make her look like a little girl, and this was the presumed intention.

No, she did not want to try the exotic *sake on za rokku*, she would have a simple lemonade with, perhaps, just a bit of gin added. No, just a trifle more. Ah—how refreshing lemons were, didn't I think so. They were, well, so *assari shita* ("simple, plain, brief" is all the help the dictionary can give with this much-used and untranslatable word)—so, well, so *shibui*, if one might say so.

Ah, a cultured young lady, using *shibui* ("astringent, but pleasantly so," also a notable aesthetic term the meanings of which are always too complicated to be gone into), using such high-flown words in much the same way as a cultured young lady in the West might speak, wide eyes on the listener, of the texture of a food or the light values of a landscape.

Content at having created a good impression, Momoko next spoke at great length with her friend about the difficulties another friend of hers, Midori, was having with the police. They simply would not, it seemed, understand. Men were truly awful, weren't they?—and, alas, all policemen were men. This was followed by a charming if vacant smile in acknowledgment of the fact that, though I might be a man, I was not, at least, a policeman.

I had several more sakès, the Child of the Peach had several more lemonades, now liberally lacing them with gin by her own hand, her friend having put the bottle within reach. Midori's problems seemed to go on and on. When I attempted to rise, pay the bill, and leave, however, there was consternation. That would never do. It was not polite to the kind young lady who had come all this distance to be with me; it was not considerate to this pleasant older friend who had arranged this happy meeting. By which I understood that I had already bought Momoko.

She, however, was in no hurry to leave and go wherever we were going. She wanted to talk more. Then a stray remark of mine suddenly led us to poetry. Poetry?—you know poetry? asked the prettily surprised girl. Oh, then you must know Elizabeth Barrett Browning.

Yes, and I recited—in English—several lines I remembered. Momoko turned around on her stool, her back to her friend, transfixed. Here of all places, me of all people—someone who knew Elizabeth Barrett Browning.

162

Instantly, we must go to her room, where we could speak at our leisure of this remarkable coincidence. I originally thought, paying our not inconsiderable bill, that this was simply a way of doing what we had to nicely, covertly. Not at all. When we had reached the nearby four-and-one-half-mat room with its few books, its several kimono, its *futon* bedroll already laid out, a box of Kleenex at one side, and when I had embraced her, or attempted to, as I thought I ought, it turned out that we really had come to speak of the poetess.

Momoko's idea of the life of Mrs. Browning was singular. She had somehow gotten the idea that the poetess had been forced into a position much beneath her, had, in fact, been obliged to give herself to numbers of men, none of whom deserved her, and had consoled herself by penning those immortal lyrics of hers.

I mentioned that the only men I know of in Elizabeth's life were her father and her husband, both of whose intentions, so far as I had heard, had been impeccable. Yes, she nodded, pensive. She had heard of them. Robert—he was her first, her true love. And she remained true to him. While in the very throes of unfortunate transport in anonymous arms she had thought only of Robert.

But certainly, I ventured, he had outlived her. He had gone on and become one of England's greatest poets.

"Did he write poetry too?" she asked, struck at the thought.

"Yes, a very great deal."

She pondered, finger on cheek, then decided how sweet it was—he, the dear man, had loved her so much he had copied her. And she, forced into this promiscuous life, remained true to him, no matter what.

And who forced her into it? Her father of course, crude man, who thought of nothing but money.

I tried to discover where she could have uncovered such a fund of misinformation. Japanese schools teach some wild things but nothing, I think, so far from any reality as this. Upon this point, however, Momoko was not to be drawn out. She knew what she knew.

Then, bashfully, a pretty smile showing, Momoko recited what I took to be one of Mrs. Browning's plaints. It was short and was executed with a few stumblings and hesitancies. It was also the only poem that Momoko knew, being perhaps more interested in Elizabeth as fellow sufferer than in Elizabeth as poetess.

She repeated the poem several times so that I might savor it, and I thought of the oddity of a girl in contemporary Japan taking up a nineteenth-century English lady for reasons that had nothing to do with poetry nor with the real Elizabeth. I thought of the trackless maze into which one would enter did one, moving backwards, attempt to reconstruct the fortuitous occurrences that had concluded with this false Elizabeth as idol. Misunderstandings, imagination, willful twisting of any fact not convenient, all conspiring to the hoped-for end, which, in its turn, became the truth so far as Momoko was concerned.

Here, I thought, is a glimpse into the real Japan. This the way the Japanese mind works. Appearances are reality without a doubt, and if the reality is not sufficient, then change the appearances. This, I decided, was what Shusaku Endo meant when he said he found Japan sinister, a swamp that sucked life from everything in it, that drained the insect dry and left only a brittle husk. Such an extreme example of osmosis as this need not, however, be merely sinister, I continued. It might, in its way, be agreeable, creative. It was in this manner that whatever Japan digested reappeared in new, marvelous, and very Japanese form—just as alive but transmuted. Gagaku, T'ang music transplanted and still heard in the imperial court; tempura, a Portuguese dish that has become strangely enriched and is still happily eaten; Momoko's profligate poetess: all of these are manifestations of an identical will.

The girl was beginning her few lines yet again. I took advantage of her babbling to put my hand on her breast. This she allowed, or else did not notice, but efforts to remove her kimono were met with a pout and a sudden doubt that I really truly understood poetry after all.

For a time I respected her feelings because they were, after all, real. Eventually, however, I hardened myself. I had bought her and —masculine thought—was not to be cheated. She was, after all, a whore, though a poetic one. Since she had so chosen to be, then she should act like one. Otherwise she would be in bad faith with herself and a cheat with others. It was possible, to be sure, to be a poetic whore or a whoring poetess, and either of these alternatives she should emulate.

This I explained reasonably, but was met with petulance and complaint. At this point I offered to leave. No, I could not do that, not when we were having such a nice time, it wouldn't be polite.

164

Though my logic failed to move her, she eventually succumbed to her own weariness. I do not know whether Momoko had ever felt less like the act of love; I certainly never had. Yet, driven on by loneliness, because I had nothing else do to, and due to the fact that I had already invested in her, I pursued and eventually she lay in her pink inner kimono, her outer garments lying in bright piles about the room. These were all she would agree to remove, and my attempts to uncover her breasts were met with struggles and complaints at a roughness she had not thought possible in a gentleman who professed to understand the finer things.

In answer to this sentiment I attempted to open the bottom of her kimono. This caused her to complain and struggle. That was dirty, I must not do that. This went on for a time until I, who had thought that Momoko was better than nothing, realized that nothing was after all superior. Feeling disinclined as well as cheated, deciding that this struggle was one I would have met from the English poetess herself, I rolled off and prepared myself for a nap.

The streets, which had resounded with singing and laughter, were now silent. Tomorrow I would leave this pirate's lair and be off once more on the kindly sea. Momoko Barrett Browning would be far behind.

But not quite yet. I felt a soft hand on my shoulder; it turned me until we lay facing each other. Then I saw what Momoko had done. Reaching between her legs, she had opened up her kimono, had raised her *koshimaki* and her stomach-band, had lowered her pants, and had made a small, quilted, nestlike burrow, very deep, that would eventually lead, had I the strength, the endurance, the sheer length, to what I presumably wanted. She lay there waiting, her face impassive, eyes closed, like a little girl making water. I could not bring myself to action. I kissed her, took her into my arms, smoothed her kimono, and fell asleep.

During the night something happened but I do not remember too clearly. Drugged with sakè and sleep I opened my eyes at the commotion going on in the middle of the night and saw her astride me. With flashing thighs and pleasurable if unpoetic sounds she was using me. But when I attempted to roll over and use her in my turn, she complained, pushed me over on my back again. Eventually the motion ceased. I fell asleep and woke to broad daylight and Momoko making tea.

165

I was expecting a cheery morning verse by our favorite poetess, but none came. She brushed my trousers for me, smiled, yawned, remarked on the rain. I mentioned *Sonnets from the Portuguese* and Momoko said that yes, Elizabeth had often gone there, had loved that country, that it must be a beautiful place indeed to have had such a distinguished lady so fond of it. In fact, she lived there, far away from home and family. It was there that she was pressed into all of those lucrative embraces. So like herself. Here she was, child of a good Osaka family, who found herself in Lisbon-like Onomichi with all of these bills to pay and all of this obligation to people, such as the old lady at the drinking establishment, who had originally been kind to her. Indeed, the coincidences of their lives, though fully a century apart and on different sides of the earth at that, were truly remarkable.

I considered asking if she also wrote, but then decided against it, afraid that this question might bring out reams of notebooks that would take the rest of the day to get through. Instead, I contented myself with remarking that I had always heard that these love poems of Elizabeth to her husband were so named because he, due to her dark complexion, called her his "little Portuguese." Her answer was merely: Oh, was that so, well she had never known that, just imagine, etc.

Now she was suddenly without any real interest in Elizabeth, to whom she apparently felt closest at night. Now she was more interested in Midori and in her various problems. I learned several of them but they were not interesting and I was sleepy and had a hangover.

I put the money under the pillow, discreetly but making certain she had seen. Then I tied my tie at the mirror while she examined what I had left. When I came back for the last cup of tea she began talking about what difficulty Midori had in meeting her bills and that sometimes her guests were not gentlemen enough to leave what was commonly considered sufficient. Then, when she went to do her hair at the mirror, I added to the small pile under the pillow, then went to the bathroom. When I returned there was no more talk of Midori and her ungrateful friends.

She came down the stairs to see me off, smiling, a bit self-conscious, tripping over the bottom stair, steadying herself, laughing at her clumsiness. She stood there smiling, a large, plain, wide-eyed, sad-lipped girl, unhappy with her life occasionally but finding solace in thoughts of that other sensitive and misunderstood prostitute, Elizabeth Barrett Browning. She stood there, anxious I should go, equally anxious that she be thought well-mannered, decorous, and —as indeed she was—sensitive.

*   *   *

I GO TO SENKO-JI in the rain. This is an elaborate temple built among the rocks high above Onomichi, said to be much in disrepair but still fine enough with its great roof and its red-lacquer balconies, its view of city and sea.

A cable car from the waterfront carries me up toward the temple. Inside the car there is Muzak, "Für Elise" played on a music box, and the hostess, in her sky-blue suit and lapel pin, whines on about the beauties of what we are seeing. She wears eyeshadow, false eyelashes, has her hair swept up. She looks like one of the night-town girls on the daytime shift. No one else is in the car. She refuses to look at me as she declaims the age, height, length of the temple I am about to visit.

It is not very old, I find, nor, actually—aside from its situation— very impressive. Nothing grand but everything quite cunning. One does not admire the maker's vision. One admires his ingenuity.

The rain drips from the pines. Small fog-filled clouds pass at eye level. In the distance the cable car jingles Beethoven as it descends. I turn a corner and there, high in the red eaves, half-hidden and only visible to me now because a standing urn of water throws a dim and moonlike reflection into the eaves, is an *ema*, a votive picture. It is of a large cat looking at himself in the reflection of a lacquer table top. He sits curled before it, not about to spring; rather, simply enjoying the sight. His tail-curled rump is thrust forward. Past and over his tawny shoulder is the reflection he is enjoying—a great cat-face with silver whiskers and enormous golden eyes.

Japan is cat country, to the extent that it is animal country at all. The Japanese have little feeling for animals, but what little feeling they have is reflected in their interest in cats. There is no real dog culture here, the recent fad being mainly an importation from the West. True, back in the seventeenth century the Tokugawa shogun Tsunayoshi showed great affection for dogs, having them palan-

167

quined back and forth escorted by an honor guard, issuing a decree that all dogs in the land must be addressed as *O-inu-sama* (Honorable Mr.—or Mrs.—Dog), and setting up reserves with elaborate feeding facilities for some fifty thousand wild dogs on the outskirts of Tokyo; but, then, his altruism becomes somewhat suspect when one learns he was told by a Buddhist priest that he would never have a male heir unless he made recompense for having taken animal life in a previous incarnation, and that he then selected his object of veneration on the simple grounds of having been born in the Oriental zodiac's Year of the Dog. There is also the bronze statue of Saigo-san standing in Ueno Park accompanied by a faithful four-footed friend, and another statue in Shibuya Plaza, meeting place for so many Tokyo lovers, showing the loyal canine Hachiko, who kept meeting his master's train at Shibuya daily for who knows how many years after his master's death, until his own death. But these are anthropomorphized animals, humans with snouts and fur and tails that wag.

The Japanese are interested in cats as cats, not in cats as pseudo-humans. True, kittens are openly abandoned and left to mew until they die, but the idea of Cat nonetheless has a hold on the Japanese imagination. They believe cats to be cunning. This is a quality the Japanese admire. The sleeping cat at Nikko, the beckoning cat of old-fashioned shop windows, the cat playing with a butterfly among the peonies as seen in countless scroll paintings, this self-admiring cat at Senko-ji—the animal would be a totem if the country had one.

* * *

ON THE BOAT to Setoda there are two girls, one in pink, one in green. They sit on the deck in the sunshine and giggle with the pure pleasure of travel. One, the prettier, is very innocent, very sweet, very open, very talkative. Her friend, somewhat less pretty, though probably equally innocent, has somewhere heard that to be aloof is to be attractive. Such is rarely the case, and certainly in her the effect is not that which she presumably wishes. The pretty one accepts my offer and looks at the landscape through my sunglasses. The other one declines with a curt nod and turns a studied but uninteresting profile to best advantage.

They are both from Kyoto and the pretty one babbles for a time in Kyoto dialect until becoming certain that I am missing half of what she is saying. Not that I have missed too much. Her talk seems to have been about her job in a department store, her day off each week, how today they got up in the middle of the night, boarded the train, how they are going to see the grand and famous temple at Setoda about which they have heard so much, how they will be returning to Kyoto just in time to get to work tomorrow morning.

Around us from time to time circles one of the sailors, a young man with biceps and acne. He keeps casting glances at me, and I eventually realize that he has decided that the girls—or at least the pretty one —were for him, and that I have come up with my foreign charms and exotic ways and taken them away. He keeps hovering about, carrying ropes and other nautical implements, his white hat at a jaunty angle. The pretty girl, however, has eyes for nothing but my sunglasses, my large shoes, my blue eyes, my white skin.

As he passes again on one of his unsuccessful forays, she makes matters worse by asking him to take a photograph. Since the language is such, he can, for a short time, believe that she wants to take *his* picture. He is pleased, smiles, comes closer. But no, she meant that he is to take a picture of *us*—her, myself, and—if she can be prevailed upon to that extent—her unsmiling girl friend.

No, the girl friend cannot be prevailed upon, nor can the sailor, who nicely pleads ropes, pulleys, and the general direction of the ship. So things are arranged that the girl friend, with great ill grace, is to take our picture and the livid sailor is to be excused.

Both are jealous. Not of me, however. The pretty girl is making the most of her outing, and I am an interesting object along the way. Yet how often one is completely taken in by these attentions, this forwardness. It means nothing, though occasionally one can make it into something. The sailor too misunderstands, as does the girl friend. When two girls are out together one will never actually leave the other for, say, a cup of coffee, or an invitation to see the interesting house of this fascinating foreigner. Occasionally, both may come. But if one of them is not interested and is also fearful—not for the other but for the success of their planned outing—then all is hopeless. I dare say the sailor could do no better than I even if he tried. For the duration of the trip, however, the pretty girl flirts. She is both both outrageous and innocent. She doesn't seem to know what she is doing.

Finally, using all her pretty ways, she cajoles the girl friend into taking the desired picture, a picture that, along with many another, will prove to fellow workers back in Kyoto what a good time was had.

We stand, arms tentatively and temporarily around each other. The girl friend, frowning, stands in front of us and peers into the camera, then snaps. I doubt anything comes of it: she didn't wind the film, paid no attention to focus, pointed at a place five feet from where we were standing, beaming, and had one finger over the lens.

*   *   *

SETODA IS THE MAIN TOWN on the pleasant little island of Ikuchi. Its location makes it a favorite stopping place for most of the traffic on this western Inland Sea. Its cultural importance, however, is at present considered greater than its maritime. For here, every year, some five hundred thousand tourists tramp the single lanelike street leading inland to the massive gate of the new temple. Setoda has become a locally famous tourist spot.

I don't know whether to begin with the physical appearance or with the history of this temple. Both are extraordinary, and each complements the other with a fidelity rare in cultural objects. Perhaps I should begin with a little of both.

The island is, like most of the islands in this part of the Inland Sea, fairly rocky and arid but with good stands of trees in spots and many bushes; it is a smaller Sardinia, a greener Corsica. Here at Setoda, in 1936, a large hill was leveled by a munitions manufacturer named Kozo Kanemoto to make room for a temple. Mr. Kanemoto's mother had recently died at the age of sixty-nine, and he had resigned the presidency of his large company, let his hair grow long, and become a priest with a temple of his own. Nothing is said of his having had a wife to abandon—or to bring with him.

To become a priest was not difficult. He approached Kyoto's Nishi Hongan-ji, one of the more worldly temples, and for an undisclosed amount of money obtained both priesthood and the rights to a small and little-used temple somewhere in Niigata. Then he transferred the temple's name and nothing else to Setoda, and set up on his own.

Since organized Buddhism can be more accommodating to private endeavor than even the Protestant church—witness the fact that a temple may be the private property of its head priest, who then

170

passes both it and his priesthood along to his eldest son (perhaps a playboy at a Tokyo university with not the slightest knowledge of Buddhism when he inherits the temple)—Mr. Kanemoto had no difficulty in becoming the reverend Kozo Kosanji, a blessed, holy man. He at once began construction of the new temple, called Kosan-ji (leaving Niigata one temple the less) and dedicated to the memory of his sainted mother.

His idea, one worthy of a Frederick the Great, of a Hearst, was that people had to go too far to see the treasures of Japan. He would therefore bring them all together right here on a single island. Since he could not get the originals, he would rebuild them, on a somewhat smaller scale to be sure, but in full detail. Further, since the originals were dilapidated, he would restore to them their original brilliance. Finally, since the imagination of earlier artisans was naturally inferior to that of our own time, he would lend from the rich store of his own fancy.

So, when one goes through the great white gate—his own invention—at the cost of one hundred yen the head, one ascends great steps leading up to a half-size replica of the Nara pagoda, flanked on left and right by replicas of the wings of the Heian Shrine in Kyoto, and, in back, a full-sized replica of the great gate at Nikko.

Passing through this—if one is not frozen on the spot by such splendor—there is an enormous island of marble and on the far side a tasteful combination of both the Phoenix Hall—the Byodo-in—and Nara's Kasuga Shrine, all in orange, green, and silver.

Rich as this holy man is, however, he cannot possibly command the craftsmen necessary for his ventures. Consequently, there are a few compromises. The Nikko gate, for example, is fabricated from plywood, plaster, paint, stencils. From a distance, however, it dazzles, and this is all that is necessary. Further, the priest himself, as the pamphlet proudly states, has overseen even the least important toe on the smallest dragon, enriching the impoverished original with treasures of his own creation.

A full description of the front view of the copy of the Nikko gate will give adequate idea of the imagination at work. The roof is green tile, modern, the kind one sees on country houses. Just under it, in the raised middle portion, is the Thunder God carrying his bag, all in plywood, painted over with gold paint. Under it is a fringe of simulated copper plates—bronze paint this time—like lozenges in a row,

171

and below that a row of small protruding eaves, painted wood, and on either end are dragons, enameled white with red lips, brown teeth, and black eyes. Flame comes from their sides in carefully painted spurts, a natural orange color. Between them is a lintel of painted dragons, smaller, and a centerpiece of wild waves, painted wave-green, made of stamped tin. At either end of this are two bodhisattvas, also tinplate but colored by hand. Beneath this are six columns with dragon heads, painted gold, with catfish-like whiskers and open red mouths. Between these are tiny figures, in painted plywood, of the *nio-sama*, angry brothers, probably war deities, and some undistinguished bodhisattvas. Among them are four large white dragons and in the middle a full-length dragon with its red mouth open. Then occurs a kind of balcony around the top of the gate, its balustrade supported by red, white, and blue lotuses. In between are gilded scenes of revelry, also animals—fox, deer, crane. Beneath these are ten pedestal heads of gods and, slanting away from them, goddesses on elephants and various minor deities of vaguely Indian extraction, also Fudo in flames in the middle and around him a frieze of realistically painted flowers. This frieze ends in a gold band running around the building like a ribbon. It is supported by bronze-painted pillars, and in between are more gods. On the pillars themselves are scenes of various angels playing or holding musical instruments among which I spy a violin. In the middle of this is the gate-opening, itself flanked, as is customary, by two great boxlike structures. Inside are not the brothers Nio, but someone the pamphlet describes as our old friend, the goddess Benten. There she sits, both of her, one in each box. Now she is Indian, however, wears a great moustache, and has no breasts to speak of. She sits behind her gold-painted picket fence and regards the pilgrims with wide, intelligent eyes.

Of course, this is not all there is to this enriched copy of the already-busy-enough Nikko gate. Inside the arch, under the eaves, not an inch has been left uncovered. The area is ablaze with primary color, with little figures, little scenes—with red and green and gold and silver. It is a sight.

It is this gate that has given Kosan-ji its popular name, Nishi Nikko, the Nikko of the West. The differences are apparent, however. In Nikko, the material is always real. If the color was white, then the material was ivory; if black, then ebony; if gold, gold. As an exercise in premeditated wastefulness, Nikko is most edifying—as,

172

indeed, it was intended to be. Levying contributions for these mausolea of Ieyasu was one way of keeping the daimyo poor and hence harmless. At least, Nikko remains, which is more than one can say of the bridge constructed by a later shogun from the then fantastically expensive commodity, sugar.

Another difference is that Nikko exists in one of the most beautiful forests in the world, a forest of cryptomeria reaching to the sky. Among these, like toadstools among giant cedars, sit its cunning seventeenth-century buildings, looking like pastry houses in German fairy tales, like jewel boxes hidden in the moss.

In Setoda there are no great trees and no inspired artisans. The people who made these buildings were local folk who had before made only boathouses—though most elegantly constructed boathouses. The setting is an apparently waterless little island, and the immediate background is advertisements for Lion toothpowder and Cow Brand face soap. Imagine, then, this many-faceted rhinestone lying in the dry arms of this island under a hot and direct sun and you will understand its singular lack of charm.

Charm, however, is not everything. The place is actually quite impressive. When kitsch becomes this grand, it becomes art. Like the Albert Memorial, like the hotels of Saratoga, like Lourdes, it transcends its own triviality through its size and its intentions.

The intentions are everywhere. One of them is, obviously, to make money. One must buy postcards, one must buy a badly printed history of the place, one must pay a bit more to see the tomb of the mother—the one responsible for all of this. If one is allowed to see the priest himself, then another contribution is gratefully accepted.

Though by no means poor, the priest has seen that an extravagance such as this is to be excused only through making it a sound economic proposition. And so, though the upkeep is expensive— crowds of local people continually washing, painting, gilding—the intake is equally so. Crowds of people from the other islands and the mainland are always ready to give considerable sums of money to see the wonders and receive the blessing. Further, since this is an accredited temple, it is tax free, and the government gets no part of all those hundred-yen coins that come spilling in daily.

At present more tax exemptions are going up. In back of the imitation of the Phoenix Hall an enormous concrete statue of Kannon, popularly called the Goddess of Mercy, is being built. At

177

the base and offering eventual egress from the statue will be a Hell Tunnel equipped with pop-up demons, spirits on strings, holes to fall into, and red cloth flames. With admissions fees of their own, both Kannon and Hell Tunnel will soon have paid for themselves.

Another intention, besides that of making money, is equally evident. It is that the old man wanted to make something beautiful. He presumably had no children, perhaps no wife, and so he turned to another form of creation—art. No less amazing than the tasteless-ness of the place is the fact that it is the visible projection of one man's imagination. He has created a world of his own, a cosmos. He no less than Michelangelo, Velasquez, Tintoretto—the difference is merely one of quality. His work, like theirs, obeys its own internal rules. It has style. The old man, quite apart from reasons of money and mother, has had the true and superb presumption of the artist. He has forced the world to recognize his vision. He has had the energy, audacity, vision to give something of himself, to insist upon it, to create it.

If one does not like it, that is really neither here nor there. For here it exists. It is. He has created, and he has done so as a Japanese. He has brought together in unlikely proximity, he has combined, and he has made different—very different.

And he is not yet finished. I hear plans of bringing deer over next year and making the Nara deer park over again, of somehow or other constructing at least several of the famous islands of Matsushima near Sendai. They will all go into the collection.

He also collects other things. The lower buildings are filled with the results. Someone had an outstanding collection of beetles. Very well, he bought it, and here it is, all dusty, with labels all written in Latin. Butterflies? They are here too, case upon gaudy, dusty case. Strange birds?—he has an excellent aviary. Here I see my first pair of scarlet-headed ibis, stalking about like tall cardinals. Here is a marvelous bevy of tea-rose cockatoos, looking like dawn on the clouds. And a series of wonderful Eastern birds with Paris hats. The collection is so fine that, upon wandering past the condor cage and seeing inside a creature as large as myself, complete with a broom-like tail, clothlike wings, stirring up the dust with what appears to be its long beak, I take it to be some interesting new creature, until I discover it is the cleaning woman.

Rare animals? They have them—brought at enormous expense

178

and difficulty. In this country where the deer roam tame, and white foxes, giant sea turtles, and large and poisonous vipers are known to the very children, exotic beasts must come from far away. And so behind strong bars sit and pant four enormous Saint Bernards, looking even sadder than usual, full of mange and Mercurochrome. And here, behind glass, lest it attack the awestruck viewer, a real, live Cheltenham terrier, looking gravely into the distance and thinking of Dickens.

And art—art, art, art. Amid Taisho-period views, postcards, late, bad prints, stands a miraculous T'ang camel, big, green glaze running down its panniers; stands an exquisite screen of iris; hangs hidden in an unseen corridor a marvelous Ashikaga picture, mysterious, a single black figure, a youth, possibly an acolyte, black and gray on gold leaf, a picture I instantly covet and consider stealing. After all, stealing from Mr. Kanemoto seems no more reprehensible than stealing from the A&P. But the picture is firmly attached to the wall.

The art stretches on, a Sans Souci, a Xanadu. The holy man has collected everything. Its presence does not contribute much to his grand design, to this Disneyland of fine architecture, perhaps, but then Kanemoto has something larger in view.

I turn back to look at it all, blinding in the afternoon sun. It is absurd, beautiful, very Japanese.

*   *   *

THE PEOPLE in the temple, the whole town, the whole island for all I know, have been spoiled through years of tourism. It always happens, though it seems to take longer to happen in Japan. But thirty-five years is a long time. It has undermined ethics. The shopkeepers have the knowing, underhanded way of those exposed over the decades to transients—moneyed transients. Like all spoiled people they are predators. One of their weapons is knowing everything about everything.

I stopped at one of the refreshment booths and ordered shaved ice with bean syrup on top. Thirsty, I also asked for a glass of cold water, using the word *ohiya*. My Tokyo accent made it come out *oshiya*.

The large woman, hearing this outlandish and foreign word, turned heavily toward me and asked: "What?"

179

"*Oshiya*, please," I said, politely. Large women in charge of things intimidate me.

There was a long, staring silence—the woman stood before me like an injured concierge. Then: "Oh—it was water you wanted." She used the generic *mizu*, which means just any kind of water, not necessarily cold water.

"I wanted cold water," I protested, faintly.

"Then it is *tsumetai mizu* you wanted," she explained, large un-smiling.

"The word for that is *oshiya*," I protested, "as well as *tsumetai mizu*."

"If you want to use that word, it is pronounced *ohiya*," she told me.

Was it me she resented, I wonder—or perhaps my speaking Japanese at all? Some Japanese resent foreigners speaking their language, and all resent it if you speak too well. Or perhaps it was the Tokyo accent—with her stuck all her life in sleepy little Setoda. She glared at me. "Here we say *mizu*."

"So I gathered," I said lightly.

She stopped, glass of tepid tap water in hand, and heavily, pregnantly, said: "In Japan we say *mizu*."

* * *

IT IS ALWAYS the same. Travel hopefully broadens those who travel. It usually narrows those who have to deal with the travelers. Maybe they just see too many people—an experience that will always make one dissatisfied and irritable. I read somewhere that we only have tolerance for about fifty new people a day. After that we become snappish.

In that case all of Setoda should be ill-tempered. It has had more than its share of travelers. It was a headquarters of the so-called pirates; then the legendary brigand Muragami Suikun came with even more. The usual number of famous people came as well. Toyotomi Hideyoshi came and so did the famous warrior Kumagai —hero of the Noh drama *Atsumori* and the Kabuki *Kumagai Jinya*. Another visitor was the famous priest Honen, pursued here by a lovely maiden with the curiously unlovely name, if I've heard it right, of Matsumushi Suzumushi, these also being the names of two kinds of Japanese singing insects. Here he finally shook this insect-lady off, and she killed herself. Then, naturally, Kobo Daishi came and created some wells. He also left behind a curious custom, observed here during the annual Feast of the Dead. Children put lanterns in the trees and invoke the saint's name. It would be interesting to ascertain whether the island's only industry—lantern-making—began before or after this visit.

Later, some Japanese Christians, escaping from one of the persecutions, came and built caves in the nearby mountain called Shiratake. The next island, Innoshima, holds the remains of a pirate king's castle. And naturally, the goddess Kannon also appeared and gave her patronage to Hinotake, the highest mountain in the Inland Sea.

All of this information was given me, not by some white-haired elder cornered in his simple hut, but by a bow-tied, white-shirted young tourist official near the wharfs. And what, I wanted to know, was the island like earlier, before such celebrated travelers came?

The beginnings were, I learned, sordid. During the Nara period it was discovered that these shallow coastal waters were good for drawing salt and, since salt was then five times as expensive as rice, this was good business; then as now, salt was a monopoly of whoever ruled the land. The salt business in this area was centered on this island of Ikuchi.

One pauses. If the etymology of a Japanese place name is too confused, it is good to pause and search further. One is likely to come across old bones, skeletons, some horrid and hushed-up affair.. Ikuchi, written with the characters meaning "living" and "mouth," can also be read Seiko, which has many meanings—a kind of cattle, a prisoner of war, or by extension, a slave.

There. Now we know who made the salt. Prisoners from the many wars always being fought in those days or, when there were not enough of them, slaves captured from the nearby islands and put to work in the roasting sun. The method of conscription was simple. Boats would pull in and a drum or a gong would be beaten. The natives—curious as ever—would rush down to the waterfront and get pulled into the boats.

My bow-tied informant, who certainly seems to know his history, wonders if the resulting sadness among the survivors—fatherless children, husbandless wives—did not account for what later became the local dance, the Kichigai Odori or Jumping-around-like-crazy Dance. Also—all of this information tumbling out, one item hard

181

upon the other, as from a closet when you pull out the bottom box—they don't eat turtles here. This is one of the few places where turtle is not considered a delicacy. Indeed, though turtles abound, they are never eaten.

Why, just the other day, the children caught a big sea turtle and then turned it loose. This irregularity was not due to any feeling for the beast. It was occasioned by the belief that the animal was not edible.

The origin of this odd form of abstinence came from ages past. There was a strait called Kame-no-Kubi, or Turtle Neck. It was so called because it was so full of turtles that boats could not pass. Then the priest Honen—the one pursued by the insect-maiden—came and found a way to rid the strait of its turtles. He preached the torpid beasts a sermon. This quickened them to the extent that they followed him inland where, he told them, he had a nice place for them. On and on he led them, up and up, the saint in the front of this lumbering procession. Finally they reached the top of the mountain. Here it is, the priest told them, the nice place I told you about. But we are sea creatures, they said, adding that they would die. The saint smiled. So they would, he told them, and then left them there and went back to the town.

The townspeople rejoiced, the strait was open to commerce. All was not well, however. The priest had done a bad thing, if by indirection, in taking life. So the god Jizo—an odd, bald, childlike deity seen in roadside statues all over Japan—came and told everyone that turtles were bad to eat. This at least, the god reasoned, would save those few turtles that had not responded to Honen's siren call.

The ruse was successful. Later I went out and talked to some children. Not one of them had anything but the most elaborate distaste at the idea of eating turtle.

*   *   *

Walking about town I passed the two girls from Kyoto. They now looked somewhat less crisp. The bright one was a bit worn, the sullen one was ready to collapse. They were sitting on a bench in the dying sunlight, apparently too tired to move.

"What did you think of the temple?" I asked.

"Well," said the pretty one, "it was very . . . very bright."

The dour one turned. "We came all that way just to see this," she said, the first words she had addressed to me. "I had said we ought to go to Nara instead."

"But Nara was so near," said the other, apparently continuing an argument that had been going on for some time.

"Nara is worth seeing," said the other.

They had one day a month for a trip, given their jobs and their wages. I had every day. Their disappointment was very real. It had taken their time and their money. The other one was not dour, I realized, merely sad.

"But, anyway," said the pretty one, "we *have* seen it."

"Yes, that's true," said the other, mollified. "At least we know what it's like now."

"True," said the first girl. "And no one else in our whole department has seen it, you know."

"That's right."

"They always go some place near, like Nara. But we went very far indeed."

"Yes, of course," said the other and she suddenly smiled, her first smile of the day. It was like sun breaking through. She too was pretty.

*　　　*　　　*

ON THE WAY BACK to the inn I stop by the harbor to check the timetable and get into conversation with a friendly grade-school teacher who is waiting for the boat to take him and his large group of very well-behaved children home to Omishima after an outing in this cultural oasis. From him I learn that little Setoda was originally the home of the mysterious principal deity of Itsukushima, that fabled waterborne, red-lacquered shrine at the farthest end of the islanded part of the Inland Sea. Here the goddess spent a rustic childhood. But, fastidious as Venus, she soon moved. The reason, however, was neither boredom nor feminine indecision. It was a certain red leech named something like *akahiru*, which greatly and mysteriously annoyed her. So much so that she left and went looking for a more civilized home—which she eventually found in the shrine on Miyajima, one of the most civilized homes any goddess could hope for.

"Who is she?" I wanted to know. "Benten? Someone else?"

"Oh, that I don't know," replied the affable schoolmaster. "No one knows, I dare say. Just a deity of some sort."

Just a deity of some sort—ah, this is Japan.

*   *   *

BACK AT THE INN, they tell me that a guest is waiting. Surprised, I climb the broad stairs and walk along the long corridor to my room. There, sitting at the table on the veranda, a cup of green tea in front of her, is a tall, large, blue-eyed, white woman with long, light hair. This visual impression is followed at once by my recognizing that I am seeing my wife sitting there, her head sharp against the blue of the late-afternoon sky, the blue of the sea.

She turned and smiled, that familiar smile that over the years I had grown to see as both welcoming and forgiving—marred now, as always when she was unsure or unhappy, by a wrinkling of the upper lip, tiny folds that constrained her wide smile.

"Hello, there," she said, words she used indicating a camaraderie she affected only when she felt unwelcome. "I was in the neighborhood, just passing by," she continued, laughing to indicate that this was a friendly joke. Laughing again at her own laughter, she again showed her uncertainty. At such times she always laughed too much.

Such a display of brave unhappiness, of smiling (or laughing) through tears, had once made me feel bad—as perhaps I ought to have, being author of those many deeds, mainly of omission, that made her sad or worried her. But, over the years, while I came to esteem a foolhardy optimism that laughed in the teeth of disaster, I also grew to feel less guilty.

In this she generously assisted me. I was not to mind her moods. I must always do what was best for me. But then, of course, she would always do things such as suddenly turning up in the middle of whatever I was doing that was best for me.

Actually, she explained, she had not just barged in. "I knew you were somewhere near here and I was in Omishima, you see, because I had just come from Nakajima. Are you going there? It is so lovely." She talked on and on about the beauties of Nakajima, anxious to be talking, to avoid the silence that always had been and always would be threatening to fall between us. "And so," she concluded, "I

184

decided to telephone over and on the very first try I called this hotel and, naturally, you were here, though you'd just gone out, they said. What's this island like?"

And then I too talked for minutes, equally anxious to avoid the waiting silence.

That we both avoided a silence so natural between friends, so much a part of ordinary married life, indicates, I suppose, that we had both expected more from marriage—a continual diversion? a continual reassurance?—than marriage can actually give. At any rate, though we had been married for three years, few times indeed had the dreaded silence actually fallen. We kept it aloft, as it were, with our exertions, batting the conversation back and forth as though marriage were one interminable game of badminton.

Searching back through my travels I told her those parts that I thought might amuse her. When I told her about Saburo in Shikoku, she at once assumed that bright, interested expression that served to cloak her deepest disapproval. When I told her about Momoko, however—speaking, it soon became clear, in much too light a tone for such a subject as love, or sexual intercourse, or, if one prefers to equate the two, both—she allowed another disapproval to show.

"Oh, that is no way to speak of a girl like that. I am ashamed of you." This was delivered with smiles and the mock-disapproving tone she invariably used when she really meant what she was saying. "A sensitive young girl like that, loving poetry."

Part of her concern was because she prized sensitive young things, part was because this was another woman and Louise had strong feelings for the more unhappy of her sex, but the major part was because she could discover in my somewhat trimmed anecdote that I had actively—rather than passively—misbehaved and this was both a novelty and an impersonal reason for her to show disapproval.

"She was a whore," I said, growing sullen, as was my way with her. "She should have acted like one," I continued. "Oh, she was more than that, I know that," I concluded, forever taking objections from Louise's mouth before she could utter them. "Anyway," I added, "I only told you to amuse you. I didn't take it all that seriously."

"I know you didn't take it seriously," she said.

But this was as far as her vocal condemnation went. Other,

stronger feelings—and they must have boiled—she hid from me, showing me only her handsome mask with its great, wide-set eyes that spoke of honesty, truth, trust.

But because I had not wanted to see her, and because she was now perhaps beginning to wish that she had not, after all, come, and because she felt her remarks about my making fun of Momoko more deeply than I had, the silence slowly gathered over us. I suggested we take a walk to dispel the gathering gloom.

This she agreed to with grace and enthusiasm. But she did not move: I was not to escape from the Momoko experience without a few more muted reprimands. Such were, however, rarely direct. Rather, and suddenly, she would find my hair too long, or too short. Attractively so, perhaps, but . . .

"Your shirt is rather dirty, you know. Didn't you bring any other? Perhaps the maid could wash it for you." Such disapproval of me was often phrased as though from mother to child. Something I must have called for, it is true, or it would not have occurred. She was, in such moods, forever making plans for me, advising me, always giving me the benefit of what she thought best. In this way, it is true, she made a place for herself as best she could in an area where I forbid her. It is also true, however, that never once did she herself offer to wash a shirt for me.

Then, that over, it was apparently forgotten. She turned toward the window, her brow smooth, her upper lip now firm, no longer puckered, and said what a glorious afternoon it was, and what were we doing here anyway wasting it inside? Louise was rigorous with herself, did not fall easily into scorn, never completely closed herself off from the man who was not what she had thought he was but, she continued to hope, would sometime, with her help, eventually become.

At such moments I always liked her. She had the strength to put aside whatever emotion was troubling her, would bravely shut it from her mind, would—rather—allow her reason to indicate, and would follow what it suggested.

Often enough I had reminded her that I was promiscuous—saying the word as though it were some kind of debilitating but noninfectious disease—and that she had known it before we were married. I also often mentioned that if she were Japanese, she would be content with the home, the name, perhaps a child, and I could

186

gallivant as I pleased upon my quixotic quests. But she wasn't Japanese, nor was I, and it was equally probable that the complacent Japanese lady I had in mind did not exist.

She would answer that she had accepted all of that—didn't I see? —that it didn't make any difference, all these stray people I met on my travels. They had no meaning for her, not any more than they had for me, nor really—she thought—than I had for them.

Now, walking along the beach, however, we did not mention such wishful imaginings. We'd said it all—all that we allowed ourselves to say to each other. Her life with me was impossible. Yet she had chosen it herself. She had known, as one of my friends had delicately put it, "what she was getting into." Perhaps she hadn't, though. That is, she accepted it, reasoned about it. It followed that a person (me) must do what was best for him. There was no question about it; her liberality toward the world and its people, her own shyness about asking for anything for herself, did not permit her to think otherwise. At the same time, approving of something attractively distant (romantic adventurer) and then living with it (philandering husband) uncomfortably near were quite different. On top of this was the ludicrous discomfort of my being such a singularly inept adventurer that I thought of possible adventures continually and actually consummated very few. She, a creature of intelligence, had not thought of her emotions, and had certainly not yet realized that emotions too are, after all, only ideas.

I suddenly thought of Momoko, poetess but prostitute in spite of herself. And I thought of Louise, forever thinking of some hopefully better time with me in some improbable future, but neglecting me and finding herself unhappy living the very life with me that she had chosen. The differences between the two women were, I decided, extreme, but so were the similarities of several of their qualities.

We stopped on a pier to watch some children playing. She liked children. Then one little boy fell off the pier, on which he had been running. He landed on a sharp stick. There was some blood and more noise. I continued to watch, diverted by this turn of events, expecting him to run home screaming to mother and a small bandage. Louise, however, turned to me at once, her eyes wide with concern and intensely imploring. Such a gaze did not believe that I could just stand there and watch the tragedy. Silently she urged me to do something, to help.

This was what the ideal husband—that man she had not married, that man she was never going to meet—would have done. I saw him bounding down among the rocks, manfully rescuing the scratched child. She did not see this. She saw, I think, some enormously kind and compassionate gentleman moving surely to the stricken child, bending over him, kinder than a father.

No such man appeared, however. I remained standing and watching, avoiding her alarmed and sentimental eyes. Then the injured child ran screaming home while the other stared after him, shocked that human beings should have blood inside them.

She did not mention the child as we walked on, the long, late summer afternoon now turning into evening. Instead, she told me some of her solitary adventures in Shikoku, where she had gone by herself, with as much determination as pique, when I had announced that I was going alone to the Inland Sea. She had been to a peninsula so wild and uncivilized that the people would not look at her and the very animals turned away. Lonely, she had walked a small stone street and said good-morning to one of the passing women. This elicited no reply, but the woman stopped an acquaintance shortly, and Louise heard her say: "Did you hear that? That foreigner said good-morning to me."

I responded with the story of the girl who played Fauré on the guitar and then she told me other things that had happened to her, to which I in turn responded, and in this way we eventually began talking freely with each other again, she leading as always, both of us mindful that we were now competing with adventure stories, but that this was better than not talking at all.

But this was not the only reason for the pleasure we took in the conversation. Both of us liked very much to travel. The trouble was that—treasuring a freedom of which I rarely availed myself—I always refused to take her with me. And both of us liked these small travel adventures for their own sake; I think they meant the same to both of us. But Louise believed that if she were with me, they would be doubled. And I believed that if she were with me, they would be halved.

Nor was that the entire reason for our liking to talk together. We each knew what the other was going to say. We could no longer surprise or unsettle each other. Here, on this island in the middle of an unknown sea, it was pleasure enough to speak English again, it was good to communicate again with all of those unspoken understandings that are the basis of all real communication, and it was almost happiness not to have to guess at meaning or infer possibilities, but rather to exchange thoughts freely with a mind you knew well, or thought you did.

I had early made it one of the more convenient articles of my married state that Louise must be strong and learn to be independent. She was learning, for I asked nothing else of her, being content to twist this small clause this way and that as it suited my plans, but I do not think either of us expected any happy outcome, at least not so far as our marriage was concerned.

In one of her rare outbursts, she had once crouched by my bed and asked why I had ever married her—a question for which I had no answer other than that I too had believed her different from what, in fact, she was. Shortly after she stood up, went back to her own bed, and did not speak of it again. Her pride, one of the few things I had left her, prevented her from speaking again. Very occasionally, upon one of the many times when I returned home very late, she would permit herself to tell me, for example, how she had almost cut herself with a very sharp carving knife we owned—but that was all.

The bloody little boy came back, running past us, now with a white-bandaged arm, and we heard the children shouting in the growing darkness as they played on the sand.

I looked over the darkening sea and wondered what Louise saw in these beautiful islands. That she saw their beauty I was certain. But I was equally certain that she did not see their promise, their assurance of bright illumination or soft caress, just beyond the horizon. Her hopes lay in me, and mine lay in this lovely land that stretched on and on and never seemed to stop. I knew that this promise was to be unfulfilled, but I continued to search; she knew that her constancy would not be rewarded, yet she continued to wait.

We returned to the hotel and the smiling, knowing faces of the maids. This was the way it should be, each with his own kind, they seemed to say.

We sat and watched the stars from the veranda. She mentioned, carefully, with no emphasis, that I had seemed surprised to see her. I answered that indeed I had been.

Next morning I put her on the boat for Onomichi, and she kept her brave smile to the end. Then I, with relief, took the boat to Omishima. I did not tell her that it was with shock rather than mere surprise that I had seen her; that for weeks I had been among people with black hair, black or brown eyes, and skin the color of Sicilians; that to come so unexpectedly upon the blond, the white-skinned, the blue-eyed had shocked rather than pleased; that, for an instant, I had known what the Japanese felt upon seeing one of us.

* * *

I LANDED AT INOKUCHI and took the bus to the other side of the island. Here at Oyamazumi on Omishima is one of the three oldest shrines in Japan. It must be old indeed. The most important shrine, that at Ise, built by the emperor Suinin in honor of the Sun Goddess Amaterasu Omikami and still functioning, was completed, if the records are to believed, fully twenty-two years before, on the opposite side of the globe, Pontius Pilate washed his hands of that other religious matter. I am also assured by the priest that this Omishima shrine remains one of the three most important in the land, on a par with those at Ise and Izumo.

Of great antiquity and so remote that it remains largely unvisited, this shrine contains an atmosphere long vanished from sacred but tourist-filled Ise, from well-tended Izumo. Distance alone, however, does not explain its neglect. Perhaps it is that the Japanese no longer expect shrines on islands. (Even Kompira-san, that great shrine near Takamatsu dedicated to seafarers, is surprisingly located in the mountains and has no view of the sea.) Perhaps it is that, in this new age of mass tourism, little Setoda drains away the potential visitors. Or perhaps it is that Japanese like their religion humanized just as they like their nature domesticated. Oyamazumi is too rigorous, too near the gods.

It is a series of low buildings among trees. Space in a shrine is horizontal and not, as in a cathedral, vertical. In a church, space is confined. It must struggle upward, having no place else to go. In a shrine, space is spread. There are no high walls, no tight enclosures. The space is a grove and this grove seems so endless that it might be the world itself.

The sky seems low, near. There are long expanses of lawn or grove

190

among the buildings. One is not enclosed, nor is one directed. One is liberated, and almost always alone.

Shrine prayer, as I have said, is not communal prayer. It is solitary prayer. It is not a state—it is a function. It lasts only a minute or so and it is spontaneous. One does not enter, as in churches, or descend, as in mosques. The way to the shrine is through a grove, along a walk, through nature itself, nature intensified. Through these trees, over this moss, one wanders to shrines.

This casual, unremarked acceptance of nature speaks to something very deep within us. It speaks directly to our own nature, more and more buried in this artificial and inhuman century. Shinto speaks to us, to something in us which is deep, and permanent.

Certainly we feel—which is to say, recognize—more here than in smiling Buddhism with its hopeful despair, more than in fierce man-made Islam with its heavenly palaces on earth, more than in the strange and worldly tabernacles of the Hebrews or in the confident, vaunting, expectant Christian churches.

This religion, Shinto, is the only one that neither teaches nor attempts to convert. It simply exists, and if the pious come, that is good, and if they do not, then that too is good, for this is a natural religion and nature is profoundly indifferent.

There is no personification. The gods have neither shapes nor forms. They are simple *kami-sama*, whose numbers are unknown but vast—so vast that they meet together only once a year, far away in Izumo.

The main shrine at Oyamazumi is plain, dark, weathered wood. It stands like a ship, austere, beautiful. It shows its age in its cracks, its blackness, its grayness. This is the outer shrine. Directly behind, painted the usual white, orange, and green, is the inner shrine.

I ask and learn that Oyamazumi follows an observance now discontinued in almost all other places. Only the house of the god is decorated. The house of the worshipers is left plain. We pray against the weathered gray pillars and beyond the barrier we glimpse the gay, candy-colored home of the deity.

The drum sounds. Its beats are slow at first, then grow faster and faster. This is the tempo, this acceleration, one hears in Noh, in the Kabuki, at country fairs, in shrines and temples all over the land. This is the rhythm of Japan. There is no droning, no chanting, just the sound of this drum, slow at first, eventually racing. It reverber-

191

ates, sounds among the pines and cypresses in the standing groves. It is like a heart pounding.

A priest and his acolyte, the former in white and blue, the other in white and dotted purple, take me around. The priest is as brisk and affable as a Protestant; his responsibility is as heavy as that of an abbot. For eighty generations the priesthood has been handed down from father to son. Yet there is no standing on dignity, nothing pompous about him. He has an awareness of his position, but his face is creased from smiling. He also has a slight tic in one eye and a massive gold tooth right in the front.

They show me the treasures. The head of a great dragon staff, left here by one of the emperors, not—not this time—Jimmu Tenno, but Saimei Tenno, who also left a mirror embossed with animals and sea creatures. And much armor, a magnificent collection—as rare and beautiful as a collection of stag beetles. The armor of Yoshitsune, given as an offering after the battle of Dan-no-Ura, deer-leather bodice worked with a chrysanthemum pattern, lacquered skirts, embroidered front, a bit of the original red left. Yoritomo's armor, purplish, shingled, red, lions on deerskin. Kono Michinobu's, red faded to pink, helmet attached. Each is arranged like a miniature castle on its stand. All have jutting shoulders, flaring skirts, hanging brocades like small battlements. The corners and angles speak directly of war. One cannot imagine any object shaped like these intended for peace.

Other treasures include a long pole, a spear, a *naginata* or halberd that once belonged to Benkei, loyal retainer to Yoshitsune, hero of a thousand stories. Mirrors from Nara; a towel stand, the oldest in Japan, that looks like a bird cage. Weapons of the pirates—bows, arrows, swords, armor—straight from the Edo period. Then Heian-period bows, made to shoot from eye level. Only later was the sight brought down and the arm stretched back. Arrows shaped like forked tongues, arrows shaped to make the wound larger, arrows shaped so that they might also be used for *seppuku*—ritual suicide, hara-kiri, slitting the abdomen.

The Mishima war flag, black waves on white muslin. The sword of Omori Hikoshichi, who went mad after killing and left behind this sword, a giant's sword, so heavy, so long, that it should have been impossible for an ordinary man to lift it.

Carvings of large dogs, *koma-inu*, from the Heian period, now all come apart. Stacks of *renga*, poems written back and forth between talented nobles. Piles of lists, missives, letters, journals—cursive script on yellowed, brittle paper.

This whole island, the priest tells me, was once a shrine island. But not now. The great waterfront torii that dominates the approach from the sea is all that is left. Yet, even now, there is no doubt that this island belongs to the gods. One sees their sign, the great white archway, from miles at sea. It dominates the island. Even if the would-be pilgrims are now seduced by the pasteboard palace on neighboring Setoda, the gods will wait.

Oh, during the war it was different, of course, he tells me. In wartime people suddenly remember their gods. Back then, people started to come—the army, the navy, people all the way from Tokyo. But in peacetime the shrine is forgotten. It stands deserted, open, waiting.

*　　　*　　　*

I WANDER OFF into a grove. The purple-spotted acolyte hesitates; then, as the priest rushes off, lacquered hat askew, bound for pressing duties, he turns and follows me at a distance. I stop, thinking I am perhaps going some place where I ought not.

I wait. He waits.

Finally, he says: "I suppose you want to find the toilet."

"No, actually not," I say.

"It's on the other side, near the gate," he informs me.

We walk for a time. It is late afternoon again. The sun is behind the trees. Their shadows are cast straight across the ground. The light is horizontal. It is the nicest time of day.

"Why did you think I want the toilet?"

"Well, for one thing, you looked like it. And for another thing, most people do."

Were they supposed to? I asked, thinking I had stumbled upon another Shinto mystery.

"Oh, no, they don't have to. They probably get excited. They use it a lot though." Then: "We have to clean it, you know."

I said that that must be rather unpleasant. The country Japanese toilet is a porcelain-topped pit. It fills over the months. Then it must be dipped out by hand, a long and messy operation.

193

"Oh, it's got to be done, can't be helped." He seemed resigned, a state often observed among Japan's young.

"How old are you?"

"I found a pocketbook once, with money in it—and half a set of false teeth. I'm twenty."

He had been at the shrine a year. As we walked along, through the sacred groves, the sun sinking, dusk gathering, I learned that this shrine no longer brought up its own acolytes, except for the single son of the high priest. They imported them. He had come from Onomichi.

I told him I had just come from there.

"Onomichi," he said. "I haven't seen it for a year now." Then he was silent. His skirts rustled as we strolled farther into the darkness. His white neckband caught what little light remained.

I was taken with this experience. It was like being in history. Here I was walking the sacred groves of Oyamazumi with a Shinto acolyte in spotted purple robes—nothing had changed for a thousand years.

Far in the distance a shrine drum began, first slowly, then faster. He stopped.

"I ought to go back, I guess," he said.

"All right," I said.

Then he did a surprising thing. He turned and looked at me, his triangular face white in the dark. "No, I won't!" Then he used a swearword—*konchikusho*. It doesn't mean anything much—the dictionary says something like "this beast"—but since the Japanese language is singularly devoid of swearwords, it carries weight. I was startled, and he went on: "Work all day long, never have any fun, no girls, nothing to drink—what kind of life is that for anyone?"

Sometimes this happens. It all comes out, all the unhappiness, all the grievances. The foreigner is chosen precisely because telling him makes no difference. He won't, can't, do anything about it. Foreigners occasionally learn a lot, being chosen for confidences no other Japanese would hear.

"Get you up at dawn and make you work all day. Don't pay you anything. It's like some kind of animal life. I'd like to run away, that's what I'd like to do."

"Why don't you?"

"Where to?" he asked. "Back to Onomichi?"

"Why not, isn't that where you're from?"

"No, you don't understand. They sent me out here. They won't take me back."

All during this his language had been changing. At first it was the ordinary, polite, somewhat formal Japanese one expects at a shrine. After the outburst, however, it rapidly became more direct, more local, more slangy. Now the r-sounds were blurred. The acolyte was talking like a *chimpira*, a tough, a gangboy.

Which was, I shortly discovered, precisely what he was. After six months in the reform school at Hiroshima he had been shipped back home. His family had—in apparent desperation—sent him off to this small island far from home to work as an acolyte.

The shrine had accepted him gladly, its stock of potential acolytes having grown low as the local young men escaped in increasing numbers to Hiroshima, Osaka, Tokyo. His clothes were taken away —he particularly regretted a new orange sweater—and he was given these (here he pulled at his skirts, laughing morosely) and so he couldn't go any place. It was like being in prison.

"How long will you have to stay here then?" I asked.

"I don't know. Until I get better, they said."

He stopped after these revelations had poured out. Now we turned into the dark and walked on. The temple drum had stopped. The sun had disappeared though the sky in the west was still light. Overhead the first stars appeared. A night breeze stirred, a mosquito buzzed. We could no longer see each other.

I tried to remember what he had looked like. A middle-sized young man, a purple-spotted acolyte, small chin, triangular face, polite, silent. But I could not associate him with the little tough striding along beside me, slashing at the bushes and blurring his syllables.

"*Bakayaro*," he said to no one, to himself. "I got to get out of here. I'll go crazy. Even reform school was better than this."

"Do they feed you well?" I asked, feeling at a loss myself but wanting to show interest and sympathy.

"What do you think? The food's lousy. I got in the shrine sakè once. They locked me up for that."

"Well, what did you do in the first place to get sent to reform school?"

He sighed and did not answer for a long time. Then: "Oh, it was just a fight. But I'd been up four times before so they called me undesirable and put me in."

"What was it like?"

"Oh, it wasn't bad. There were lots of other guys my own age there. And they taught us things. I learned how to make bird cages."

His skirts swished. We had left the grove and were in a small field. The sky was filling with stars. In the distance I heard a rhythm that I at first thought was another drum until I realized it was the sea, lying out there somewhere in front of us.

"Oh, look at them," he said, stopping. He looked up, his profile black against the night sky.

"You'll miss dinner," I said.

"Well, I won't be missing much."

We walked on. The pattering steps of the acolyte, which he had learned well, I now realized, had given way to the stride of the *yakuza*, the responsible gangster. He suddenly stopped. "I come here a lot," he said.

The field ended in darkness. Beneath us was a faint, moving line of white, then another, then another. We were at the edge of the field, standing on a low bluff. Below us was the sea, the tide coming in. The waves hissed on the sand beneath us, their white catching the light of the stars. He suddenly sat down, his legs over the edge.

"In the daytime you can see Osakikamijima, but not at night. Sometimes you can see the lights at Kinoe, but not tonight."

"Can you see Setoda?"

"No, that's behind us, over on the other side of the island. I got that far once."

"What happened?"

"I hung around that crazy temple there. Everyone thought I worked there, the place is so mixed up. I took people around and they paid me. I got me a girl too—on the second night. Told her it was holy and so she let me. Cried a lot afterwards though."

"Why didn't you stay?"

"Oh, someone caught on after about a week. You can't hide any place around here. And the shrine here, of course, had the cops out. They caught me and brought me back. In these crazy clothes you can't get far anyway."

He kicked his heels, his skirts above his knees, and pulled at the summer grasses. A mosquito buzzed near, then was carried away by sea breeze.

Suddenly he stood up, black against the sky, and began pulling at his skirts, his kimono top, his sashlike obi. His skirts fell, he threw off his kimono. He stood half-naked.

"There, that's better," he said and sighed, adjusted his loincloth *fundoshi*, and sat down again. "It feels good to take those silly clothes off sometimes." Then: "I wish it was light." Then: "You got a light? I'll show you something."

I felt in my pockets, produced my lighter, held it out to him. "Go on, light it," he said. I did. "Look here," he said and turned his near shoulder to me.

The sudden flame blinded me, then I saw his bare brown shoulder and raised the lighter. The skin was marked, beautifully traced with blue and red. It was cherry blossoms, extending from his neck down half his forearm. "I was going to get a big carp going up a waterfall on my back but I ran out of money. Tattooing is expensive and it takes time. Just this here on my arm took almost a month. The reason is the red. It's poison. You can only do about a square inch every other day or else you get sick—throw up."

I put my hand on his traced shoulder, ran my fingers over the skin. It was smooth, warm.

"That cost a lot of money—got it done in Hiroshima. They don't usually do it so well nowadays, but this old man, he was a real master."

The tattoo was beautifully done—it looked like a woodblock print. Each petal was formed. The lighter hissed, the flame died. It was black again, my fingers still on his warm shoulder.

"Look," he said and lay back. "Can you see it in the dark?"

I looked, my eyes becoming again accustomed to the night. He lay black on the black grass, his loincloth white. Then I saw white above it. A high wide band extending from his loincloth halfway up his chest.

It was a *haramaki*, a length of muslin wound round and round, tightly, a style still worn by gangsters. "You know what it is?" I told him I did. "And when I used to have my knife I kept it right here. Here," and he took my hand and guided it in the dark to his right side, halfway up. I felt the tight cloth, layer upon layer.

"You're a real *yakuza*," I said.

197

He laughed at the compliment.

"Not really, I was just a *chimpira*. That was the life though. Gambling, lots to drink, all the girls you wanted. Ugh, it's too tight."

He stood up, looking tall against the stars, and started turning round and round, the *haramaki* unwinding as he did. After he had taken it off, he punched it all together as a pillow and lay back.

"I got a scar too," he said.

"A knife scar?"

"It's just a small one," he said modestly, "but it's deep."

I tried to light my lighter. It would no longer work.

"Here," he said, took my hand, put my fingers on his chest, guided them under his right breast. I felt an irregularity in the smooth skin. "There it is," he said and pushed my fingers so that I could feel it, a small ridge. "Much deeper and it would have gotten my heart," he said.

I ran my finger back and forth over the small scar, the warm, soft skin. He lay back, eyes open. I could see the stars reflected in them. He stretched his legs and sighed.

"You're not the first foreigner I ever knew," he said.

"I'm not?"

"No, I met a foreigner in Kure once. He was nice to me. Couldn't speak the language very well, though. I was in the gang then. He liked my tattoo a lot."

"Oh?"

"Foreigners are nice. Lots of people don't like them. But I do. You can say anything you want to them, tell them anything, and that's nice. And then they're interesting. They'll do things that Japanese don't do." He yawned loudly.

*   *   *

LATER, I LOOKED UP, feeling chilly in the sea breeze, and saw that the moon had come up behind us. The gangster-acolyte still lay beside me. Now he was silvered in the light of the newly risen moon. His head cast a long shadow over his chest for the moon was low. Each nipple cast a small shadow. Every hair was silvered as though with frost. His legs, bent at the knee, disappeared off the bluff as though into the sea itself. A mosquito buzzed.

I sat up and looked down at him. His tattoo now shone, colorless, all the red, all the blue, lost in the light of the moon. It was a tracery, a black-and-white photograph. He laughed and I saw that his eyes were open.

"I look like I'm covered with snow," he said. Then he yawned again, stood up, retied his loincloth, put his kimono on, then his long *hakama* skirt. When he was dressed he found he had forgotten his *haramaki*.

"*Konchikusho*," he said. Then: "Oh, well, I'll carry it."

We walked along the sea back to Miyaura, the town where the shrine is, scuffing the sand with our feet.

"How long will you stay here?"

"Not long. I'm going to run away."

"You can't hide in Japan," I said. And it is true. There is no place for the fugitive in this well-run country. People are curious, everyone is registered, the law is thorough.

"Then I'll go abroad. I'll come stay with you."

"All right."

"No I won't," he said. "I'll stay here. Then I'll get a job back in Onomichi and I'll get married—if I can."

The moon sailed higher. It was a long way back to town. The lights were small in the distance, then larger. Mosquitoes buzzed. He slapped them. "They get bigger and bigger," he said. "Here it is almost autumn—they are enormous."

Back in town I asked him to have an ice with me at one of the small shops still open.

"No, we got a morning service a dawn. I better go back." Then he smiled and shook his head. "But that's not it. I got a bad reputation here. They don't like me in town very much. Then they see me come in with some foreigner and that would make it worse."

I smiled at this.

"But," he said earnestly, "I enjoyed meeting you, I don't mean I didn't. And talking with you and everything was really nice. It does you good to get things off your chest, you know. I feel a lot better, relieved."

I smiled again.

He turned at the corner to wave, carrying his *haramaki* in a folded ball, his stiff skirts swishing, his kimono tight at the neck, the living

199

Heian period, a vision from history again. The moon was now half-way up the sky. I yawned, felt suddenly chilled, suddenly very much alone. And it had been so warm. Autumn was on its way, though it was here still dead summer. I ate a strawberry ice by myself, shivered again, went back to the inn and felt asleep at once.

*   *   *

ON THE BOAT to Mebaru on Osakikamijima, I sailed through fields of oysters and pearls, the sun rising, making the mountains golden, cragged, shadows spread across their face. The boat cast its shadow behind the ship, darkening the wake. The farther shore was dark, as though still asleep. Then, slowly, in the shadow of the mountain, the small port appeared.

Poor, a single street, the eaves almost touching, the street a cool ravine, the stores—clock store, food store, beauty shop—like caves opened in the latticed and wooden walls of this man-made gorge.

On the way to the bus station I am seen by a mother. She averts her face, as is customary this far from the big cities. But then, in a quiet imperative, she calls to someone: "Midori-chan, Midori-chan, come here."

Midori—evidently a small girl I guess from the name and the use of the diminutive *chan*—is summoned more urgently several more times. I am about to pass; the girl is almost too late. The mother casts a quick appraising glance and risks: "Midori-chan, come quickly and look."

The child appears, stares. I am almost past. The mother turns and is not so ill bred as to point but instead indicates with her chin. The child goggles.

I stop so that the she may enjoy a longer, better view. I smile, mother smiles, Midori smiles. I say a few words, but Midori is mute, tongue cloven to roof of mouth, astounded at the speaking apparition. The mother smiles and nods. She is a good mother, giving her child all the educational advantages she can.

*   *   *

THE BUS RIDE to Kinoe is long and dusty and dull. This is an agricultural island, all tangerines and a lemon-like citrus. No fishing—the

200

seafront is deserted. No houses along the shore—they are all in the mountains.

The bus stops, for no apparent reason. Here a gravel road straggles away from the sea road and staggers over the mountains. Here, also, they are repairing the road. It is shortly before noon. The local workers, having worked all morning, are preparing for their noontime meal. They are stripped, and women—wives or daughters—are pouring buckets of seawater over them.

They stand by the edge of the sea, on the far side of the road, where a small pier has been allowed to fall into ruin. The women, bare to the waist, scoop up the sea and pour it over the glistening bodies of the men, who shout at the cold, shake themselves like dogs, then stand for more.

They pay no attention to the bus and the few passengers pay no attention to them. I, however, get out, sit on a rock, and discreetly stare.

The Japanese are sometimes very beautiful. This is not generally known. First, as in most countries, Japan does not send its beauties abroad—people in a position to travel are, for some reason, rarely attractive. Again, the beauty occurs where we do not think to look for it—the skin, for example.

Japanese skin—why has no one ever properly celebrated it? One would not expect the Japanese themselves to. They, after all, live in it. But we the coarse, the hairy, the heavy-pored—we might have been expected to make much of this finely spun, hairless covering, reminding of some half-forgotten childhood friend.

That is what the skin is like, the skin of children. Faintly translucent, which is why the Japanese get red when they drink; lightly perfumed, the odor of rice, because of the diet; and smooth—not smooth as leather is smooth, but smooth as some fabled Asiatic cloth is smooth to the touch.

The skin of children, the skin of animals. To us in the West who revere anything more innocent than ourselves, this is what the Japanese skin is like. To run the hand along not a leg but a flank, to raise the wondrous and silken texture of a haunch, a forearm—there is in this skin a natural perfection that seems untouched, as though we are the first to touch it.

Such perfect covering makes it seem as though we can feel deeper than the skin itself. The skin is not a barrier. It is yielding, it invites.

It is possible, says the skin, to know more, to enter more fully, to understand more deeply.

There is no hair on this skin—just the blackly shining hair of the head, the eyebrows. Under the arm is not a bush but a small shrub. Japanese girls do not show the triangle. Rather, something like a cornice and two pillars, a small torii, a holy gateway. Japanese men do not have that inverted tree the roots of which clutch the navel. Low, like a hip-hugging belt, the hair stops straight, as though shaved. It is the pattern of the ideal, seen in early Greek statues.

The bodies, too, are early Greek. The breast is small, comely. The thigh is short, lowering the body. It destroys our Renaissance ideas of human beauty. It restores that of the Cretans. We remember these proportions and respond to them. The long legs of the Hellenic era, of all Western culture afterwards, are forgotten. These short thighs, the texture of this skin—they retain the matrix in our memories. To cup a hand over a breast we would call immature, run a hand along a thigh we would name adolescent—these erase experience and recall innocence. It makes the Japanese seem sometimes childlike. It makes us, once again, for a blessed and horizontal moment, children.

*　　　*　　　*

Kinoe, like Mitarai farther on, was once a pleasure town. It was not so large, but was well known all over the Inland Sea for the attractiveness of its site and the quality of its attractions.

Here, where the great boats from Kyushu and Osaka used to pass, where there were two tides and two winds to wait for, this pleasure village grew up and prospered. During the nineteenth and early twentieth centuries, the Meiji period in particular, the time of the wars with China and Russia, the town was at its liveliest.

A great sailing ship would glide into the harbor, a red flag would run up its pole, a lookout in the city would ring a bell, and the girls would set off in their boats. For this was what the town was famous for—those girl-filled boats called *ochoro-bune* or "honorable prostitute boats." So when the bell sounded—it was replaced by a smart and military trumpet in the later years of Meiji—the long boats, each holding five or six girls and their boatman, would glide from the slips of the town and approach the waiting ship. The girls would board and politely inquire among crew and passengers. Once agreement was reached, the girl would either stay aboard or, more often, return home and make her room ready for her customer.

It seems coarse to say customer. That was, of course, what he was, just as a whore was what she was. But it sounds sordid, and sordid is one thing a Japanese cannot be. He can be a number of unpleasant things, he can even be some unpleasant things that we cannot, but he is, I think, incapable of sordidness. Rarely looking further than the surface, usually unmindful of consequences and implications, he retains good will and innocence. The whores of Japan remain pure, their customers innocent.

And so they came together, one place or the other. It was important that the proper contacts be made on the ship, however, and for this reason the girls got all dressed up and comported themselves as ladies. They dreamed of a steady patron. They would not then have to peer into the equivalent of steerage, nor linger noticeably about the scuppers. They could, with the assurance of welcome, ascend directly to the main deck or—joy—to the bridge itself.

One hears many stories of the girls' generosity. Not only was credit extended, money was actually loaned. Knowing the state that men get themselves into when cramped up alone, a girl wore pretty things, respected her patron's privacy, cooked beautiful meals, the kind you look at before you eat.

She would do his washing, would—between kittenish turns in the bath—manage to get him very clean, would wake up early to make certain that his clothes were in proper order, would make light of his not having enough money, would say that next time was fine, would —in fact—behave with a delicacy and ardor that, among the whores of any other country, would have put her straight into the madhouse.

Because she was this kind of girl, the sailor would approvingly call her his *ichiya-zuma*—his one-night wife. She, smarter than the sailor, knew that she could hope for more. This she usually received in the form of presents from the grateful men—silk from China, coral from the southern islands, a clock from Amsterdam. It was also not unusual for her to be further rewarded by an offer of marriage.

A sailor makes a good husband, just as a whore makes a good wife, and it is not in the least paradoxical that this should be so. It is precisely what, if one bothered to think about it, one would expect.

Then, too, the island was a nice place for the sea-weary sailor to live. There were lots of fish, lots of fruit, not much work, low prices. Many were the sailors who settled down with their ex-whore wives and prospered.

That, on the whole, the town did not prosper was no fault of the whores. After the introduction of the steam engine, waiting for tides and winds was no longer necessary, and thus one of the pretexts for stopping at the island was lost. Others could, however, be found—a faulty windlass, a loose gasket.

The smaller ships, the freight boats, continued to stop, though the large passenger ships now steamed past. This did not bother the island. The grand hotels became less grand, the town became more rural. The flag went up, the trumpet sounded, the girls, giggling, jostled their way into the boats. The patrons were fewer, but the inns still filled up.

They were all made for accommodating the major industry of the place. In my room I noticed that the *fusuma* doors could be locked. This is not common in Japan. Usually a soft-stepping maid can sidle up inaudibly, have the *fusuma* open and herself inside before you are even aware that she is up the stairs. Here, privacy, that rarest and most expensive luxury in Japan, was common.

But then the boats went out again, the lovers parted—with, one may imagine, what murmurs, what brief tears, what waving of bright handkerchiefs, what crowding of pretty sandaled feet on the piers, what half-hours of disconsolate grief upon the oh-so-pathetically-tossed-up bedding.

But worse than this gentle grief was in store. The Pacific War— that near-religious exercise of *yamato-damashii*, the "Japanese soul"— banned all natural frivolity, including, in spirit if not in letter, sexual intercourse. The girls were restricted, the boats were turned upside down, the flag was taken away, the trumpet confiscated. From their lonely windows the girls saw the troopships filled with open-mouthed, khaki-clad youngsters being led off to slaughter. From the ship the boys saw, with giggle and nudge, the infamous and attractive island town that a seafaring uncle had once spoken of.

After the war the girls became big business. They had always belonged to houses, some twenty or thirty to a house, but now they became corporate members. Each house became a private company. Their pretty Meiji- and Taisho-period ways, their credit-extending, did not suit the expanding economy. Soon they came to resemble more closely their sisters in Tokyo's grand and incorporated Yoshiwara, though never have the whores of Japan reached those heights of impersonal rapacity that their cousins in New York and London think not only right but proper.

Pimps were, as yet, unnecessary, but each house had its bully-boy, used mainly to keep the girls in order. This was, alas, necessary for the reason that not all of the ladies liked their Calypso-like life on the island. Some had, indeed, not liked it from the beginning. Too often they were sold by indigent fathers and were committed until they, with unremitting labor, might buy themselves out. All of them were outlanders, strangers to the island, as the local women never became whores—or if they did, they went elsewhere.

The whores of Kinoe were, in the present Showa era at any rate, from Kyushu or Shikoku. Many were the children of coal miners, in all times and places a particularly penniless folk. The more attractive were bought, sent as children to the island, where they attended school and patiently awaited puberty. Shortly after this, and graduation from middle school, they were put to work.

It is easy to wax sentimental over these poor children, destined for a life of social shame if not sin, poring over their first-grade readers, little guessing what was in store—though it must have been a dull child indeed who did not guess. It is easy to become sentimental over this scene, and a number of people have—most beautifully, Ichiyo Higuchi in her novel *Takekurabe*.

Still, it would, I should think, have been a most willful and misguided girl who would have traded this interesting life of comparative ease for the back-breaking boredom of life in the mines, a life that would have been her lot had not providence made her prettier than her sisters. It is said that when girls did want to run away and had to be restrained, it was usually because little Kinoe did not give enough scope to their talents. They lusted for Onomichi or Osaka—brighter lights, better pay.

Tradition has it that the original women, the ur-whores of the island, were no less than those Heike women who apparently spent the better part of their adult lives fleeing from the Genji. Having

205

somehow to make a living, they settled down at Kinoe and at Mitarai and learned their trade.

Scholars—there are a few on the subject—seem universal in their condemnation of what they call this myth. It is quite after the fact, they say, and point to respectable Meiji as having been the period when all manner of nonsense was made up and called legend. Momotaro, they will tell you, is a Meiji invention. So is about half of Kobo Daishi. So, certainly, are those fleeing Heike women.

During the middle nineteenth century, the scholars continue, Japan suddenly discovered that it had no history that accorded to any known Western standard. The Japanese suddenly felt their history, like their old-fashioned buildings, their funny ways, disreputable. The West had descended upon their land. It is possible for a well-integrated person to receive a shock so great that he begins to doubt himself, and it can happen to a country as well. Just as a person may then develop a neurosis, so may a country. It was from Meiji onward that Japan became schizoid, the common reaction to two irreconcilable forces at work within the same body, both mutually contradictory.

An early symptom was that everything somehow had to become respectable—not according to Japanese standards, where everything was already respectable, but according to the half-understood and even then dissolving standards of the West. This is why trousers were put on what the West still insists upon calling coolies, why phallic stones were uprooted like so many perfectly sound teeth, why local festivals were clothed and toned down to their present state of insipidity.

And when a local bad habit was too firmly entrenched, or too lucrative—the whores on this little island for example—then it was dignified, it was given a legend. Attention was called to a certain red handkerchief worn by the girl. Aha, red! You see? Heike! This in spite of the fact that for centuries red or pink has been the traditional color of the looser women just as diamonds and silver fox used to designate the expensive ladies of Atlantic City, and as the see-through blouse and the beehive hairdo still serve to identify the whores of New York.

But worse, far worse, was in store for this once attractive little town. Over a decade ago a group of energetic and militant lady

Diet members, after years of perseverence, managed to ram through the Anti-Prostitution Bill. It was ratified, approved, passed—and the whores of Kinoe, as elsewhere, suddenly found themselves illegal.

This stupid law has changed the face of Japan. Prostitution was as necessary a social ameliorant in Japan as it is elsewhere. Prostitution, of course, continues. But it is driven underground, into the world of gangsters. Not only are there new numbers of unhappy, bored, unsatisfied young unmarried men, there is also a new connection between illegal prostitution and other forms of illegality—blackmail, drug-pushing, etc. After the law was passed the country was engulfed by pimping and syphilis, those diseases which thrive only in secrecy.

The law had an equally disastrous effect upon one of Japan's favorite art forms—the geisha. After the passing of the Anti-Prostitution Bill, which naturally did not discriminate against these high-class entertainers, the whores discovered that they too could claim immunity by calling themselves geisha. And the geisha discovered that there was no way to stop them from doing so.

In the popular hot-spring resort of Atami—a place resembling Miami in its high prices, Atlantic City in its varied attractions—the Geisha Association (there is one) got its members together and created a by-law: to call yourself a geisha you had to know at least three songs, had to know how to sing them, accompany them on the samisen, and dance to them. This, they thought, would keep out their less talented sisters.

Not at all. The more enterprising whores got to work at once and in a very short time the Geisha Association was treated to the sight of large-wristed farmers' daughters, all bound up in kimono, singing and plunking away while others shuffled about the room in approximation of the niceties of classical *odori*. The unwelcome but perservering newcomers had to be admitted: the by-law said so. One of the results was a fall in prestige for the geisha, at least the Atami variety, and another was the popularity of such pejorative phrases as *makura-geisha*, or pillow-geisha, and *daruma-geisha*, the reference being to that roly-poly toy (made, in Japan, in the shape of Daruma, the Zen saint who sat so long in meditation that his legs withered away) which lies down when pushed, only to roll upright again, ready for yet another shove.

In Kinoe, however, the effect of the new law was strong enough

207

to kill the town. It might, of course, merely have driven the girls from the main street into the side streets, as it did in the majority of Japanese cities. But the mayor of Kinoe had been mayor for a long time and did not want to risk his chances of reelection, did not want to forfeit prefectural favor; nor were there any side streets. Kinoe is an *ippon-michi* (one-street) town. The mayor's office and the police station are one. The day the law went into effect the mayor and the chief of police obeyed it. The girls were packed up and sent away. Their boats were sold to various small transport agencies. Their houses were turned into small hotels, restaurants. The only reason Kinoe had ever had for being was no more.

The town, though large as these island towns go, is dead. No one stops. Few leave. My inn, a big one, is empty. No one ever has happy occasion to lock his *fusuma*. The girls all went to such non-*ippon-michi* places as Osaka, and straight into the arms of shakedown-men, crooked cops, pimps.

A few of them, however, have settled here with their former sailor boy friends and are treated with that affectionate respect that a town traditionally feels toward its most famous local product. My informant, an old man who knew everything and probably invented what he didn't, said that just such a couple ought to be coming along any minute now.

We waited. He was drinking sakè, I was drinking *ramune*, a straw-colored, straw-flavored soft drink bearing in both taste and name some distant relation to lemonade. It comes in a green glass bottle with a marble imbedded in the neck. Its own fizziness shuts the bottle. When you push in the marble, and it takes a strong little finger, it explodes and boils over like champagne. A Meiji drink, it is hard to find in the cities now; indeed, it is only such small and neglected places as this that—

"Here they come."

I looked up. A well-dressed matron in a light summer kimono, blue and white, was strolling toward us, walking three or four paces behind a pleasant-looking, middle-aged gentleman wearing a hat, open-necked white shirt, business suit, and the cloglike *geta*. She had her arms full of parcels. He was carrying nothing but was fanning himself with his handkerchief.

They walked slowly by. She was fat and pleasant. She smiled at her difficulty with the parcels. She looked like any of the local women except that she was dressed up and had taken trouble with herself. Her hair was neat, she wore a discreet amount of lipstick. She walked past. Her profile was full, even florid, but she had once been beautiful, I saw. And in her dignity, her good humor, her humanity, she still was.

*   *   *

THERE WAS LITTLE ELSE of interest, but the sakè-drinking old man did not allow this to deter him. I learned with delight, however, that I had at last reached an island that Jimmu Tenno had not, though Empress Jingu had, on her way to Korea, and so had Sugawara Michizane, presumably on his way into exile. And there were pirates, though the old man insisted that they were not really pirates, not actually *kaizoku* because they used different characters for the word so that, instead of meaning "sea robber," it becomes something like "red clan." Aha!—the Heike again. A suspiciously late-sounding reading, I observed. Well, you never know, was his opinion.

Then I learned that Urashima Taro is said to have come from here. I have always liked him, the hero of Japan's single lovely fairy tale. Carried off under the sea by a grateful tortoise, he lived for what he thought was a matter of days in the bright-red-lacquer T'ang mansions of an undersea kingdom, in the Palace of the Dragon King. But upon returning, he discovered, like Rip Van Winkle, that years had passed. Here, in Kinoe, continued the literal-minded old man, there were lots of turtles, big sea turtles, always had been, still were. Perhaps that is the reason for the story.

When I think of Urashima Taro and the great undersea palace, however, I think of Miyajima, that fabled place to which I am getting nearer each day. It is the end of the islands of the Inland Sea, though the sea itself continues on to Kyushu and Shimonoseki. There, at Miyajima, the Palace of the Dragon King actually exists, reincarnated as the great shrine of Itsukushima—corridors of red lacquer, dark and sea-green roofs, the great torii standing in the surf, the whole built over the waves. I mention my thoughts to him.

This, it turns out, is a remarkable coincidence, my thinking what I thought. Why? Why, *she* came here too, you know. Who did? Why,

209

the goddess of Miyajima, of course. I at once asked her name, hoping to hear it at last, thinking that he, like all the others, would probably not know it.

"Was it Benten, perhaps?" I ventured. It would be pleasant if it were my favorite goddess that I had, after all, been following.

"Not at all"—*chigau*—was his terse reply. "It was Itsukushima-hime. Why, they named the whole island after her."

I felt surprisingly, absurdly pleased at finally having heard the name of the beautiful and mysterious goddess toward whose final abode I was traveling, the beautiful companion whose route I had also traced. It quite consoled me for the loss of Benten.

"She came here," he continued, "because she was looking for a place to live, you see. She wanted her shrine to be at some pretty place. But back then this island was full of snakes. Of course, being a goddess and all, she didn't mind them, but what disturbed her was that the island was also full of pheasants, you see."

The pheasant is the deadly enemy of the snake. They fight, and he told me about the hissing and cackling, the writhing and the fluttering. "Well, she just couldn't stand it, so she just up and went off"—*dete shimaimashita.*

Unfortunate goddess, I thought, remembering her troubles with the red leeches at Setoda. Her difficulties were over, however. At Miyajima she found some birds and was suspicious for a time, but they turned out to be merely *yamadori*, which look like pheasants but have no strong feelings about snakes.

This reminded him of another bird. It lives here, on this very island, but is mysterious. In what way? Well, a long time ago, when a Korean embassy came with tribute for the emperor, their boat sank right here in this bay. And it was on New Year's Day at that. And so this bird— What bird? The bird they were bringing, of course. And so this bird escaped. And it flew out to that little island out there and it still lives there. How does one know? Why, because every New Year's Day it suddenly flies up, remembering its fright of some time back, and disappears. But it always comes back. It likes the place.

Has he ever seen it? Oh, no. Has anyone ever seen it? Oh, no. But that doesn't prove it isn't there, does it? No, it doesn't.

Perhaps it went this way, he said. Some old crow or seagull lived there and the first rays of the sun would naturally gild it. Or maybe it was some kind of flying chicken because the island is named Niwatorijima, or Chicken Island. Now, if it were a gold bird, it would be called something like Kinnotorijima. "Every summer a few little boys go out and look. They want to rouse the creature, you see. But they never find anything. No gold bird; no chicken."

"Is it maybe a phoenix?" I asked using the word *ho-o*.

He thought I had said *hyo*. "No, no, it's not a leopard, not a cat at all. It's a bird we're talking about; a bird, you see."

He suddenly stopped, put down his sakè cup. There was confusion in his eyes, and he seemed to be tracing our conversation back to discover what was wrong. "Now, wait just a minute there"—*chotto matte yo*—he said.

I waited.

"I would have sworn her name was Itsukushima-hime. But wait just a minute now."

"Maybe it was Utsukushii-ma," I said, *utsukushii* being a word meaning beautiful, "because she was very lovely, they say."

"No, no, not at all"—*chigau, chigau*—"the *shima* means 'island'; you can't do that to it. Now, just let me remember for a minute. What *was* her name now?"

I despaired. I would never hear it.

"Let me see now." He thought for a while, then remembered that one of the Shinto gods, Susa-no-o no Mikoto, had three daughters, princesses (*hime*) all. And their names were Tagitsu-hime, Tagori-hime and...and...ah, he had it: Ichikishima-hime. Well, it must have been this last one.

"Why? It could have been any of the others," I stated.

"No, I don't think so. Itsukushima and Ichikishima sound a little alike, you see."

I didn't like the idea of three goddesses crowding around me. I wanted my old traveling companion back. He noticed my dejection.

"Oh, well, it's only a goddess, you know," he said, kindly. "There are lots and lots of them. You can call her anything you like, I suppose." He smiled and finished his sakè.

*   *   *

LEAVING ON the early morning boat I pass very near this black little island of the golden bird. Every tree is sharp in the still air and stands against the silver background of the morning sea. I see a crow, a

211

small crow on a large branch, quite black, as though cut from paper and hung there. He will not answer my amiable cawings. Farther out, the day becomes overcast, the sky is a lead color, the waves are green, like beaten bronze.

*   *   *

AT IMABARI STATION, where I wait for the train, a couple, middle-aged, are sitting across from me. They are working the puzzle in a weekly magazine.

Its construction is such as to appeal deeply to the Japanese. On the last page of the magazine is a picture, a cartoon showing a street scene, a family scene, some sort of everyday scene. Appended, to be torn out, is another picture that looks just like the cartoon but isn't. There are, in fact, a number of minute differences—the laces are missing from one shoe, the creases in a suit or dress are left out, etc. One must find all the differences and encircle them with a pencil. When it is completed—and it is difficult to complete, for some of the differences are indeed minute—it is mailed to the magazine and the winners are sent something or other.

This kind of puzzle is of an enormous interest to the Japanese. To take something nearly finished and finish it, to find an original work and go over it hunting for errors, to take an edition of something and smother it in annotations—this is the Japanese way.

The man puts his pencil tip into his mouth from time to time, bright eyes working, then pounces upon a tent pole that is in some way different from the tent pole in the original. His wife is not so quick. She suggests the left ear of a small boy who is eating an ice-cream cone. Her husband is properly indignant. Not at all, they are identical, are you blind?

She is silent but not hurt. Japanese women do not take refuge from rebuff. Suddenly he senses a difference around the mouth. Aha—one dimple is missing. Didn't she see that? No, she didn't see that.

"Oh, these are tricky. You got to keep your eyes open," he says, licking his pencil.

"There," she says, "his little toe."

"What about it?"

"There isn't any nail on it."

"There isn't any in the original either, silly."

"Oh," she says.

"They try to trick you, these puzzles. You got to keep your eyes open."

I have seen Blake subjected to the same kind of scrutiny at Tokyo University. They count the adverbs. The professor who first discovered that Proust, toward the end, says fork when he means knife is still living in the glory of his scholarly achievement.

*   *   *

A LONG AND EVENTUALLY TIRESOME train ride from Imabari all the way to Matsuyama. It begins well, however. I go to the end of the last car and stand hanging out the doorway, enjoying the wind. Even on the smallest American railways you cannot do this anymore, I should guess. There you are well taken care of. You cannot even open a window. You enjoy the air conditioning until it breaks and you roast. Here, however, off the main lines you can still open windows. Anyone who wants to may lean from the door of a moving train. Anyone who cares to may fall.

Back in the car some children stare at me. I stare back and eat the grass-green caramels I bought at the last station, bought mainly in order to enjoy the delights of a transaction through an open window. The caramels taste like the waxen penny candy I bought when young—a sickly peach-pink taste. Japan is the land where penny candy should come from, even if it doesn't.

I watch a train boy on the platform house across the track. He is drinking tea, staring straight ahead. He does not see me. He is thinking. The train jerks. I hope he will see me. He does not.

Travel in Japan is pleasant because of the sense of accomplishment it gives. I look at my map and discover that if I had gone the same distance in another direction I would be in Korea. Japan is not small. It is a full-sized country with more variety than most. Japan is thought to be small mainly because the Japanese want it to be thought small, just as they themselves want to be known as a small people. They feel that it is gross to be large. Actually, Japan does not feel large or small. It feels just right. It is the ideal size for human habitation.

The train passes a small boy playing with his dog in a field. The train goes through a long tunnel. It comes out. And there is another

213

boy playing with another dog in another field. The two will never meet. A mountain lies between.

Later, however, after Miyawaki, the land turns flat and the weather turns rainy—and I have run out of things to read, having given my much-read copy of *Emma* to the old man at Kinoe, who thought he would like it since it was about a girl, even though it had no pictures and he knew no English. So I spend the rest of the day looking out of the window of the slow and dirty local train, sweating in the wet heat, and watching the raindrops course down the pane.

At such times one becomes lonely. Usually I make a distinction between being alone and being lonesome—a distinction that Japan both fosters and observes. Today, however, I welcome loneliness and would probably have resented a book. It would have distracted me from my indulgence.

At such times one feels very much the foreigner in Japan. I could have spoken to any number of people and been again assured of my being equally alive. Rather, however, I was silent, would not answer the friendly stares, gave way to my emotions. I wanted to be unhappy and so, naturally, I was.

Yet, if there is one thing that Japan teaches, it is to distrust the emotions. They are, after all, only ideas, like any other. You can change your mood as you can change your mind. I see people doing this every day. Japanese have a particularly taking way of doing so. After an emotional excess of some sort, they will shake their heads as though just waking up and say, well, that's enough of that now, and turn their minds to other things. It is not a question of ability—anyone is able to do this—it is a question of volition. Today I have decided to be unhappy just as I might have decided to spend the day in bed.

It is, to be sure, very easy for the foreigner to give way in this fashion. If he thinks about it at all, he cannot but realize that he is regarded as unreal by the Japanese. He is too curious, too strange, to be taken seriously. His sorrows are not theirs, nor his pleasures—at least, so their attitude suggests. The friendliness is real but it rests upon simple curiosity. Most Japanese will go out of their way to help a foreigner in some kind of trouble, but this does not mean that he is any more authentic to them, nor that they find him emotionally understandable. And if a foreigner gets into a kind of trouble that the

214

Japanese think is bad, then heaven help him, because they won't.

One lives with that knowledge, however, just as one lives with the knowledge of gray hair, wrinkles, and never becoming rich enough. It is not an important consideration and not one truly responsible for the funks in which foreigners find themselves in Japan occasionally, like that I have made for myself today.

Why am I on this train, creeping through the rain, on this dismal island? I asked myself. What possessed me to forgo what civilized qualities Tokyo offers—books, friends, food—and exchange them for this misery? What do I want, where am I going?

Such went the funk, and, as always, the malaise of being alive was diminished to this small puffing engine and its toy cars with me in one of them creeping along a dank seacoast. I didn't see, refused to see, that it was the voyage of life I was questioning and not the voyage through the Inland Sea. It is always so much easier to blame the more apparent, the lesser.

Then there was no food on the train, and since it was raining, they were not selling any at the small stations where we stopped for long periods before sighing and puffing onward. Certainly, I told myself, this is redolent enough of old Japan to suit me—I who have this argument with the new, this quarrel with my times. If I don't like the speedways and hamburger stands, the pizza parlors and parking lots, if I do not agree with the hordes now covering the face of the earth, surely then, poking along an absolutely deserted stretch of coast in a coach possibly constructed in 1900, saved from hamburgers, pizzas, anything edible at all—surely, this might please me.

Such are the vagaries of the romantic temperament, however, that it is never satisfied. While believing that such a temperament— mine, for example—is the only thing that can save the world, I was nonetheless morose, bored, and unpleasant with myself.

At this point, however, tired of my emotions, I fall asleep.

Then I wake up. It is growing darker. The pines are black, the sky is a deeper blue. The clouds turn pink, then gray. The smoke from the stack rushes close by the windows, then fans out to the ground like a fog, catching at the lower branches of the pines. Lights in the distance, then a town.

It is supper time. Glimpses into window after window, one family succeeding another. A mother holds a bowl in front of her child,

215

changes to two children eating, to an old woman with her chopsticks in the air, to a father standing and stretching. Then the town, the people, the lights all vanish, sucked into the night.

Beneath the failing sky a new moon. Bushes, trees, indistinct flashes, like static on the radio. Then a new scene. A small field and a single lamp on a pole which illuminates an old man. He is still working in one corner, still tilling the soil. The field is finished but for this corner.

All day long he has been tilling this field. All day long I have been traveling this island. He too started early this morning. This is what he has been doing all day long.

*   *   *

In Matsuyama it continued to rain. I did not again visit the castle; did not go to Dogo, city of hot springs; did not have any adventures. Instead, to punish myself, to make myself feel more badly still, I picked the cheapest and most unprepossessing inn I could find. It was so cheap that, as I soon discovered, there was no toilet paper in the lavatory, or else they had forgotten to replenish the stock—at any rate there was none. I never remember to carry a stock around with me—really a necessity in Japan, where it is but rarely found in public conveniences—and always have to ask for it.

I asked for it here in the cheap inn and at once the two silly maids set up a merry noise. The thought of a foreigner coping with the Japanese toilet is a happy one, and to be thus informed in advance seemed to double their enjoyment. With my simple request, squeals of merriment began and continued for an hour or two, fresh bursts of delighted laughter echoing from corridor and kitchen.

To be sure, it doubtless *is* amusing. The Japanese toilet is notoriously difficult for the uninitiated. One squats over this enameled hole in the floor that—if there is no plumbing, and there seemed to be none in this inn—leads directly into the noisome pit itself. One hangs there, legs aching, awaiting deliverance. It is strange that a people who have without a murmur relinquished their own architecture in favor of plastics and prefabs, who have cheerfully cut down their forests, leveled their hills, and dirtied their seas, who have turned their entire country over to that modern juggernaut, the automobile

216

—that these these same people should with such stubborn tenacity cling to such a medieval, even barbaric, device.

Yet they have, and the two maids all but loitered in front of the door hoping to hear if not actually view my exertions. It had obviously made their day, and I went to bed grumpy and sour and fell instantly asleep.

In the morning, however, I felt much better and, anthropomorphically, the sky had cleared to that of a brilliant late summer. I did not, however, feel like staying in a city where I had treated myself so badly. So I took the trolley down to Takahama, the port for Matsuyama, and got on a boat going, I thought, to Mitarai. It wasn't, but that was fine too.

It was fine because it was a brilliant day, the kind of day one thinks impossible until it occurs, and because I was on the sea again.

*   *   *

THE ISLANDS OF NAKAJIMA, a large island and several small ones, lie at the northeastern edge of the Iyo Nada, that portion of the Inland sea which separates Shikoku and Kyushu. They have been inhabited longer than the islands in the middle reaches of the Inland Sea. They are consequently both mainland and island in feeling.

Walking along the wide main street of the major port, open to the sun, deserted, I came upon a beautiful house. It was eighteenth-century and was designed in the most restrained, the most severe Naniwa-style of old Osaka.

The facade was of white and black plaster, black lozenges laced with white, broken by wide windows covered with vertical bars, and a large doorway that led like a gate into the house itself. Wood and plaster were balanced, not symmetrically, but so that the facade was a series rather than a single pattern. The plaster was raised, as in a bas-relief. The moldings cast shadows under the noon sun.

The entryway stretched into the house, like a long mouth. At the back were more vertical bars. Then the house proper began—probably rooms on either side, grouped around a small inner garden, perhaps on different levels. It would be cool inside, with a breeze blowing through the bars with their effect of privacy. Corridors would separate parts of the house, which, like so many of these old

217

country buildings, would continue on, room after room. It is as though these marvelous old houses can breathe. Everything is light, open, yet decorous, partially hidden.

People's houses are like the people who own them. The people who lived in this house were, I found, open, gracious, reserved. They asked me in and brought out tea. They were an old couple, their children long well-off in Osaka. Here they sat every day in these long, cool rooms. When I praised the house's beauty, they smiled. Yes, it was rather beautiful. Oh, yes, it was rather old too. Three hundred years perhaps—that facade was a bit later. It was as though I had complimented them on the beauty of their children. Yes, it had long been in the family.

In the next room, high on the wall, were large old-fashioned oval portraits, early photographs retouched with oil. A young man in a celluloid collar and a spotted cravat, staring with black eyes at the camera. A young lady, eyes averted, hair elaborate, in a checked kimono (the kind young women wore in the Meiji period), cheek resting on closed hand—following instructions from the photographer, who had seen French portrait bromides. Another picture, the couple again and two children, both in kimono, both in caps, looking bleakly ahead, the smaller holding a toy animal.

These were they, the old couple, when they were young, and these were their children, now old and married and parents themselves. The first was taken just after they were married—on their honeymoon as a matter of fact.

Another picture. A young man in a cadet uniform, looking straight at the camera with black eyes, his face pale. Their youngest son, very young. He died on Leyte.

The garden was very simple. A pomegranate tree, a lantern made of stone, three maples in a group, a fish pond with two old carp in it. It was small, they said, but they had lots of room. There were no children now. It was quite a waste, but, on the other hand, it was quite nice.

They were open, contained, assured old people. They were well made, like their house. Perhaps their house had helped make them so. In that case, what of Japanese now who live in tiny cramped concrete apartments with a square of imitation tatami, crowded in with their formica breakfast-nook table, their TV set, their washing machine? Will they be as contained, as decorous, as these two old people on this little island? I cannot believe they will.

I sat and enjoyed the cup of green tea in this house where I wanted to spend the rest of my life. Then I thanked them and left. It was not until later that I recalled that Louise had been on this same island only a few days earlier. Had she seen this house, talked to this old couple? Our years of sharing made me hope she had; my feeling that I, Balboa, was discovering the Inland Sea, that it belonged to me, made me hope she hadn't.

* * *

THE SEA FLAT, a blue plain; beyond, the rising green mountains of Shikoku, blue at the shoreline; behind, the tan islands of the Nakajima group, low on this motionless sea; ahead, the shimmering outlines of the islands we are approaching; and above, the wonderfully blue sky of late summer with clouds like more islands at the farthest horizon. It is very beautiful.

If I were to tell a Japanese that it is very beautiful, he would ask what is beautiful, and I would select the clouds or the far islands or else say that everything is beautiful. In Japanese it is always *something* that must be beautiful. Though the language has many abtract nouns, I have rarely heard the one for "beauty."

Beauty is then not a state, but a quality. It is like strength or width or weight. It implies that there are many kinds of beauty—not just one ideal beauty. Everything is real; therefore everything has its own form of beauty, and beauty exists in it and not outside it.

Beautiful islands, beautiful sea, beautiful sky—a whole world of varied beauty.

* * *

THE OLD TOWN of Mitarai lies at the eastern tip of the island of Osakishimojima, facing a narrow strait between this and the next island. A white-stone pier, a lighthouse at the end, marks the entrance to the harbor, the town lying beyond. There is a small pine-surrounded shrine, black on the light sand, then a small stone bridge connecting it with the waterfront street, a street that turns and am-

219

bles in front of houses, behind them, wanders past the hillside temple, that single boathouse, the restaurant, before turning away from the water and becoming a fishing-village road.

It is the kind of street one could have found in Tokyo before the earthquake, or before the war. It is like the street-alley-lanes still sometimes stumbled upon in Asakusa or Ueno, its turnings created through the years by someone who built a house here, a store there, forcing the street to narrow, to widen, to turn here, circle there. The accident of its corners created the town, just as the placement of the houses created the street. It occurred to no one, either there in old Edo or here in Mitarai, to make a street that was straight, efficient, expedient. It occured to no one to complain that it took twice as long to go through the town. No one wanted to go through it. Everyone lived there.

The houses look like old Edo, the streets look like Genroku prints. Black-laced white plaster, lozenge patterns, gray-tile roofs cemented with white, windows and doors fronted with tall, narrow, vertical bars. It is like backstage at the Kabuki, like wandering in the world of the woodcut artists. Mitarai is like a town that fell asleep in the Genroku period and never woke up.

I stepped off the boat and into eighteenth-century Japan. There are now electricity, bicycles, small trucks, a shipping yard, but the place is otherwise unchanged. I am surprised, then enchanted. Nothing had prepared me for Mitarai, no one has written about it, the travel books do not mention it. I feel I am discovering it—stumbling upon all that is left of the once-flourishing world of Hokusai, of Saikaku, of a great if short age, as frivolous as that of the late T'ang and as endearing. It is a pocket in time, now dusty, forgotten, small, sleepy, but real.

Later I learn Mitarai's history. The eighteenth century was its period, just as the nineteenth century was the period of little Kinoe back among the islands through which I had come. It belonged, like the rest of this part of the Inland Sea, to the daimyo of Hiroshima. He used it for entertaining officials from Edo and the more deserving of his own retainers. It was a lovely island, exotic in itself to palace people. There was always something to do, something to see, and it was a rare pleasure for government officials to be on an island vacation with an expense account from the vast coffers of the daimyo of Hiroshima.

One of the rarer joys was that the place was so far from Edo that all of the things so often forbidden in that sporadically puritan capital were tolerated and even encouraged in Mitarai. This included gambling, drunkenness, bright clothing, and girls.

There were many girls, but these young ladies were quite different from the farmers' and coal miners' daughters in plebeian Kinoe a century later. And they were not called *joro* or prostitutes. They were called *oiran*—a charming euphemism written with characters meaning "flower leader"—and they were the ancestors of the geisha, for whom we have only the ambiguous English term "courtesan." (As someone has remarked, the Japanese have fifty-three words for "prostitute" and yet do not distinguish between "lock" and "key" —which must be a commentary of some sort upon the importance they assign to things.)

Even today the Japanese insist upon a rigid distinction between the *joro* and the geisha, and this is a great practical distinction if it makes no ethical difference whatever. The geisha may be kept, but she is kept as a mistress. She is not on call. This the law respects. In contemporary Japan the *joro* are criminals, the geisha are not.

The geisha have, over the centuries, created their own myth. By being able to dance and play instruments, through their supposed conversational prowess, and because they are terribly expensive, they have convinced generation after generation of Japanese males that they are attractive.

Thus it has come about that every civilized nation in the world has its mental image of the geisha. These may vary, but the general impression is that the geisha is a rare, talented creature, someone to be approached slowly and with tact, a fragile and flower-like being who wilts at a glance, and whose favors, by reason of their supposed rarity, are to be treasured and sought after at any price.

This is the reason that geisha parties are so expensive. If they cost that much money, they must be fun. Yet, as any one knows who has attended a geisha party and endured their company, it is not the geisha who are fun. On the contrary, one is oneself supposed to amuse the geisha, to be rewarded by their shrill and birdlike screams of simulated merriment. After an evening in their company one is exhausted, quite ready to agree with gruff Henry Adams, who, on an early trip to Japan, said that for an exhibition of mechanical child- ishness he had never seen anything to equal the geisha party.

221

The *oiran* of Mitarai was not like the geisha. Like the great eigh-teenth-century courtesans of Europe, she knew precisely who and what she was and turned wanton provocation into an art. She en-joyed a real cachet. Though she may have had intellectual preten-sions, they were not those of the contemporary geisha, who is sup-posed to know how to discuss baseball, the *sumo*, and the stock market. Her pretensions may have been equally limited but were much more suited to her. She knew all the gossip from the mainland and could tell you just who was with child by the daimyo of Hiroshi-ma, just why the daimyo of Satsuma would travel nowhere, not even here, without his little pages. She knew whose stock was up, whose down, who was in favor, who not. She had her friends, her protectors, and she had a taste for the intrigue that naturally flourished here on this little island, where there was little else to occupy the mind.

She also had the *oiran dochu* to get ready for and to recover from. This was a grand parade of all the *oiran*, a copy of the even grander cortege that took place in Edo's Yoshiwara. It had to look impromp-tu but also had to be as grand as possible—the ladies taking the air while the locals stood around to gape. The Yoshiwara *dochu* might have been impressive, but here on this little island the provincial parade of the *oiran*, against a background of sea and shrine and ships, must have been charming. Its atmosphere probably resembled those of the Kabuki performances given here by traveling troupes who came to the island for a weekend and, knowing their audience to be undemanding, could relax, have a good time, and strive for charm rather than high art.

Mitarai's *dochu* likewise had its pretensions, but on a modest scale. The city then had only four houses for *oiran*, the kind called teahouses in later literature, but each contained a number of girls and they all appeared during the *dochu*, strolling back and forth a good many times in their gorgeous kimono, brought all the way from Osaka, if not all the way from Edo itself, teetering seductively barefoot on their high, three-toothed sandals of lacquered wood, preceded by their little-girl servants, whose shoulders served as an occasional crutch as the gorgeous creatures balanced themselves gravely along the country roads, followed by their umbrella-bearers, local boys magnificent in scarlet breechclouts, all hands and feet.

The famous walk of the *oiran*, that slow, pigeon-toed, fastidious,

222

and charmingly awkward gait, was copied straight from the Yoshi-wara, as were the little pauses, hand delicately fanning neck when the exertions of moving became too great, or when the stroller wanted to peer with her great, shy, deerlike eyes at someone worth cultivating.

Occasionally, however, the *oiran* of Mitarai had niceties of their own invention. One girl, perhaps reasoning that the general effect of the *dochu* might be heightened if she were to wear *tabi* on particular-ly muddy days when this stocking-like footwear was certain to be splattered, appeared one day with an old lady in attendance and a strong young man carrying an enormous lacquer box. Putting on her white *tabi*, slipping into her high sandals, she joined the procession that was beginning just after a heavy rain.

One step, two steps, three. "Oh, my *tabi* are dirty; I must change them." The old lady bustled over to the burdened lad and from the box drew forth a new pair of snowy *tabi*. Then and there, supported by her umbrella man, her little girls, she bared her feet, extended them, first one, then the other. The new *tabi* were fastened, and then she, looking at the old, which did indeed carry a few marks of mud, threw—positively threw—them away, into the road.

Finally the whole procession, the rest of the jealously livid *oiran*, could move again. One step, two steps, three. "Oh, my *tabi* are dirty; I must change." And the whole thing began again.

After the parade had passed, and it must have taken considerable time and occasioned much envy among the less inventive *oiran*, the roadway, as a record of the period relates, marveling, "was strewn with *tabi*." It must have been, because now that nothing else is left, that the combs have fallen apart, that not even a towel rack or a teacup is left, several of these *tabi*, black with age, are still shown, are unwrapped from their tissue and, delicate as old parchment, laid before you.

Nothing else remains from these brave days when the *oiran*, pretty as a picture against the sea, against the pines, trod the pier, stepping expertly among the ropes from the ships, the baskets full of fish, the crates of tangerines, bringing to little Mitarai a heady whiff from elegant Edo.

Nothing else except, miraculously, an entire teahouse, the Waka Ebisu-ya, the largest *chaya* in the Inland Sea, which in its time housed a hundred girls, where Hosokawa, the daimyo of Kumamoto, spent a thousand gold pieces in a single night, where the the girls collected the big Edo posters—now called woodblock prints—and where even now the walls are covered with their poems, written in long, elegant, flowing, cursive script, black on the plaster, the poems falling down the wall like curling ribbons. This great house—one of the handsomest Edo-period structures to be found anywhere in Japan—also enshrines the favorite local legend.

Here during the middle Edo period lived a famous *oiran* named Yae Murasaki. She was queen of the courtesans and what she said went. One day she was in a great hurry, guests were waiting, and the *haguro* just wouldn't take. This was the mixture of lacquer and iron filings with which Genroku beauties painted their teeth, making possible the black smile that Edo found just as attractive as we, presumably, find eye make-up.

No matter how much the mixture was boiled, no matter the attentions of the *kamuro*, the girl servant, this one named Shige, it would not stay on. The guests were impatiently calling, the blacking wouldn't take, and Murasaki became hysterical. With a degree of petulance, she turned upon the *kamuro* and in a single movement poured the boiling *haguro* down young Shige's throat.

She instantly regretted her action, particularly when Shige, strangling, began to vomit blood. It got all over everything, and the unfortunate child, dying, hands and clothing smeared, reached out against the wall, raised herself, gazed long upon the unkind courtesan, and then expired.

Murasaki was of no use to her guests after that, though toward evening she became more quiet and decided to make herself presentable. She took the mirror . . . and there was the face of the dead child looking at her. In terror she turned, caught the reflection in another glass . . . and there was the dead Shige again. She whirled and saw the wall where the unfortunate girl had supported herself. There was the hand mark, all red blood mixed with black *haguro*, and there it was to remain.

Murasaki quite lost her reason but had wit enough left to realize that only a great penance would atone. So she took the boat for Shikoku and began the long and difficult eighty-eight-stage pilgrimage from temple to temple. When she had reached the first she heard a voice. She turned around, but no one was there. Still the voice con-

tinued. It said: "Now, sister, you may go alone. I leave you in Buddha's care."

Thereupon, the spirit flew straight to heaven, and the impetuous and unfortunate Murasaki passed into indifferent immortality on the pages of local history.

But the hand print remains. No matter how often the wall is re-plastered, eventually the hand print shows through. I saw it there, still preserved, the red against the black, now chipped and faded, but still the hand print of a child.

*   *   *

THERE ARE OTHER RELICS, less picturesque but no less unpleasant. These are the chapbooks of the house. One reads; one's heart sinks.

Young girl, Komi, abandoned by mother, child employed in kitchens of Waka Ebisu-ya from age of eight. Then, in different writing: Komi, death of. Age fourteen. Reasons unknown.

Or: Yumi, age fifteen. From Shikoku. Bought. Then, later: Yumi, age sixteen, escape of. Capture on board ship. Repatriation. Then, still later: Yumi, punishment of. Age seventeen. Death of. Reasons unknown.

Amid these remains there is one scholar, a mild man with glasses, who reads me the chapbooks. He runs the single inn. When he is not working the garden or helping the maids clean the fish, he writes up some of the local history. If there were enough historical interest in the island—and he sighs and says there isn't—then the publication of a pamphlet might be subsidized. He always wanted to start a museum—it could contain those old *tabi*—but there is no money.

He has, however, just discovered something that pleases him. There was a Dutch doctor who traveled these parts in the very early days and wrote a diary. He came to examine the girls of Mitarai, and, among others, a sixteen-year-old in an advanced state of hysteria was brought to him. The islanders thought her possessed.

He made a long and careful examination and then said that he was of the opinion that nothing at all was the matter with her. She simply ought to be married. You run along now and find yourself a man and you will be all right. The girl, already half-cured, wreathed in smiles, thanked the kind, wise doctor and left.

The scholar tells me this, smiling himself the while. But he had

229

been saddened to discover another detail. This same winning doctor was later murdered—or executed: he was found with a map in his pocket.

This scholar-innkeeper is also compiling a collection of the songs and poems the girls used to write. He has taken them from the walls, has found some in the back pages of the chapbooks, and has heard some from now-dead women when he was a child.

They are all more or less what one would expect, though not devoid of literary merit. The Japanese are such that even the school-girl's diary, the businessman's haiku, are often truly artistic. The content of the songs and poems are, however, expected:

> Look how the pine needles
> Always join in twain.
> Even they . . .

Which is, of course, the Tokugawa equivalent of ladies'-magazine fiction, pathetic fallacy and all. Others are more realistic:

> If you truly love and go to him,
> No matter how short the way,
> When you come back, it will be
> All the longer.

This is a wiser woman writing. She knows that things being in twain is not, perhaps unfortunately, the natural state. And, as the writers move from preconceived notions of love and begin writing from experience, the poems naturally become better:

> The big ships
> Sail past Mitarai now.
> It must be because
> They have no money.

Even more enjoyable are the frankly disillusioned, probably older women, who wrote lines like this:

> Remembering,
> Love is sad—
> Yet not to remember
> Is never to forget.

But this translation does not strongly enough suggest the irony, the paradox, the all-illusions-gone feeling that is the great charm of the original. It is a carefully worked out, popular plaint of the kind called *dodoitsu*, which have a syllable count of 7-7-7-5. This one has a late-Restoration feeling about it, something like good Dryden. The carpentry is all and the phrasing is cunning. It is like an aphorism, a little package, all tied up with bright ribbons as though it were a cake. It is impossible to take disillusion seriously when it comes like this. The original Japanese will give an idea of its civilized plaint:

> *Omoidasu yoja*
> *Hore yo ga usui*
> *Omoidasazu ni*
> *Wasurezu ni.*

One can see the pensive gaze with which the lady began her poem, began it with a well-known opening—the first two lines. Then one may imagine the industry of her fingers as she counted syllables, the busy hand with the fresh-dipped brush. Then, her eyes flashing as form took over and she saw the possibilities of those last two lines. All disillusion—the original inspiration perhaps—gone, she tried various combination and, finally—

> *Omoidasazu ni*
> *Wasurezu ni.*

One may imagine the triumph with which, initially not without stumbling, she read the completed poem. Then the sound of joyful hands clapped once and the compliments from smiling friends; then the charming complacency with which she sat to make a fair copy, perfectly happy, content, her original heart-sore inspiration quite forgot.

*   *   *

I ASK THE SCHOLAR about love stories. Certainly there must have been at least several celebrated *oiran* who loved well but none too wisely; surely there must have been a suicide, perhaps out under the pines near the shrine, where, in the morning, the corpse, still warm, had been found; perhaps there had been a brigand whose rough exterior hid an all-too-human heart, which he had entrusted, just before that fateful final voyage, to one of the local beauties; certainly there must have been— But, no? Nothing of the sort?

Nothing of the sort. For a place so ideally suited to the creation of romantic history, Mitarai is strangely lacking. If ugly little Shimoda can have an Okichi pining for love of Townsend Harris, if Nagasaki can manage the original who later became both Madame Chrysanthème and Madame Butterfly, one would think that Mitarai— But no, nothing.

"I've looked all over," said the mild innkeeper, glancing up from his manuscript. "Perhaps the reason is that Mitarai was always given over to nothing but making money, and money always drives out romance."

Agreeing with this pithy aphorism, I bent over the manuscript and we began to speak of other things. During our talk, however, an idea formed and became more and more visible to both of us. His book needed just such a love story, and most other noted places already had theirs. It was too bad that Mitarai didn't. Perhaps we could just...

"We need a monster," I said. "Let's do one about a monster." And I started outlining a beautiful story built loosely around Perseus and Andromeda, with a lovely *oiran* offered as sacrifice, and a sudden and horrid monster who stalks from the sea, and just then—

"A monster, eh," he said, rubbing his chin. "That would have to be pretty early. Almost pre-Nara. That's not a very popular period, you know."

I hadn't but, undeterred, outlined another. The lovely someone-or-other, against her will working in the brothels of Mitarai, meets the captain of the good ship something and they fall in love. He will have to go back home—Kyushu seems a proper place—and bring the money to buy her out. But there are typhoons and perhaps an earthquake or two and it is some time before he gets back. And it is then that he learns that she went to the pier every day, scanning the horizons for his ship. This made her ill and finally she died. No, she killed herself. And she killed herself just as his ship was finally sailing over the horizon, but she didn't know this because all ships look alike. And when he sprang from the deck, her body was still warm though her spirit had fled. And he made a vow of some kind or other (this part to be worked out later) and became either a pious monk or else a brigand, terror of the seas.

The innkeeper liked it very much but decided for a double ending. "It makes it sound more natural that way. And so he became a pious monk and also a terror of seas."

"But," I said, having thought of the final touch, "it was only later that they discovered why she had killed herself and he discovered this too and this is the reason that he became a pious monk, terror of the seas. She had worked too long in the houses—she had contracted syphilis."

He looked doubtful.

"But don't you see? This makes it realistic. It makes it sadder too. Think of her, poor thing, beautiful, in love, and with syphilis."

"Did they have syphilis back then?"

"Oh, they've always had syphilis."

"All right, but I somehow liked it better before. It was more beautiful."

"But this way it is more meaningful."

"Well, maybe, but . . ."

"All right. She doesn't have syphilis. But why does she die then?"

"She kills herself. You said so yourself."

"But why? If she doesn't have syphilis, then there isn't any reason."

"Precisely. That is what makes it so lifelike."

"But if she waited all that time and then, just as his ship was on the horizon—"

"Just so. That makes it more pathetic. So close, and she did not know. I particularly like his taking the still-warm body in his arms. Maybe he should weep and make his vow right then."

"Maybe—but this way there isn't any reason for anything."

"That's right. It sounds like a real legend."

He began to write it down while it was still fresh, but it took a long time: he was apparently embellishing it. I fell asleep and in the morning he was cleaning fish and so I was not able to hear the final version. Soon it will enter folklore and be told to inquiring tourists. I doubt I would recognize it.

*　　　*　　　*

233

THE ISLANDS on the way to Kure and Hiroshima—these have other memories, different memories, more recent memories. Many of them are war islands. I am told about them by the captain of the ferryboat taking me to Kure, a tall, kind man with an absent air who contains a fund of information about these, his islands.

Here, on these islands we are approaching, during the Satsuma Rebellion, during the Russo-Japanese and Sino-Japanese wars, during the great Pacific War, the Japanese Navy and the Coast Guard had their bases and camps and fortifications. Then came the Americans and the Australians during the years of military occupation. And now the Japanese Navy is here again, though disguised under the name of Self-Defense Forces.

The largest island in Hiroshima Bay—some call it Etajima and others call it Nomishima, a confusion harking back to the distant days when it was actually two separate islands—is again filled with cadets. It probably looks like Annapolis, much as it must also have looked before the war as well, having been the site of the Imperial Naval Academy since 1889. There have, however, been changes. In 1960 a five-year plan was announced: the place would be made more attractive to tourists. At present it contains, besides the sailors, a large cactus garden. Also, something is being made of local history. The etymology of Katakikubo (Revenge Dale) is explained by a tale of a group of evil samurai who, having ravished the beautiful daughter of a local farmer, were set upon—successfully, in a dale— by her vengeful brothers.

Next door, the largish island of Kurahashijima is advertised as the home of dragons. They still show pictures of the tusks, though authorities have cast cold water by identifying them as the tusks of a mammoth. This, however, would hardly disappoint me: I find the idea of a mammoth on these tropical isles quite as exotic as the idea of a dragon.

As always in Japan, a little scratching under the asphalt highway or the concrete high-rise apartment house brings history bubbling to the surface. Here among these islands with their new factories, their piles of industrial waste, their television sets and cold-drink vending-machines, history and folklore lie just under the rocks. On the nearby twin islands named Upper and Lower Kamagarijima—upper being the one nearer the capital Kyoto, not the northernmost—a pirate named Taga built a large and now-vanished castle. But before that the strong Benkei came and lifted something or other heavy. And before that Kobo Daishi came and, since it was windy, put up a number of rocks as a screen. This titanic windbreak he called the Eleven-Faced Kannon, and then he changed his story, saying that really it was not because of the wind but because he thought he wanted to offer the image in hopes of the Genji's eventually winning their protracted conflict. And before him came Jimmu Tenno, who arrived sleepy and had himself made a carpet of rushes to rest on—hence the name of the islands: Reed Cutting. Even earlier, however, came a deity who lost his comb (*kushi*) on the local mountain (*yama*), a small hill now called Kushiyama. It was this same deity who found the neighboring island miserable (*nasakenai*) and so named it Nasakejima.

On and on these small islands continue, crowding into the Bay of Hiroshima, each one holding its own history, its own folklore, some of it old, some of it new. I hear about Hoborojima—is it here in Hiroshima Bay or somewhere farther back? But my informant is an indifferent geographer, seeming to feel that one island is much like the next. In any case, this tiny island was once considered beautiful. Then she (the island) somehow fell into disgrace and tried to escape but could not because to the north was Hanagurijima (Nose-Pulling Island), to the south was Tosenjima (Chinese-Ship Island) and also Oshima (yet another Big Island, but so small I can find it on no map), all standing in her way; so she was caught and now pines away.

And here too is little Ninoshima, whose history is fairly recent. It has a small mountain shaped, the locals say, just like Fuji. It was here that some of the victims of the atomic bomb were taken because it was thought safer than the city, where they expected another bomb. And it was here that an orphanage for the children of the victims was later built.

My boat moves slowly from one tiny island to the next, bound for the terminal, Kure. The seas here are crowded with cargo vessels, the shores are lined with factories, and smoke drifts across the face of the sun. Some of these islands were once submarine bases, cruiser slips, lighthouse stations, bunkers, and are not now often visited. The boat stops at one.

Away from the little town are the ruins—new ruins, ruins just twenty-five years old. They are chalk-white against the blue sea. They are also barren, as though trees will no longer grow. They look mineral, like islands of salt. The dust rises. One bends to pick up bits of metal, shells, spent bullets. Even the birds do not come. There is little for them to eat. Only the insects, only the basking lizards. Overhead hangs a single gull, supported in the hot, ripe air of late summer like a fish in water.

Some of these islands are warrens of tunnels and stone-ridged caves, with alleys like trenches, and sunken stone rooms, now empty and so deep they are cold. It is difficult to imagine that all of this once had a purpose. But it did, and the purpose was war.

Here at Ondo was a bunker for a machine gun. Here is the bolted plate for a cannon. Once these tunnels led some place. They were filled with running troops. Now, in ruins, they lie half-open to the sun. They are like a pleasure maze, like the ruins of Knossos.

There are names, hundreds of names, written, scribbled, scrawled. Suzuki Ichiro—a name like John Smith—who was a private, first class; Watanabe Sumire, a schoolgirl who came here ten years ago; Lt. Gordon Robbins, who came from what looks like Lancaster; Sgt. Warren Peabody, from Council Bluffs, 6/25/46.

There are other marks on the walls too. Here an explosion tore away the stucco, exposing the brick; there is a large red stain, but blood could not have made it because no one has that much blood and so it must have been chemicals. Some of the walls are marked with fire, others with boredom—aimless scrawls, little pictures, girls with large breasts, a kind of ticktacktoe. In some of the rooms there is seaweed, now dried, crisp, powdering underfoot. Was the water ever this high? I wonder. The seaweed festoons the walls. It looks like an underwater ballroom, the first-class lounge of some great and sunken ship.

*   *   *

IT IS NIGHT. We pass islands that are great collections of shining standing tubes, clusters of enormous aluminum balls, covering the land with their metallic undergrowth, and whose purpose I do not know. They puff and sigh as we pass, reflected in the endless rows of perfectly spaced lights, the illumination for those straight industrial blocks, geometrical, perfectly spaced units of land in which I see nothing living, not a man, not a dog, not a tree.

I turn and walk to the stern. There lie other islands, forested

islands, uninhabited islands, farming islands, fishing islands, stretching farther and farther into the sea. The nearer are now black, almost
invisible. Just an hour ago, as afternoon faded, they were dark,
almost black, but those behind were slate gray, separated by silver
inlets leading to a farther island, dove-colored. Then, those behind
turned blue, as island after island, like a range of peaks, stretched to
the horizon, a faintest violet that was almost not a color at all.

Now, at night, those islands, far away, are black shapes riding the
lighter black of the waveless sea. Each is sprinkled with lights: a
village, a town, a city—spots of light, tiny halos no brighter than the
overhead stars. Shikoku is a cloud in the distance, low on the horizon,
dim lights at its base. Is it a city? What city?

The boat whistles, the wind is cool. At the port a new collection
of aluminum stacks slowly rises, as though from the sea itself. I
wonder what I am approaching, what I am leaving. The land is
turning mineral. I look and see island after island approach, but all
of them silver and illuminated to an almost hallucinatory clarity.
Not a tree, not a bush, not a blade of grass. Extinguishing the stars,
they rise like sculpture, sigh, blow smoke or steam, pass.

Is it all gone? I wonder as the cool wind reaches me, something
sharp in it, like a knife wrapped in silk. I remember once, near my
Tokyo house, some workmen were constructing a wall for an apartment house. They came to an old tree with a low overhanging
branch. After some consultation they put a hole in the wall to accommodate the branch. It is still there—or was last month—a small
and unthinking reminder of a way of thinking, a way of living, that
is right.

The Japanese are the last people who stand in reverence of the
natural world. Rather than attempting to eradicate it, they have
successfully adapted themselves to it. They have offered themselves
to it, have come to terms with it. I am reminded of Robert Frost's
words about those who "found salvation in surrender." There is
something larger than man, though this the West denies. It is nature
itself, the way things are, have been, and always will be. The white
man's most daring and foolhardy feat is mere rapine. All of his glory
is merely brutality. He doesn't know how to live in the world he was
born into and so he will destroy it and build another that will destroy
him.

Japan had this gift of surrender. In backward sections of the land,

237

it has it still. But as I move from these islands nearer the shore I see that it is going, gone. Japan has learned all too well—the virus of glory is catching. *Shikata ga nai*, it can't be helped—that lovely and accepting phrase will soon be as extinct as the cry of the nightingale and the blinking of the fireflies on these shores. And with it will have gone a kind of hope.

*   *   *

KURE. I AWAKE COLD. The sheet, too hot last night, is icy. I pull it over me and shiver; then, thinking I must be ill, I sit up and look out the inn window. The sky is gray and white, a winter sky. I stand up and hang from the window. The green of the garden, only yesterday the tropical green of deep summer, is now grayish, as though covered with pumice. The tree trunks, yesterday a rain-forest black, are now pale. The earth itself is no longer brown. It is tan, and a cold breeze stirs the bamboo as though it were January.

Autumn has come, with the appalling suddenness that is its way in Japan. The long, hot, rainless summer is over. And it is over instantly. One morning it disappears. The leaves hang, and the sky—in the middle of September—looks like snow.

Like evening in the tropics, autumn here is sudden, unequivocal. You wake up and have winter as though you awoke and had pneumonia. Those summer insects that sang beneath my window last night are now stretched on the underside of leaves, trying to escape from the cold earth with feeble claws. The lizards that ran yesterday among the rocks, the birds that panted with open beaks, the busy wasps reveling in the heat—all are still and cold now.

I touch a mosquito on the *shoji*. It does not move. It is as though frozen. In my room, though, it is still summer, because there are my striped shirt, my bathing suit, my sunglasses. But they are no longer needed. I will have to discard them as though I had outgrown them, as though they were things left over from childhood.

The mosquito does not know it and may not live to see it, but in a week or so will begin that most miraculous of seasons—Indian summer. It is false and lovely, perhaps lovely because it is false. And it is loveliest of all the seasons in Japan, where, for two, three weeks, it is suddenly summer again—a deep summer with the sky an impossible

238

blue and the sea the color of jade. It is one long and lovely respite before the winter.

*   *   *

HERE, SOUTH OF HIROSHIMA, there is still more industry. Shipyards pound all night. The colored skirts of the refineries, red, green, yellow, stretch far into the sea. The chemical plants belch colored smoke, and sulphur-colored plumes stand against the sky. On the horizons there are more of those great collections of shining standing tubes, those enormous silvered balls, covering sea and islands alike with their metallic undergrowth. I still don't understand their purpose and probably never shall.

The deity who had difficulty first with red leeches and then with snakes and pheasants—I've now decided to call her Utsukushi-hime, liking the overtones of beauty in this version of the name—she would not recognize the place now. She came rather near here, but something was always wrong no matter where she stopped. Toda, south of here, was beautiful, but then she noticed that the mountain was too low. That would never do. She moved again. Then she went to miserable Nasakejima. She liked the scenery this time. But the mosquitoes!—millions of them, teeming. And, in the morning, she discovered there was no drinking water anyway. Perhaps I'm wrong in some of the details—maybe she liked mosquitoes and didn't need drinking water—but the fact is that she kept moving until, eventually, she discovered the perfect Miyajima, which is also where I am heading. So she too always kept moving on.

But at least she missed Kure—she would have hated it.

Quite a number of other famous people apparently also managed to miss Kure. The most famous of these was Kiyomori. He was later to rise to fame as the leader of the Heike, but in his younger days he lived in the fiefs of Bungo and Aki, now parts of Hiroshima prefecture. It was he, say the records, who built the grand shrine at Miyajima, making Utsukushi-hime, now located after her long travels, move over to make room for some local gods from Otsu, his birthplace. It was also he who widened the strait at Ondo.

This is the narrow stretch of water that separates the peninsula upon which Kure is located from the island of Kurahashi. In those

239

days it was so full of reefs and dangerous whirlpools as to be all but unnavigable. According to legend, Kiyomori had discovered a very beautiful girl on this island. She was a *jokan*. *Jo* means "woman" and *kan* means "official," and she was probably some kind of shrine maiden. He wanted to marry her, but she made the condition that he must first widen the strait to make it safe for small boats, and must, moreover, do this in the space of a single day, between sunrise and sunset.

This seemed fair to him. He called his men together and they set to work. But as the sun slowly descended, he realized that they were not going to be able to finish in time. So he climbed a nearby hill— it's still there, just where the new bridge now begins—and fanned the sun with his large war fan. Slowly the celestial body came to a stop. Still fanning, he called out: "*Nichirin yo, kaeshi tamae!*" which might be translated as, "Ho, you sun, go back please." Obligingly, the sun reversed its course and rose in the sky long enough for the men to finish their work.

Joyfully, he hurried to claim his bride. She, however, far from being overjoyed, far from being willing to marry him, laughed scornfully and stuck out her tongue. (The locality of this affront is known—in Japan such localities are always known and may be visited: ask for Shitazaki, or Tongue Point.) Angry, he put his hand to his sword and was about to draw it. The maiden, in turn, became a *jatai*, an enormous snake or some kind of water-dragon, it is not certain which. He at once set sail, the monster in close pursuit.

He set his course for the strait of Ondo, which he had so lately widened. The maiden-monster swiftly followed, wallowing, making waves and noises. Drawing closer to the strait he saw that the mighty whirlpool, Niramijio (still there today) was already in action. He cried something to the effect of, "Oh, water—widen your path; have you no sense of obligation?" Hearing this, the whirlpool quieted, for the water was grateful that he had so widened its passage, and he sailed safely through. But the way was far too narrow for the monster. She snorted and puffed but could not get through. So she went back home. End of legend.

Another who did not come to Kure was Jimmu Tenno. He got as far as the Mebaru Strait. At this point, however, his bird flew away. This was a golden dove that always traveled on the tip of his bow.

240

Heretofore it had always returned. Now, however, it did not come back. Jimmu, the first emperor of Japan, waited patiently in the vicinity for many days. Eventually he caused a shrine to be built, then passed on. The shrine is still there on a hill behind Kure called Takagarasu-yama (Hill of the Swallow)—the golden dove having been changed through the centuries into a more familiar bird.

Apparently it was no accident that so many people did not go to Kure. There were a number of reasons for not going. Chief among these were the spiders. There was a hill called Kumotori-zaka, so named because it was the lair of these monster creatures, which made their webs cunningly across the valley mouth Unwary travelers would be caught and the spiders would rush down the hillside, secure the unfortunates, then carry them off and suck them dry. One day—naturally—a brave hero (whose name I did not catch) passed through, stopped, and said: "I will kill them all with my sword and my *bushi* spirit." And so he did, all but a few. These remain to this day, it is said, great hairy creatures, big as automobiles but still too frightened to make an appearance.

Farther up the local river is the scene of a domestic tragedy—the kind of which the Japanese are most fond. The river is very deep and has many pools in it. One of them is called Yoshigafuchi, the Pool of Yoshi. This Yoshi was a beautiful handmaiden who worked at the local castle. Every day she went to the pool to wash the dishes. One day she dropped a plate. It fell to the bottom and was not to be recovered. Very unhappy, she commited suicide and since she was so good and so beautiful, this made everyone in the castle very sad. They named the pool after her. Her memory lives. (The new tunnel is, I note, called the Yoshigafuchi Tunnel.)

In many countries this would be considered one of the less interesting legends. Not in Japan—this is the kind that is most repeated and lives longest. That the beautiful but stupid lady ought not have killed herself at all, much less over a plate, occurs to no one. On the contrary, her tawdry little tale is found, somehow, just like life. Well, I suppose it truly *is* like life, come to think of it. Even now the company secretary in Japan leaves the company payroll in the taxi, is unable to find it again, takes too many sleeping tablets; the student fails an examination, goes out, disrupts the railway line for hours by jumping in front of one of the engines. It is presumed that these folk are to be pitied, that they could not help themselves, that mysterious are the workings of fate, that life is like that. Just like poor Yoshi—and, sure enough, her story has never been forgotten.

With famous people going out of their way to avoid the place, with all sorts of horrid and pitiful tales surrounding it, one comes prepared for Kure. It is not a pleasant place—though, of course, being in Japan, not nearly so unpleasant as the two places it most resembles, Norfolk and Galveston.

It is, like these, a honky-tonk port, the economy of which is geared to the fast turnover, the inhabitants of which are a third navy, for this is the place of the great Japanese naval yards—just as Etajima out in the bay is the place where all the naval cadets are trained. It looks rather like a frontier town in the American West or, perhaps, what the Klondike villages looked like in the days of the gold rush. It is a city of transients, of bars and girls and pachinko parlors. By night it is a baby Ginza with lots of neon and flashing lights.

The sailors come to town at night, all dressed in their blues now that summer is officially over, their wide collars and ribboned hats making them look like little boys from the nineteenth century on their way to a band concert. The sailors are bored, as they always are in sailor towns. They are allowed out every third night and have always seen the movie, have always been to the bar, have always tried to pick up the girls, have always failed. There are too many of them. They get in each other's way.

Then, the Japanese are not, in peacetime at any rate, particularly nice to their servicemen. Given the never-again attitude of the Japanese toward war, their ambitions toward being a little Switzerland, given their proximity to that horrible object lesson, Hiroshima, the people of Kure are impatient with the navy and are apt to be short with it.

This, the country being Japan, is not to be glimpsed in any overt action. Rather, as always in this country, the true state is seen in reflection. The townspeople show no open hostility, but the sailors have been taught to be especially nice, to please.

A taxi backs up and accidentally knocks over someone's standing bicycle. Instantly, two sailors are there, righting the machine, politely directing the taxi so that it will cause no further accident. Any place else, of course, the overturned bike would so have remained until its owner's return. Here, if a blind man were to attempt to cross

242

the street, he would be mobbed. So attentive are they that only a major calamity—earthquake, typhoon—could take sufficient advantage of their benevolence.

They have been trained well. They perform their good deeds with no self-consciousness whatever. They are like particularly conscientious Boy Scouts. I see several who appear to be actively looking for kindnesses to perform and seem disconsolate at finding none.

For the most part, however, the sailors wander or lounge. I fall into conversation with several, then several more, then a solitary one here or there. But soon I quit, discouraged. The conversation always goes the same. After some preliminaries—the weather, the fact that they are Japanese, that I am not—my friendly question of "Where are you stationed?" or "What kind of boat is it?" brings narrowed eyes and shorter answers.

It is not that being inquisitive is bad manners. Actually, this is the proper way to carry on a conversation in Japanese. The three initial questions asked foreigners are, in order: What do you think of Japan? Are you married? How old are you? One may be as personal as possible, and the more inquisitive the better. Rather, the difficulty lies in my being foreign. After a few more questions from me I hear them murmuring among themselves. Perhaps he is a spy, sent by a foreign power to root out secrets from simple sailor boys.

This is frustrating to conversation. More, it is irritating. In itself such a reception is not pleasant, but worse still is the comprehension that this attitude—that of the sailors—is that of the country at large regarding foreigners. No one except sailors would say spy, or even think it—but for all Japanese, sailors included, the foreigner is as different from themselves as a spy is from the common, decent, hardworking non-spy. This is absurd and foolish and true.

*   *   *

WALKING BACK to the inn through the cool autumn-like wind, following, followed by, sailors returning to their ships, I am reminded of that ex-sailor, the virtuous young man with whom—how long ago? it seems very long—I spent the night at distant Honjima.

Japanese puritanism. It is difficult to convince the newly arrived, newly infatuated foreigner that such a thing exists in a land he pleases, and even needs, to find permissive. This is because, being a Western rather than an Eastern puritan, he is thinking about sex.

But there are many kinds of puritanism. The enthusiastic new-comer may, for example, find it singular that in Tokyo, the largest city in the world—and consequently in all smaller Japanese cities and towns as well—the buses stop running after ten or so in the evening, the subways at around eleven, and the trains stop just after midnight. There are still taxis—if he can get one to stop—and so he might not at once notice this anomaly, but a few moments of thought will reveal its significance.

The millions of inhabitants of this great metropolis are systemati-cally and nightly deprived of public transportation. The implications are plain. They should be at home, asleep. That thousands, indeed, are not is indicated by the packed snack bars, the after-hours places, the all-night movies, and the general lack of taxicabs. Nonetheless, says custom and mores, they should be.

This nightly closing of all forms of public transport is, I suggest, but one of the many forms that Japanese puritanism takes. There are others and my sailor friend has already indicated a few.

Yet the strain is different from that we know so well in the West; the virus is—from our point of view—mutated. Webster's indicates the genus nicely: "*puritan*: one who practices or preaches a more rigorous or professedly purer moral code than that which prevails." The difference between East and West is that, in the latter strain, the impetus toward purity, having been early inculcated, rises from the inside and may or may not be seen on the outside; in the former, the impetus comes from the outside—society—and may or may not reach whatever dwells within. When such a code is transgressed the Westerner feels a private guilt, the Easterner a social, or public, shame.

One need not search far for respective reasons. What John Calvin with his belief in the total depravity of mankind is to the West, Confucius with his vision of an ideal society is to the East. The French reformer believed in the superiority of faith to good works, since man has no free will of his own, and that all of those due to be saved were already so predestined; the best one could do, therefore, was to act as though salvation had already occurred. The Chinese reformer believed that the five ethical relationships in life (subject to emperor, child to parent, wife to husband, brother to brother, friend and friend) were quite capable of regulation; the best one could do, therefore, was to act as though one believed they had been. Neither of these gentlemen—a millennium apart in time, very close in spirit —were to realize that their various idealizations were fanciful, ludicrous, inhuman. This discovery was left to their later adherents.

One detects, however, a difference in these varieties of puritanism. Calvin was writing about private morals, the practice of what he considered conduct; Confucius was writing about public moral ethics, the theory of what he considered right conduct. The Japanese, as heirs to the Chinese code, were given a fuller escape clause.

Of which they continually avail themselves. Nonetheless, the code is there: it accounts for the less workable parts of the government, for the rigidity of ward official and Customs officer alike, for the condemnatory attitude of most policemen, for the suspicions of sailors, and for the somewhat spotted purity of the boy on Honjima.

Cheered by these dismal reflections I gained my darkened inn and climbed under the chilly comforter vowing to leave on the next wind.

*   *   *

I DO NOT, however, leave immediately. Perhaps it is that I am feeling the mixed revulsion and fascination at finally going to Hiroshima that must afflict all Americans. I explain to myself, however, that it is because I want to do some shopping.

I cannot find what I want. I never can; it always infuriates. At present I am searching for a silicate filter for my cigarette holder. Until last month they were readily available. Now, however, a new kind of cigarette holder has appeared that requires another kind of filter. The manufacturers have, with great foresight, seen that the tobacco stands carry now only the kind of filter useless to my holder. At the same time they cunningly display the new holder in order to tempt me. But I am firmly attached to my old. Impossible to find silicate filters in Tokyo, I agree—but surely here in the country...

Not at all. The giant hand of enterprise covers the land. The tobacco stands of Kure are as naked of the desired filter as are those of Ginza. And all of this overnight. Two months ago kiosks all over Japan were stacked with my kind of filter.

The same is true of everything else. I keep photo albums and have for years used a certain kind. Last year I suddenly found that no one had them any more. They were no longer being made. Shortly it developed that the kind of album in which you paste the pictures was likewise unavailable. Now only the new kind—sticky silver paper covered with thin veneer—is available. It is new, therefore it is good—supposed to save you time or something.

More seriously, when a Japanese publisher issues a translation of a Western book he prints only a certain number of copies and no more. Second printings are almost unheard of, no matter the continuing demand. If the edition sells out in a week or in ten years, it is all the same to him. It takes a monumental demand—*Gone With the Wind*, *Lady Chatterly's Lover*—for him to consider further printings. The same is true of phonograph records—and the same, naturally, is true of shops that sell books and records. They order one of everything, and when it is gone it is as though it never existed. There may be talk of having to order it from the publisher, but this does not mean that such will indeed occur, it is merely a phrase indicative of the impossibility of your project.

One detects a paradox here. Japan, the land that loves time, has a dizzying rate of turnover in small things like photograph albums and cigarette filters, the life expectancy of each model of which must be measured in mere months; Japan, land where tradition is respected, cannot even keep its books and records in print. But I know perfectly well that footwear (*geta*) in use since the Middle Ages are still sold on every street; that kimono in almost no way different from styles five hundred years ago are still to be bought; that, indeed, the only kind of saw you can buy (one that cuts when pulled rather than pushed) is one perfected in the mists of antiquity.

Then it strikes me that naturally this would be so. *Geta* and kimono are Japanese; cigarette filters and photograph albums are not. Though I dare say there are many more people using my kind of filter than there are using *geta* at this late date, nonetheless, the mystique holds—things Japanese, no matter how useless, are important; things foreign, no matter how useful, are not, not really, that is.

And if I want to find a book or a record it had better be Japanese. I had been looking for Jane Bathori singing Satie, had been trying to find for a friend the superb Japanese translation of the *Memoirs of Hadrian*. If I had been looking for everything ever written by some local Kenneth Roberts—Eiji Yoshikawa, for example, author of

Musashi Miyamoto and other claptrap—or all the recorded songs of Kokichi Takada, croaking ladies' favorites of decades back, purveyor of *ryukoka*, ersatz folk-flavored "popular" tunes of a nearly violent insipidity, these would have been there, hundreds of copies of them.

There are areas, however, where some things foreign remain. One wonders at this, and then realizes that a subtle change has taken place in the objects, that they have been japanified, and that some fancied resemblance to something already in the culture has proved their unhappy saving, and—finally—that they have not been saved so much as preserved, like flies in amber or, more fitting simile, like the mammoth in the ice.

An example is to be found in any department store. There is a section, rather near what is called the young-miss corner, where what appear to be cakes are being sold. But these are not cakes. Rather they are quaint little clocks in the shape of snow-covered chalets or vermilion-turreted castles, music boxes built to look like windmills and waterwheels, wooden letter-holders that appear to be mailboxes or dog houses. Nearby are flounced French-flapper dolls to decorate the virginal bed, a variety of cute accessories including hair barrettes in the shapes of Mickey and Minnie Mouse, and bracelets on which are imprinted, in English, such harmless if redundant phrases as I AM A GIRL.

There is no generic name for this assemblage, unfortunately, but it is at once apparent that the objects are all for young ladies. Further, for young ladies of some means if little discernment. They are for the *ojosan*, the young lady of good family who may be exposed to things foreign but never in their possibly dangerous and original form, who must, on the other hand, be continually reassured that such are, after all, despite their charming novelty, really, somehow, Japanese.

Take the clocks and music boxes. They are always in the Swiss style, such being thought of as the safest since the least exceptional— the Swiss being moderate, hard working, and not overgiven to innovation. At the same time, the style of carving is quite Japanese— it is of the variety known as *Kamakura-bori*. And though the music box may be in the form of the exotic windmill (the Netherlands is another safe choice, it is the most unexceptional country in Europe, think the Japanese, next to lovely Switzerland), it will sound, if wound, that beautiful old Japanese favorite "Moon on Ruined Castle."

Such objects now belong to the Japanese *ojosan* and exist no place other than in her world. Her life is one of exclaiming with delight at the more gooey deserts and crying with innocent if nonetheless Lesbian pleasure at performances of the Takarazuka—the all-girl "opera" that manages to preserve all the amenities of the old-style Shubert Brothers musical (glimpsed by a Japanese director in the 1920's and never forgotten) with most of the originality and wit of production numbers of American films from the 1930's.

It is she who presumably rushes through the stacks of charming frocks to sate herself with Mickey Mouse barrettes and cunning Bavaria-inspired weather forecasters in which the pretty couple safely wear kimono. Without a thought in her charming head, she hovers, hummingbird-like, over the arrayed treasures and finally makes a choice that her chairman-of-the-board father or flower-arranging-teacher mother will happily pay for. All of these girls are virginal, all of them are as pretty as flowers, and all of them have vegetable intelligences.

Of perhaps more import, however, is the fact that Mickey and Minnie are thus, and in typical Japanese fashion, saved for the ages. Long after their celluloid originals have turned to dust, long after every reference in Western literature is free of their names, they will remain in Japan, Mickey and Minnie together, and though possibly no longer to be recognized as mice, they will have taken on an autonomous existence simply because they have endured and will confront us from watch-face or hairpin with that implacable air of mystery which we now find in pre-Columbian sculpture or the artifacts of Etruria.

Wandering through the varied cultures of Japan or—better choice —climbing about among the different strata of civilizations on this island plateau, one comes across such fossils as this continually. This one—made of chalets and French-flapper dolls—is still soft to the touch as it were, but the one containing, say, T'ang music and dancing is hard as rock.

There is none, however, for cigarette filters. These remain foreign, intransigent. I ask at one last kiosk. No, the old lady knows what I mean but they stopped selling them last month. "But how about this?" And, with the air of unveiling the latest invention, she reveals a tray of brass pipes, long, attractive if filterless. These are those traditional pipes, once smoked by men and women alike, each holding a pinch of tobacco that went out after one puff, with which lovers of the Kabuki are quite familiar, which have been in evidence for the last two centuries, and which, though I have not seen one used for years, are still quite available. It is because they are Japanese, you see.

*   *   *

I LOOK FROM THE BUS WINDOW and again notice that with the land come the trees. The islands have many bushes but woods are relatively few except on large islands like Ikuchi. Here, one would have thought them destroyed long ago, the commercialization of life is otherwise so evident. Even here, along this road over the pillaged land between Kure and Hiroshima, there are hills with crests of trees, and groves remain here and there.

At the same time I notice that there is no field, no hillock, no convenient turn in the highway without its advertisement. Lion Tooth Powder—this I make out as the bus bounces by. Then something about the new Toyopet—legend and happy picture—natural in this automobile-ridden land. Then, suddenly, I decipher: Cancer Cured! And this also one expects in a country where patent medicine is gobbled like candy.

The next four or five signs I cannot read. I am relieved. Since I do not read well, these millions of advertisements are not actually offensive to me. Rather, they are pretty. They add to the general air of the unkempt picturesque. Japan can be very beautiful to us illiterates.

*   *   *

HIROSHIMA. The historical fact of the city lives only in the imagination. "There!" one thinks. It was right there—the great fireball, the terrible wind, that high cloud, mushroom of death. Right there—the skeleton of the Industry Promotion Hall, the only solid building that survived, rising above the plateau of this delta city of bridges and waterways—right there it was dropped.

I stand in Peace Park, on the balcony of the museum, and look at the spot where massive death was. This is where concrete crumpled like paper, where iron smoked and twisted, where annihilated humans left their shadows etched in concrete.

Trying to visualize, trying to imagine, as though I had myself been there, I fail. The immensity is impossible to reconstruct and con-

249

sequently to comprehend. It was chaos and our minds are too orderly to comprehend this.

Hiroshima itself has not retained the experience. The park, the museum, the paper cranes, the memorial statuary, the ruined promotion hall—they are there. But the city is, after all, the largest in southern Honshu. It is too important to be merely museum and memorial. It is many things to many people now, and few indeed must be those to whom it is just the city where the Americans dropped the first atomic bomb a quarter of a century ago. Life, as the typically Japanese phrase has it, goes on.

This is also one of the facts of death—that one forgets it. One may disapprove of oneself for forgetting, may have wanted to keep the fact green, tended like a grave. It is impossible. Life is too strong. Death loses on every occasion except the last.

And Hiroshima has other things to think of. The people find their city neither a place of past horror nor a shrine, just as the Romans—who have had to live with the Vatican in their midst—do not find their city particularly holy. Besides, only twenty persons remain out of each original wartime one hundred. The rest were either killed or have moved away. With house gone, family gone, city gone, there was no reason for survivors to remain.

New people came in. They were, as was to be expected, people with few former roots in the city. They were also, to an extent, profiteers and speculators. That was over two decades ago. Now they are respected; some are councilmen, others run the city government. Not so long ago the local Chamber of Commerce wanted to tear down the ruined industry promotion hall because it was not good for the image of their bustling, up-and-coming city. All those dead memories of death and destruction—they were bad for business. That this was not allowed was the doing of the country, not the city. The national government would not permit it; the local government was all for it.

The bomb is not spoken of except by those in the tourist industry and, presumably, among those very few wounded survivors who remain alive. These few are hidden away, are not spoken of. They linger unseen in homes or hospitals; they are relegated to the slums of the city, then disregarded. The bomb has become tiresome, except as a propaganda weapon. Consequently, its victims are no longer interesting. Recently one of these survivors—a man with keloid scars, a beggar—was run off the streets and no longer appears on the bridges and street corners in the city where he was once, perhaps, a happy and respected citizen.

This indicates one of the most terrible facts of being human. The unfortunate are, try as we will not to do so, further degraded by us. We take from survivors what humanity they have managed to retain. Though we look with conventional horror at pictures from the German concentration camps, a part of the horror that we feel should lie in the fact that we certainly think, and just as certainly refuse to acknowledge, that these unfortunates are somehow no longer human and that this makes it all, somehow, not as bad as it might be. The man who divorces his innocent wife after she has been raped by someone is behaving in an all-too-human manner.

The bomb is therefore forgotten except when useful. Otherwise, it is old fashioned, a serious defect in modern-minded Japan. It is unfashionable. This does not show itself in cynicism as it might in a worldly city, but in apathy. It is understood that the period is over, that it is now history and that history is not interesting.

*   *   *

THE FOOD IS SOUTHERN in Hiroshima. I met *unagi-domburi*. In Tokyo this would be grilled eel over rice. Here it is eel grilled and sweetened and covered with rice to which a vinegar sauce has been added. It tastes Chinese, like sweet-and-sour pork. Also Chinese in appearance are the great butterfly prawns I next order. They are so large that I pick them up with my fingers to eat them.

This excites the interest of the waitresses, who talk among themselves and eventually call the manager. He stares at me for a time and then politely approaches my table.

Is this then, he asks, the proper way to eat prawns? His manner is properly respectful, he intends no irony, he really wants to know. Perhaps the Japanese, using their chopsticks, have been eating prawns wrong over these hundreds of years.

"Not really," I say, "but it is *one* of the ways to eat them."

Are there then several ways of eating them? He wants to know. Perhaps the Japanese might avail themselves of these new ways.

"Yes," I answer, though I had not thought much about the

251

problem. "There is this way, with the fingers, and the other way, with chopsticks, which is also correct."

He is not convinced, lingers. Maybe, he suggests, with a diffident smile, it is merely a provincial custom, something that occurs only in my esteemed home-country but is not to be seen in the world at large.

I put down my bitten prawn. Service is so uniformly exemplary and at the same time so impersonal that, though I have on many occasions interrupted waiters in their work to talk to them, this is one of the few times that anyone has interrupted my eating in order to talk with me. Delighted, and not yet detecting the faint animosity in him that later became more apparent, I said I did not know much about the proper way of eating prawns but that I had been surprised at Hiroshima, had not expected such a bustling and business-like city, and had not expected so strong a Chinese influence.

"Chinese?" he asked, smile fading at the corners.

"Yes," I continued, dilating on the subject. I compared Hiroshima with Nagasaki in this regard, mentioned the fact that before the war there were many Chinese businessmen and sailors, spoke of the way my eel had been done, glanced around, and added, "That painting there, for example."

All Japanese restaurants of this order have murals, just as all public bathhouses have murals. They are all done by the same man. He has a very oily brush, uses very bright color, and always does the same scene: lake or sea, islands, pines, boats, little people, big clouds —occasionally a railway train, more often a steamboat. They look Chinese to me because they are so garish, like pictures in Chinese restaurants.

He looks at the painting, then back at me, face blank—the expression of a polite Japanese disagreeing. Then, this being south and the people more open: "You're wrong" (*chigaimasu*). "It's Japanese— not Chinese at all."

I meant that it was so loud (*hade*) that it looked Chinese to me; Japanese art is much more nicely subdued (*jimi*).

He was not mollified by my explanation, but continued to stand there, began to bite his underlip. Finally he surprised me with a cold "*Do itashimashite*." This one of the more unsatisfactory polite phrases in Japanese. It is used to mean something like "You are welcome," but a more literal translation might be "What makes you say so?" I am never certain whether it is being used literally or figuratively.

Consequently I didn't know what he meant. I suspected, however, that rarest of commodities—irony.

Perhaps it was the Chinese reference that had irritated him. Most Japanese dislike Chinese. They also hate Koreans. The majority here is convinced that these neighboring peoples are hopelessly inferior. To be sure, so, in a way, is everyone else in the rest of the world, but these two are more so.

The belief is surprisingly widespread. Good friends inform me that the Chinese are untrustworthy and the Koreans naturally have a bad smell. We find this shocking, remembering all too well the now-hopefully-vanished attitudes of our own that were prevalent in the era of the Kike and the Nigger. But we—remembering—should also find it, however lamentable, natural.

Actually, the Japanese go further than most peoples in discrimination of this sort. Anyone not Japanese is, naturally, in some way inferior. Those who maintain that the Japanese themselves are victims of what they call an inferiority complex are themselves victims of an elaborately sustained illusion. Actually, like the Germans and the Americans, the Japanese suffer from a very advanced superiority complex. This being so, anything not Japanese is so different that it may, in various ways, be discounted.

The commonest way to discount is to dismiss. The Japanese dismisses the entire remainder of Asia, for example. He has no real interest in India, China, Korea, Southeast Asia, though he may take advantage of these countries. During the Pacific War he simply took those lands he wanted; now, after the war, he simply takes the money he wants out of those lands. His attitude is shown in his apparent disinterest. Japan, civilized, will bring its civilization to these inferior peoples who do not enjoy and perhaps indeed are incapable of enjoying the higher life that Japan represents.

One may also, however, discount by appropriation. Europe, America—these lands are also inferior, but their ideas and products may be put to good use if they are first run through the Japanese mill and emerge unrecognizable and therefore very Japanese. This results sometimes in a watch or a camera that is, in all but a few, if telling, ways, identical with some Occidental original; it also results, however, in such fascinatingly monstrous transmutations as the Japanese idea of Humanism, or Democracy.

It follows that all foreigners are stigmatized, but some are stigma-

253

tized more than others. At the bottom of the heap are the poor Koreāns. Even those born in this country, whose families have been here for generations, are denied citizenship. I knew a Korean man, born and raised in Japan, who, weary of life here, went to America. There, running foul of America's law against aliens working in the country, he was told to leave. But he could not return to Japan, his own country, because he was not a citizen, and the Japanese would not have him. He was sent to Korea, a country to which he had never been, the language of which he did not know, and where he knew no one. I never heard from him again.

Americans are near the top of the pile. Nonetheless, I have found it expedient to tell curious strangers, inquisitive tradespeople, and cab drivers that I come from such safely neutral lands as Sweden, Switzerland, Canada. This is because I do not want to defend (indeed, cannot defend) America's policies, both domestic and foreign. And I would be expected to. I am not actually myself—not to the taxi driver, nor even to acquaintances who should know better. I am, instead, a typical representative of my land and my people. No matter my protesting that if indeed I were, I would still be there among my own kind; still I am forced into first explaining and then defending "my" country. Since the Japanese do not truly believe themselves to be individuals, they refuse to allow anyone else to be.

Sitting here in this restaurant in Hiroshima, under the eye of a piqued manager who guesses my nationality, I refuse to give in to that easy and sentimental feeling of guilt in which Americans specialize and, at the same time, I refuse the equally easy thought that the disapproving manager is not after all representative, but merely a single man among millions. I can, it is true, attempt to be myself, attempt that divorce from country, but few indeed are the people who attempt this and fewer indeed are those who succeed.

At the same time my journey, my quest, strikes me as quixotic. I want to find the place where the real Japanese live. But are there any?—any other than those I already know? Is not what I really want a place where I can find my own individuality? Is not that what the search is about? And is it likely that there is such a place among these lovely islands?

I am looking for a land where people will accept me; I am not looking, as I had thought, for a land where I could accept them.

Turning to stare at the mural again, I find that it appears now very Japanese—it is an unlikely country, a strange place in which I am engaged in such a venture.

Finished, I stand up, pay, tell the tight-lipped manager that the food was good.

"*Do itashimashite.*"

*   *   *

TO DISTRACT MYSELF I went to the Hiroshima post office and asked after a letter from Saburo. None was there. This disappointed me out of all proportion. Though I had forgotten what he looked like, he had belonged to an earlier, a more innocent part of the voyage. He, at least, I felt, knew me, which was certainly something no one else in Hiroshima did. His letter would have helped remind me of myself.

So I walked around a while.

There is never enough to do when you travel.

This must be one of the reasons why travelers the world over are known for their attempts to pick other people up. It is not that they want sex so much as it is that they want something to fill the emptiness that their very freedom has created. And what else can you do after the coffee shops, the zoos, the museums, and the libraries are rifled?

Too—another factor in favor of seeking sex—there is no more personal undertaking. Naked, lying down, one is resolutely oneself, the person one otherwise left at home. The freedom to lose yourself, one of the great attractions of the sexual encounter, is based, after all, upon the assumption that you have first found yourself.

At the same time—tips for the traveler—there are few better ways of learning the language, of taking the temperature of the land, of measuring the inner states of its inhabitants. Also, there are few more attractive memories to take home with one. Sex makes, in its way, the ideal souvenir.

I thus cogitated in a small coffee shop near the park named, appropriately, Heiwa (Peace). I hadn't really enjoyed much sex on my journey, I thought, being inclined to discount the selfish endeavors of Momoko and my other fumbling attempts. But I was thinking of it in the way common to tired travelers: I wanted to have had sex. Therefore, not feeling like sex or, in any event, not feeling like the

255

long, tiresome, and hypocritical endeavors that might—or, more likely, might not—lead to this faintly desired end, I decided to divert myself in other ways.

* * *

IN THIS I FAILED. One nearly always fails. The fact that one is driven to diversion indicates, perhaps, a frame of mind which ensures such failure.

Seven in the evening found me standing in a chill wind surrounded by the blinking bulbs of Hiroshima's considerable night-town. It stretched into the distance in all directions, very large, seemingly as big as that of Tokyo's Shinjuku, certainly as lively.

Just as lively for everyone but me, I thought. Being in one of these exciting warrens of pleasure always brings out the most morose in the white man. He feels neglected and incapacitated; at the same time— and this is one of the greatest of Japan's many attractions—he is sensible of a permissive atmosphere, the very lure of promise. Just now, just around this corner, just on the other side of that door, surely awaits the one for whom you have been searching so long, throughout all your life. There, just there—only turn and smile and you will have happiness forever.

This marvelous illusion is based, in part, on the people who throng the streets, eager for a good time and almost frenetically happy; in part it is due to those others who will serve this mood: the sandwich-board man who winks and smiles, the kimonoed girls who stand just inside the big plate-glass door and open it invitingly and seductively as you pass, the uniformed doorman who grins and wants to shake hands, the dressed-up hostesses who are lined in the entryway, smiling, shifting their feet and dabbing at their makeup, casting glances the while.

And it is an illusion, though one wonderfully sustained. These people belong to the world of *mizu shobai*. This is an interesting phrase, perhaps a poetical one. The *mizu* is "water" and *shobai* is "business." But there are other connotations, particularly in the water aspect, which not only suggest the unstable world in which entertainers have to make their living, but also the stream along which we all drift, the *ukiyo*, the floating world. All these people, from the lowest bobbing barboy to the grandest geisha left, are united

256

by a common skill: the art of pleasing. Japanese, particularly women, lend themselves well to this. It means that even if you are right and the customer wrong, you apologize prettily; it means greeting joyfully customers you particularly dislike; it means using heightened pronouns for the visiting farmer and lowly pronouns for yourself; it means pleading prettily and politely when the oaf is messing your best kimono; it means an almost complete abnegation of self; and it means utter hypocrisy.

I have watched *mizu-shobai* girls by the hour, wondering at their strength, at their ability to endure and continue. Then, eventually, I understood that, in its way, the art of pleasing is sincere. I thought of the probably apocryphal story of the great tea master who, having practiced for an hour an aestheticism so great it seems almost self-indulgence, stopped on the way home to urinate in the street. It is not the incongruity that should claim our attention, but rather the fact that each of these seemingly disparate acts is what we would, with our limited vocabulary in these matters, term as sincere. He means this artful discipline and he means this gratifying voiding.

When with the customer, the geisha or the bar-girl means everything she says, even the most extravagant flattery. The reason is that sincerity comes with the role. This she puts on as she puts on a kimono. It may bind a bit but it is both pretty and proper. It does not, however, follow that she means it forever. No one means anything forever, but this is something only Asians seem to admit.

It all becomes very clear, standing there in the cold, windy, lighted streets. The Japanese are a people who have managed to retain, right into the latter half of the dehumanized twentieth century, a very human, even primitive, quality: their innocence. While this does not prevent great subtlety and a degree of sophistication, this mighty innocence—one that the Japanese share with those the white man elsewhere calls natives—rests upon an uncompromising acceptance of the world as it is. The innocent does not look for reasons behind reasons. He, secure in the animal nature that all of us have and only half of us admit, is able to see that all reality is what the West finds merely ostensible reality. Reality is skin deep because there is only skin. The ostensible is the truth. There is no crack between the mask and the face because the mask is the only face anyone ever has—that crack, which contains irony and wit as well as cynicism, does not exist.

It is not perhaps, then, the contrast between the old and the new that so attracts in Japan as it is the contrast between innocence and experience. What I flee from in the cities is the beginnings of something new: cynicism, that big-city vice, and with it that great and final breakdown—occurring here, finally—between man and his own nature; that neurosis which creates great cities and occasionally great art.

This native innocence results in ignorance on the one hand, mere knowledgeability on the other. It accounts for the almost absurd atrocity of the Japanese at war, the Japanese at business. At the same time it allows the Japanese to live in peace with himself.

They are not perhaps natural in the sense of Rousseau's noble savage, but they are nevertheless natural beings in their own way. They know what all natural men know: that life is here and now, not in any further state, either theological or financial; they know that death is certain and this they accept with a grace almost shocking to the struggling West, which must retaliate by calling them suicide prone or death oriented; and they know perfectly well that reality is that which is apprehended and nothing more. This does not make them pragmatic, because no one would think of constructing a rationale to support such a natural observation, but it does make them empirical. And we of the West find it difficult to live in a land of one dimension such as this. We must always have the further lure and promise of something more, something better, whether it be heaven or a yet higher standard of living, because we must think of ourselves as somehow more, somehow better.

But I am speaking of the people of the Inland Sea; I am speaking of old Japan. Already the change is upon us—already the innocence is fading, going, gone. It lingers here, in these islands that I have so recently visited, but only for a time. I'm fortunate to have seen it.

Feeling much better after such thoughts—it is always surprising what a tonic mere thinking is—I decide to go and have a drink on it.

*   *   *

I WALKED INTO the nearest bar. It was tiny, was in a basement, was named Kibo (Hope), and had, I thought, a curiously reluctant door until I discovered that someone on the other side was pushing as hard as I was.

Standing to one side, I let him come out: an older man with a crocodile belt, a red face, a hat, and an angry expression. He brushed past me, violent, eyes fixed and furious, and stamped up the stairs. Not too hopeful a place, I thought, for the quiet drink I had been contemplating.

Entering, I saw the young woman in tears behind the bar. Another woman, older, was looking into the depths of her tall drink, displaying that polite, disinterested, unseeing air that Japanese cultivate in the face of embarrassment.

"Please come in," sobbed the young woman, dabbing at her eyes with the bar towel. I hesitated. Noticing this, she managed a crooked smile and said: "No, no, it's nothing at all—please come on in."

I seated myself somewhat awkwardly on one of the stools and looked at the bottles stacked in front of the mirror-backed farther ledge.

"I'm very sorry this happened," she said, mainly to the older woman. "It was very rude."

This was met with reassuring sounds. "*Do itashimashite*," said the older woman, smiling, adding: "These things happen from time to time."

"So they do," was the answer, "but usually they happen some place more private."

"Such things happen," was the wise rejoinder, "no matter where." Then: "I suppose he was your special patron."

The young woman nodded, briskly smoothing her cheeks, turning to look at herself in the mirror behind her. The other made a few subtly uncomplimentary remarks about him and then, leaning forward, asked how long it had been but in a tone that wondered how awful it had been. This the young lady did not answer. She turned to me with a smile and asked what I would have, stopping in mid-question when it occurred to her that I might not speak Japanese.

I, using my most polite grammar, said that I would have a whisky and water—"*Mizuwari o itadakimasu*." Then I continued to stare. I admired her.

This feeling perhaps originated with her so resolutely drying her tears, putting her troubles behind her, facing the further demands of life, and doing so with a smile—a rare quality that I completely admire. But also admirable was the polite way she had silenced the older woman, who, herself too well-bred to continue prying, was now forced into compliments about the coziness of the place. Though a part of the warm feeling I felt toward my hostess originated in the loneliness of the solitary traveler and his need for affection, probably foremost in my admiration was the simple fact of the woman herself.

She had perfectly set wide eyes, black, flecked with gray, a completely straight nose, a full but straight mouth, skin like satin, still slightly rouged by recent emotions, and a way with herself that was deft, assured, and faintly humorous, yet affectionately so, as though she did not really take herself too seriously but at the same time recognized her own worth. I saw her as a very rare creature and she, smiling, perhaps at my stare, put the glass in front of me and said: "One whisky and water."

The older woman opened her mouth, probably to ask another personal question, and the young woman turned to me with: "Have you been in Hiroshima long?" While we talked, she did the things other girls who work in bars do. She smoothed the neck of her kimono, a dark gray tinged with rose, put one hand to the back of her neck from time to time to touch her long, upswept hair, smiled and nodded—but she did it all with a grace of her own, and a slight stiffness, as though we had just met at a party, did not know each other, and she was politely trying to think of something interesting to say. She was far from the fluent airs and graces of other women in other bars.

The older woman finally got a word in: "But you can't have been in business long," she said, using the term *mizu shobai*.

The other smiled and shook her head: "That's just the trouble"—*sore de komatte iru no desu*.

"One must be careful then," said the other darkly, finishing what looked like a whisky sour.

But this beautiful and charming young woman was not to be drawn into a further discussion of the interesting scene I had just missed. And, in any event, two more customers—businessmen, they looked—came in and had to be served.

One of them was talkative and began speaking of a certain bar hostess of his acquaintance who was no better than she should be but a good girl for all that, speaking in a presumably conversational but actually well-thought-out manner, using the apparently lightly interested but really earnestly involved tone that one recognizes the world over: the man on the make.

She answered in the somewhat mocking tone of the professional hostess, assuming that air of innocence which is always canceled out by what is said, an air playful but guarded. This is the tone of the *mizu-shobai* women when speaking to men. The difference was that this young lady did it so badly. She rattled on when she should have merely prattled; she tended to shock when she intended, perhaps, to titillate; and she became earnest, heavy—a quality I felt could not be truly hers.

She ended by driving the men from the bar. It was not that apparent. They had another drink apiece but, second time around, the interested man was not so interested and soon there was a polite looking at watches, a civilized remark on the lateness. This was met with simulated distress and assurances of the almost unreasonable earliness of the hour. Nonetheless, they went, and, the older woman having gone somewhat earlier, I was left alone with this fascinating and direct young woman.

So she indeed proved herself to be by saying, as soon as they left: "Well, I didn't do *that* very well, did I?"

She did not expect an answer and was smiling to herself, hands on the counter, when I answered her: "No, you didn't do it at all well—you made them go."

She looked up, surprised. "Did I? Well, I suppose I did." Then, smiling to herself, looking at her nails: "That must be the reason, then."

"The reason for what?"

"That the Kibo is not what is called a successful bar. I don't have what is known as an established clientele." She was speaking lightly, ironically. "A person in my position should be welcoming them instead of sending them."

"And making them angry too if I am to judge by that gentleman with whom I collided at the door."

"Oh, him—he's different."

By which I understood that he was, indeed, her special patron. A businessman of some kind, someone with money, will—now, as in the Japan of two hundred years ago—put a woman up in business, buy her a bar or a geisha house, give her something to do. Sometimes it is because they both want to make money, but this, I think, is rarely the real reason. She is his anyway, though he may be married to someone else, almost always is, and she must be kept busy and relatively happy. This then is a patron, and women of the *mizu shobai* have for centuries competed for the best.

"No," I said, draining my second drink, "it's you who are different."

She turned and looked at me. "Well. . ." she said, half smiling at my declaration. Then, dropping her gaze, she added, with a smile: "And it's true too—I know it's true. I shouldn't be here." She shrugged, a delicate, expressive gesture, and said: "I don't know how to do it." She turned and smiled—a wide, friendly smile.

And I knew then who she was like, why I felt I knew her already, yet why she remained mysterious. She looked like that beautiful fifteen-year-old girl I had spoken with on Naoshima, who had found me a room at the inn, who had come in the morning mists to say good-bye.

Finishing my third whisky, drinking rapidly, as though I, her only customer, were going to make up for all those who had not come, I was already thinking what life with her would be like.

"I came into the business late, you see," she said, explaining. "My husband died, and—"

"I'm going to be divorced," I announced.

"And so," she continued, smiling, "I found that there was not much else for me to do."

"Where did you meet him?" I asked.

"Him? Oh, he was—and it's funny to remember it—an older friend of my husband's. He sometimes came to the house when we were married. I remember—isn't it strange?—I remember cooking for him. He always liked eggplant baked with bean-paste. And I never thought of him as anything but a friend of my husband's, or—perhaps—some kind of uncle."

"You're young yet," I said.

She didn't ask me to guess and then refuse to say. Instead, she said: "I'm thirty-two and that is not young."

"I'm forty-six," I said, anxious to give information.

"And that isn't young either," she said.

Just then two more men came in—men in Japan so often drink in pairs—and I sat and watched her cope with them. She wasn't any better, but then this couple was considerably worse. They were tipsy and inclined to be amorous in a mindless kind of way. They wanted to play games—real games with matchboxes, suggestive ways to open cigarette packages, and so on. They giggled and tried to hold her hand.

The women of the *mizu shobai* put up with a great deal. They are leered at and pawed over from seven in the evening until the early hours of the morning. In Tokyo I knew a young man, a great womanizer, who found the perfect way to get what he wanted and yet avoid this tedious preamble. At just seven he would appear at a bar where there was a girl he had seen and liked. He would have a drink or two and carry on a light, interesting conversation, to which she, still fresh this early in the evening, would lend herself with pleasure. Then he would go home, set the alarm clock, and go to sleep. At two o'clock in the morning he would be awakened, would dress and return to the bar. He appeared, fresh, rested, completely sober, as charming as ever. She, having been through seven hours of slobbering and pawing, tired, disheveled, discouraged, would see him there —like a vision from her youth, some trusted friend from her own childhood. His tactfully expressed concern, the fact that the bar was, finally, closing, would land her, first, in some small and intimate restaurant for a quick bite and some more quiet charm, and then— invariably, he said—back in the scarcely cold bed and into his arms. If I had been earlier, I thought, I could have perhaps tried the same thing. But then I *had* found her in tears and that had, perhaps, softened her sufficiently.

Now one of the men had hold of her little finger and, with the infuriating stubbornness of a spoiled child, was refusing to let go. The other was involved in a long joke about an overflowing toilet, both the point and the conclusion of which he had forgotten, and kept shaking and rubbing his head over.

I ordered another *mizuwari*.

She turned, smiled, and said, rather loudly: "I am so sorry but it's closing time. The police, you see, are rather strict in this district."

This had, at first, no effect on the two other drinkers, but after it had been repeated several times, they paid and left. I also stood up and paid, and then didn't know what to do.

She smiled and told me to wait outside, considered, then said I should wait at the corner, at the far corner, by the noodle shop. I was witnessing a rare sight—a woman of the *mizu shobai* deserting her post.

Outside, the street looked brighter, livelier than I remembered

263

from seeing it sober. The girls lined up in the fronts of the cabarets seemed charming, even—or especially—one with a silver incisor and a single dimple. Men striding along in tipsy couples seemed definitely worth knowing, and a solitary girl standing just behind the door of a coffee shop and opening it gently when anyone at all passed by seemed full of mysterious beauty. I was drunk.

The young woman joined me, having put a light summer-kimono jacket, a *haori*, over her shoulders, put the key into her small, black purse, and said: "You don't want to drink any more. What about some coffee?"

She looked around as though expecting to find her crocodile-belted patron standing guard, then waved at one of the taxis and named the place we were going—some place far, apparently. Actually, it was only several blocks away.

"Did you think he would follow us?" I asked.

"One never knows," she said. "He was angry enough to do anything. He's an unreasonable man," she added, mildly.

"He's probably tired of you," I said, already seeing myself happily working beside this beautiful and honest girl, already running a wildly successful Hiroshima bar, the only one with an American bartender.

She shook her head. We were in a small coffee shop, the kind that stays open all night, with white-faced waiters who never see the sun and heavy curtains that never get cleaned. "No, nothing like that. It's just that we haven't argued for a week or two now." She sat beside me, warm, close, smelling of hair, of fresh, soft skin. "You see, I made a joke this evening. I said I should call my bar Kibo Nashi"— here she paused a moment to make sure I had caught her meaning of "No Hope"—"and he took this as an excuse to become angry. He can work himself up like that." She smiled, sipping her coffee.

"Is he jealous?" I asked.

She turned to me. "You said I was different. What did you mean?"

She gazed at me and I felt foolishly happy, about—finally—to embark on the great adventure that I had not yet had, about to discover truths I had as yet merely glimpsed. I wanted the night to last forever and talked on and on. At first I spoke and she listened, but then she began talking too. We began by talking about her, but we continued, somehow, talking about me.

"It's always like this with Japanese women," I complained. "I wanted to talk about you and now we are talking about me." She gave me a straight look that cut through my cant, a look that contained a smile and the knowledge that I much preferred talking about myself.

"You are better at *mizu shobai* than you think," I said.

"This is what I like about foreigners," she said, laughing. "You're all so open. I feel that you're always really telling the truth. Are you all like this?"

"Not actually. I'm really the only one like this."

"Well, what about me then?—since you so much want to talk about me."

"I've never met a girl like you before. I didn't think that any existed in Japan. You are the only girl in the country like you," I said and wondered what would happen if I put my hand on her knee.

Later, tired of coffee, of the stale, cigarette-smoke-heavy air, both of us a bit weary of talk, I suggested a walk. It was past midnight. The air was cool and the stars were out, millions of them.

"The moon's set," she said. "In a day or two it will be full. It will be *jugoya*"—the full moon, a word used only in the autumn. Then: "Where did summer go?—it seemed so short."

We walked on, walking through the darkened streets, surrounded by the sleeping in their shuttered houses.

When I was on Onigashima, she had been to her father's grave; on the day she had to call the police to help get rid of a drunken gangster, I had been in Mitarai; cold and lonely in Kure, she had been lonely in Hiroshima and had not even opened the bar that evening, she had felt so alone. When President Kennedy was assassinated I had been in Paris and she had been with her husband in Osaka; the day the atomic bomb was dropped I was on the China Sea and she—eight years old—had gone with some schoolmates to Kabe deep in the mountains: which was why she was here with me now and not dead and forgotten among those other tens of thousands.

We had reached the park, the Peace Plaza. The hotel and museum were dim in the distance; the small paper-crane-filled chapel was nearer. I was in Hiroshima, walking in the night with a beautiful, intelligent, independent woman who might have been killed.

"Oh, it's not all that hopeless, I suppose," she said, meaning her patron, her bar, her life. "Still I envy you. Here you are in the middle of your journey. You will be here for a day or two and then you will go on and everything will be different, for you."

"I won't forget you," I said.

She stopped suddenly. "I didn't mean that. And that was a silly thing to say. Everyone always forgets everything. I know that. I've even forgotten my dead husband, and I loved him and thought that I never would. But I did." She stopped, then continued. "No, what I meant was that—that I envy you, I suppose. You don't have any responsibilities, you can go where you please, you must make money enough somehow or other that you can do this. It is a nice life. I'm envious, simply that."

And I was, I realized, in a way envious of her. She had a place of her own, she had something to do, she belonged somewhere.

"We can go part of the way together," I said, referring to my trip, my voyage, my quest, anxious to be with her but not anxious enough to relinquish entirely my worthless freedom.

"Yes—that hadn't occurred to me. I was so busy being envious that I didn't think of how lonely you must occasionally be."

"But you're lonely too," I said, remembering that late twilight in far Naoshima, and the girl who had wanted to know all about the Ginza, had wanted to travel. She was enough like this woman to have been her younger sister. "You don't have anyone but that old man with his—crocodile belt."

She smiled. "He has a lizard one, too—and one he insists is genuine rattlesnake."

It was nice walking in the dark with her, feeling sentimental about her, knowing I could walk away from her whenever I wanted. It was like...was like brother and sister.

"Let's go some place, just the two of us," I said, having decided that what I really wanted was to be lying down rather than standing up.

She looked around the deserted park. "But here we are just the two of us."

"I mean some place more private."

She looked into the distance—there was no one in sight, no one would come all night—then turned to look at me. "Why?"

Apparently seeing nothing romantic in our being together in the

266

dark of the deserted Peace Park, she continued to gaze at me. I didn't tell her the truth—that I wanted to have had my adventure.

"Why not?" I parried.

She appeared to consider, then smiled and shook her head. "No, it's not right—you're not right...I'm not right."

I took her hand and she let it lie there. Now that nothing was going to happen, I grew bolder. "Here you are," I said, "out in the dark with me. Why did you come if it wasn't all right?"

She smiled and tried to remove her hand from mine. "I was feeling sorry for myself; you were sympathetic—very sympathetic. You are not like all men, you know, and so you shouldn't try to act like them."

Again I felt her trying to withdraw her hand but I continued to hold on to it.

"It isn't that you want me, you see," she said. "It's that you're lonely. Almost anyone would do. And I don't want that. I want someone who wants me."

"I think I do," I said doubtfully, remembering suddenly the man in the eel-shop and what I had comprehended, that I was not looking for a land which I could accept, but one that could accept me.

Again she pulled at my hand. This time I let her go, also remembering the drunken customer who had refused to let loose of her little finger.

"Thank you," she said with dignity.

And I was reminded of Louise—honest, frank, thinking eternally of what was best, best for everyone, straight, true, sincere, and, consequently, beautiful.

"And besides," she continued, "it's not true. It's not me you want. And as for me—well, I too want something different." She went on and told me about what she wanted. If we had earlier spoken too much about me, we now talked too much about her. What she wanted was a perfect marriage, a meeting of minds, an identity of wills; husband and wife were to become one in a perhaps ideal but equally incestuous liaison for which all endings were happy.

It was touching, her speech, because such a marriage is impossible. It was also both prim and based, I felt, on a kind of desperation. Just like Louise.

And I realized that, until I did something about it, I would always be attracted by these noble, honest, hopeless women who would

begin with these straight and sincere feelings and would end—
because nothing else was left them—wanting to mother me. My
wife, the girl on Naoshima, this woman in Hiroshima—Momoko as
well—unhappy creatures all, attracted me because of their straight-
ness, because of their beauty, and because of the looming failure of
their desires. It was hopeless.

"*Kibo nashi?*" I asked.

"Precisely, *kibo nashi*," she said, smiling.

We had been walking in the dark. Now we reached a streetlight. I
looked at her in her gray kimono, shaded with rose, her feet in *zori*
and white, split-toed socks, her obi humping her back, and I realized
that for the last some minutes, for the first time on my journey, I had
forgotten that I was speaking to a Japanese.

I stopped, elated. The barrier I had known, the one that they and
I had erected, the very distinction between "they" and "me," was
gone. It was to be found only in small differences—her *zori*, my shoes;
my coat, her *haori*—differences I knew, familiar differences.

I turned to her with a smile.

"It's all right now?" she asked. "We can part friends?"

I nodded. She smiled, shook her head, and said: "When I do
escape from this life—and I will—it is going to be with a man who
isn't at all like me. Us, you and me, we are rather alike, I think."

"Like brother and sister," I said.

She considered for a moment and then agreed. "Yes," she said,
"like brother and sister."

Later, at one of the all-night cafés in Hondo she was sipping
iced tea, I was drinking a Coca-Cola. We were playing a game.

"How does a foreign dog go?" she asked.

"It goes bow-wow."

"'Yes, that's right. We always say that ours go *wan-wan*. Our cats
go *niao-niao*."

"Ours go meow-meow."

"They're fairly close, aren't they?" She considered, then added:
"And our pigs go *bu-bu* and our goats go *me-me*."

"How do your rabbits go?" I asked.

She thought for a time and, then, with the most beautiful smile,
said: "Rabbits don't make a sound, do they?"

Then the waitress came and said that the sun was coming up and that they were closing. We went into the street, somehow colder now that it was light.

"*Kibo nashi*," she said, smiled, hesitated. Then we embraced, and she stopped a taxi, got in, and was driven away.

I stood looking after her. She really did have whatever *mizu shobai* really means. While she might be poor at match games and playful repartee, she had mastered the more important skill of guessing the degree of a customer's interest, of divining her own.

Turning my little adventure over and over in my mind, I discovered several unexpected angles. She had been, perhaps, as ready as I was for something new—had been, perhaps, even readier, since she had something real, Mr. Crocodile Belt, to escape from. While I saw in her something I already knew, something already familiar—a new Louise—she was looking for something impossible but at least something she did not already know about.

But what, I now safely wondered, if I had swept her off her feet, had smothered her protestations with kisses, had— No, I'm not the type, and this she knew.

Becoming rapidly soberer in the growing light, I still fantasied on. I imagined taking her—what was her name? but we hadn't told each other our names—with me through, let us say, Europe. There she was in her gray-and-rose kimono standing shyly in the Piazza San Marco.

But when I looked more closely I saw that she had changed, that she was no longer herself. The Japanese are like that. They do not travel well. The men are embarrassed, shy, sad, or else—the obverse —so miserable that they become rude; and the women—they turn more and more into themselves until they close completely.

The Japanese is all Japanese and he must be seen in his own context because his mountains, his forests, his seas are also him. It is not that he does not have individuality, for he does. It is that he has more than individuality, he has his context—and he has never been taught to foster a strong personality, has never been told that each and every person must be, somehow, different, unique, only himself. He has never found that necessary because his strength comes from his land and from his people. This is why the Japanese are most themselves among others of their own kind. The Japanese—

I stopped.

269

Already "they" and "me" had returned. But after a few more thoughts I wondered: And why not? I could now ask myself this because the distinction no longer seemed important. We'll be "they" and "me" part of the time, and part of the time we won't.

*   *   *

AND I REALIZED that my quest was over—at least part of it. Sitting in the sunny Hiroshima station, a freshly bought paperback *Persuasion* in my pocket, I understood what I had guessed earlier: that the voyage had not been to find them, but to find myself, and that—to an extent—I now had.

In the train, looking at the flat, bright coast, traveling to the ferry station, I suddenly, and for no apparent reason, thought of Lafcadio Hearn dying and penning a few last bitter pages. The book was called *Japan: An Interpretation*, but he, like all of us who come to this land—attractive, mysterious, and impenetrable as a mirror—was writing about himself; the tender, myopic, beauty-loving Lafacadio was being, finally, interpreted.

I mingled with the others who left the train, waited for the gates of the ferry to open. This disillusioned end I would be spared, I thought, I hoped. I would never find them, the real Japanese, because they were always around me, and they were always real, but I might at last decide what my own real self was, and hence create it.

But it was too nice a day just to sit and ponder. So, for the first time in my life, I was able to achieve the feat I had so long admired in the Japanese: I shook my head and put aside perplexing thoughts. Then I turned with a smile to the waiting, open day, and—along with all the others—boarded the boat.

*   *   *

THE ITSUKUSHIMA SHRINE at Miyajima—a floating orange-lacquer labyrinth, a series of pillared pavilions connected by roofed and railed corridors, lying white, orange, scarlet between the green of the forested mountains and the green of the sea. It is low, a rambling single story, like a great summerhouse. The rush roofs, low against the green mountains, flat against the sea, stretch, cross, intersect, one behind the other, so like the palaces on early screens that one expects those knobbed and formal linen-white clouds to come sailing by at eye level.

There is no general view. One can never see it all because it was not designed to be viewed from outside. It—like Venice, of which it somehow reminds—is not a view; it is an experience.

One is meant to wander, turning at random along these straight and open corridors filled with the rustling of the forest, the whispering of the sea. There are no walls. One looks through the shrine as through a forest of lacquered trunks, contained and guided by these gleaming corridors.

It is like someone's house, filled with peace, with the peculiar restfulness that only the nearness of water can bring. It is like that other great house, the Byodo-in at Uji near Kyoto, floating over its pond. But here, as one turns, expecting the lotus pond, one finds the sea.

A number of people live in this house. There is not only the staff of white-robed priests, garments fluttering in the sea wind as they walk along the corridors, turn corners, and abruptly disappear; there are also a number of spirits.

The first of those of whom I think, however, is no god. He is a mortal, Taro of Urashima, who voyaged beneath the sea and came upon the Palace of the Dragon King, which must have looked much like this. On a sunny day the light filters among the columns as though through the sea itself. One expects to find sea urchins in the corners, an octopus slowly slithering along the corridor ahead. Though there are gods in large number at Itsukushima—among them the three princess-daughters of Susa-no-o no Mikoto—it is so human a place that I remember mainly Taro, who wandered, marveling, through a labyrinth much like this.

It is T'ang, as is the Byodo-in, but it is Japanese T'ang, which is to the Chinese original as rococo is to baroque. It has been made human. The scale has been reduced. It seeks not to awe but to charm. It is like a miniature replica—large as it is. It is like a doll's house of fabulous ingenuity and miraculous workmanship.

I turn yet another corridor and am free of the labyrinth. I stand on a wide veranda facing the sea, and there in front of me, standing thigh-deep in the water, is the great torii, bright red, enormous, far away but so large that it looks near. It is the water gateway to the shrine.

Japan is a sea country. Many of its most beautiful shrines face the ocean and this, the most beautiful of them, opens directly onto the sea. More, it goes to meet it. It stretches itself out, like a waiting hand, open, both inviting and accepting. It is like a mudra, one of the positions of the hand of the Buddha himself. The sea-borne pilgrim is welcomed and enfolded in this shrine.

It is, of course, very old. The plan was first laid in the ninth century, was added to in the twelfth; and, though the buildings have in the course of time been often reconstructed, this purpose remains, this gesture to the sea, this metaphor of faith.

*   *   *

I CLIMB THE MOUNTAIN behind so that I can look down on the shrine. From here, however, it shows nothing at all. It is a collection of roofs with a tiny torii in front. It could be a small village collected at the base of the mountain. One expects a fishing fleet rather than pilgrim boats. The same is true of mountain shrines. They reveal nothing of their nature from below. Rather one must—by ascending, by descending—approach shrines at their own level. Only then, like caves, do they display their true nature, show what they really are. They are made for humans and so they are humanized, but they are only for those who have gone through something—the mountain climb, the ocean voyage. Only then may one see them as they are.

Here is where she came, the deity whom I have been following— Benten, Utsukushi-hime, Ichikishima, whatever name she is to be known by. After the leeches, the snakes, the mosquitoes, the pheasants, after all of her other adventures, she came at last here. The gods in Japan are, like the other inhabitants of the country, great tourists. Every year all of the deities make the the grand pilgrimage, if so it may be called, to the Izumo Shrine in Shimane, near the Japan Sea coast. Everyone goes, the grandest (from Ise, I suppose) and the most humble (little household deities, all grimed with soot from the household fires of farmers' huts in far Tohoku), because they are, after all, Japanese, and so everyone must do everything together.

I look from my vantage point out over the clear morning sea and watch the next loaded ferryboat slowly sidle into the slip, then watch the black dots, pilgrims all, spread over the pier, through the town,

272

into the shrine. The lacquered floors must be creaking with their weight now; standing in the corridors, one could watch the tourists shuffling among the pillars like hunters in a forest. The gods of Miyajima must be pleased today.

*   *   *

SUDDENLY I REMEMBER my letter, picked up at the post office this morning, put in my pocket, and forgotten till now. It is postmarked Takamatsu and was sent only three days ago. The envelope is rice paper, bought for the occasion I would guess. It contains two sheets, one heavily written on, the other perfectly blank. (The height of rudeness in Japan is to send a letter with but a single sheet, but the second sheet need not be written on: again the form, the appearance, is preserved.) The paper is pink and this letter, written expressly for me, sent directly to me, suddenly becomes precious and I wonder how I could have forgotten it so long in my pocket.

Saburo, in laborious *romaji*, Japanese expressed in our—for them —cumbersome alphabet, first speaks of the weather. All Japanese letters first speak of the weather. This, however, takes me some time to comprehend because Saburo, like everyone else, writes an unreformed *romaji* that does not correspond to Japanese sounds. Fuji becomes Huzi and Shimbashi becomes Sinbasi. There was a famous example of this misuse. A ship, the *Chichibu-maru*, had to be renamed after its maiden voyage to Seattle, where the locals laughed to see a boat named *Titibu-maru*. Nonetheless, this humiliation was not strong enough to change the ways of the Ministry of Education.

The weather has turned cool in Takamatsu. This must mean, Saburo sagely ventures, that autumn is at hand. I am to take care of myself under such treacherous climatic conditions. Then, as always in a Japanese letter: *sate*—which word indicates that the felicities have been observed and are now to be put out of the way as we get down to the business at hand.

The business had not turned out well. *Kanojo wa iya datta*—she didn't like it; *nankai mo yatte mitara*—no matter how many times he tried—*asoko made wa misete kurenakatta*—she wouldn't show him what it was like down there. (I must say that she had her reasons. Saburo was presumably attempting this private endeavor in a public park on

273

a Sunday in broad daylight, having brought her to the very spot where he and I had talked, hoping that some of the magic still lingered.)

Worse, she told him that he was perverted (*boku ga hentai da to itta*) and that she wasn't that kind of girl (*so iu onna ja nai to itta*) and that they needn't meet again (*mo awanakutemo ii to itta*).

Well, it was too bad (*zannen deshita*) but couldn't be helped (*shikata ga nai*). I was to have a good time and not forget my friend Saburo, and (in English) good-bye. Then, at the bottom, a scribbled post-script. One week later (*isshukango*), it all turned out all right (*yappari umaku itta*), though whether it turned out all right with the young lady in question or one of less invincible virtue he did not specify. Perhaps he had chosen his time and place with more wisdom. At any rate it was really great (*honto ni saiko*) and I was deeply thanked (*kokoro kara domo arigato gozaimasu*) for my part in this successful venture. Also, he was pleased to say, her parts (*asoko*) were just like I had said (*sono tori*), and he ended with several compliments upon my powers of observation and the hope that we would once more meet again, and then, in English, a letter-writing manual having apparently, at this late date, been brought in: "I remain, with the most sincere expression of good will, your friend—Saburo."

*　　　*　　　*

As I WAS REFOLDING the letter and putting it back into my pocket, I heard voices behind me. "You see," said one of the voices. "He has just received a letter and has come up here to read it. It is probably from a loved one and he wanted to get away so that he could read it in private."

"I see," said the other voice.

I turned around and there, directly behind me, stood a small, old lady in a kimono, and a boy, a middle-school student, black in his uniform and a cap too large for him.

"Good morning," said the lady, bowing.

I bowed in turn and she remarked on the weather and the view and what a nice place Miyajima was. "Oh, look at that bird." she suddenly said, indicating with a finger. "That was a sparrow."

"I see," said the boy.

"Sparrows are nice birds," she added. Then: "Oh, look, you can

274

see the cable car from here. See, it is just now beginning to go up the mountain."

"I see," said the boy, looking in the other direction.

"This boy here is my grandson," said the old lady, smiling at me. "I have brought him to Miyajima to show him the sights. He is old enough to be impressed now and remember."

She stood, small, bent, her hair silver in the sunlight, pulled back tightly into a bun, each strand like wire, her hands in front of her holding a large black bag. She smiled again and her face crinkled like paper. Then she sat down on a rock and patted one side of it to indicate that I was to join her.

One sometimes finds this directness in old people. One also finds it in the Noh drama, where the first character comes onto the stage and directly tells you who he is, where he is going, and why. Old people have gone through all the polite shufflings and mute longings of youth, all of the inarticulate and confused reasonings of middle age, all of the false politeness, the hanging back, that shyness creates and manners sanctify. Old women in Japan can do anything they please. They can be rude in bus or train, can pry into any matter, no matter how private, can be outspoken and impolite if they like, can wear the brightest colors without fear of censure, and can be so bawdy as to make their children blush. This was just such an old lady, and she was out showing her grandchild the sights.

She chatted on, pausing in her recitation of their adventures from time to time to point out a distant boat, a crow, a tree that had caught her fancy. It had not apparently occurred to her that I might not be able to speak Japanese—few foreigners do, despite the fact that it is among the easiest of languages to speak, if not to read. But then I remembered that once I had met an old man who had much pleased me by beginning at once in his native tongue, taking quite for granted that naturally, being here, I spoke. I was grateful to be spared the usual hesitancy, so often prolonged to the point where one begins to believe that they are seriously considering whether you can even think, much less speak. This I confided to the old man's young-ster—old people in Japan always travel with children—and was told that it was not so much that he knew I could speak Japanese as it was that he was certain there was no other language on earth.

"And you," she was saying, "you must have come from far, far away. Where is it you come from, now?"

275

I told her I came from the distant and snow-covered province of Ohio.

"There, you see?" she told the schoolboy. "Just think of that. He came from some snow country far, far away. Consider that, now." Then, to me: "Why?"

"Why what?"

"Why did you come?"

No one had ever asked me that before. How did I come, that I sometimes heard; or, since I had come, how did I like it, that I always heard; but why, why had I come?—I didn't know what to answer.

"There, he doesn't know," she said, turning to the boy and nodding to emphasize her words. "He came all this distance, and he doesn't know why. Isn't that just like people though? You see, everyone is alike, really."

"I see," said the boy and looked at me with guarded black eyes.

"Perhaps he did something bad," she said, looking directly at me, her eyes smiling, her silver hair shining in the sunlight.

I opened my mouth, but no words came.

"Oh, if you did, you should be able to tell me. I'm no chatterbox. I'm able to keep a secret, I am. There, you see," this to the boy, "he did something bad and so he came here to the shrine."

"I don't think I did anything bad," I began.

"Oh, we all do bad things. Here." She reached into her black bag and produced a rice ball covered with seaweed. "Eat this."

"I've had breakfast—" I began.

"Eat it, eat it. One can't eat too much. Do you like rice balls?"

"Yes."

"Then eat it up." She put it into my hand. It was very heavy.

"Once when I was a girl," she said, "I liked a boy who did something bad. Can you guess what it was? You can't? Well, when I was a girl I lived in a fishing village over near Ise—you know where that is? Good. Well, this boy, his name was Ichiro, and he used to go out fishing like all the other boys did. And then one day he did a terrible thing." She went on with several sentences of explanation.

But I could not understand what the terrible thing was, though the boy did and nodded soberly. I tried to think of all the terrible things that a boy could do to a girl—getting with child, deserting, raping. I tried them out.

"No, no, no," said the old lady, shaking her head. "You men always think of things like that. Eat your rice ball." She rephrased the description, and this time I understood that Ichiro had cut something he wasn't supposed to.

"Is the rice ball good?"

"Very good," I said, my mouth full. I had reached the middle, where the sweetly sour pickled-plum lay.

She tried various words to tell me what she meant. Finally, the boy supplied one.

"Oh," I said, "he cut the nets."

"That's it. He cut the fishing nets. It was a terrible thing to do. They were all we had to get our food by."

"But why did he do it?"

"Well, it was terrible. They had a ceremony and then turned him out of the village. He had to go away and no one in the whole peninsula was supposed to ever help him or talk to him or speak about him again."

"Where did he go?"

She shook her head, smiled, her face creasing.

"But why did he do a thing like that?"

She smiled again and shook her head.

"Did he do it for you somehow?" I ventured.

She laughed, a dry little laugh, like husks shaken. "Oh, no. Not for me. This was for something in himself, deep down in himself. His name was Ichiro," she added. Then: "Shall we be going?"

Going down the rocky path in her kimono and slipper-like *zori*, she managed much more surely than either I or her grandson. She turned, offered the boy her hand, and said: "They didn't use to allow women here at all. I remember when I couldn't come here. And, oh, how I wanted to see it, mainly because I couldn't, I suppose. . . . Why not? I don't know. Women were supposed to be unclean—not dirty, you understand, just somehow unclean. Men were supposed to be somehow clean."

"Even now you can't die here," suddenly offered the boy.

"That's right, I just told him that and it impressed him. If you feel that you're going to die, then you have to leave the island. I don't know what would happen if you didn't. Probably you'd just cause a lot of bother. You're not supposed to be born here either. Even now.

I've never understood. I can understand about dying and disturbing people, but being born is such a happy occasion. Everyone likes to be born."

How old was she, I wondered. It is always difficult to tell, but with her it was almost impossible. She looked seventy but was descending the difficult path as though she were half that. Emulating her directness, I asked her.

"Me? Well, I was born in Meiji, I'm one of the last people from my year of the Meiji era." That is, she was born sometime between 1868 and 1912. In any case, she must be near seventy, I decided.

"Do you want another rice ball?" she asked as though this vertical, slippery path were the most logical place to eat it.

"No, thank you. It was very good, though."

"Very good indeed. Oh, see that bird? That was another sparrow."

"I see," said the boy.

Off the mountain, walking along the pier, she suddenly stopped. "Well, this has been very nice. It isn't often you meet a person you can talk to. We'll see you this evening. It's time for his nap now."

"No, it isn't," said the boy, whining, as is the way of Japanese boys forced to something they don't want to do.

"Well, it's time for mine," she said. "It's past noon." Then she looked up at me. "This is our hotel. Please come about six and have something to eat with us." She bowed.

"Is this your first time here?" I asked.

She looked at me, her head to one side. "Now, how did he know that?" she asked her grandchild.

"I see," said the boy.

*   *   *

I TOO TOOK A NAP, in part recovered from the night before, and awoke to the late-afternoon sun covering me. It was warm in Miyajima. I listened and that familiar whirring sound began in the distance—the cicadas. It was summer again. It was as though, like Taro of Urashima, I had slept away a part of my life—the fall, the long winter, the spring—and here it was summer once more.

But it was deeper, mellower. The sky was a deep blue, as deep as the sea, and the air was thicker, it caressed the skin. It was not really summer, it was that miraculous counterfeit, Indian summer. I lay back on the pallet, the sun covering me like a blanket, and realized how happy I was. Then I got up and went to the shrine office.

*　　　*　　　*

SHE AND HER GRANDSON were sitting at the table in their small hotel room facing the mountains and she greeted me with: "Who was that letter from?"

"It was from a boy in Takamatsu."

"What did he say?"

"He said he was well, and hoped I was."

"It was written in a foreign language," she said, looking up at me.

"No, it was written in *romaji*."

"Well, that is almost a foreign language. We Japanese can't say very much in *romaji*."

"He didn't really say very much, just that he was well and hoped I was."

"That's about all it's good for. Have some tea. Do you like *yokan?*"

I picked up a piece of the sticky bean-paste cake on a toothpick and ate it. It was sweet, cloyingly sweet, sweet beyond the dreamings of all the children in the world.

"Good, isn't it?" she asked. "Nothing like *yokan*. Have another."

We talked on and on. There was no problem talking: we spoke of the habits of certain fish, of the magical properties of monkeys, of the grandchild's ability to draw (which resulted in a demonstration that produced a large cat with seven whiskers), of Momotaro, of the correct way to play the samisen, of the Yomiuri baseball team, of what my mother was doing at this very minute, of life on other planets. When she asked after my wife, I said she was dead. During this we ate soup, more rice balls, of which she had brought a number and they would spoil if they weren't eaten, and spaghetti, the last being for some reason a speciality of the inn. We finished off with a tangerine and talk about the rabbit in the moon.

"But you don't see a rabbit, do you?" she asked, remembering.

"No, we see a man's face."

"Now, however do you see that? I heard that once, that you see

283

a man in the moon, and I went out in the garden and spent about an hour looking up at it, and I still saw the same old rabbit. Oh, look, that was a shooting star."

"Yes," said the boy.

I looked at my watch and suggested a visit to the shrine.

"But it's gotten dark," she objected. "We wouldn't be able to see anything."

"Let's go anyway," I said.

Her grandchild was also taken with the idea. "Let's go, Grandmother, let's go," he said.

She shook her head, two children being too much for her. "Very well, but I think it's stupid to go and leave this nice room and all this tea."

We walked along the dark sea wall, past the lighted hotel fronts and onto the small path that led around the tiny bay. She was no longer spry. She could not see. She held out her hands from time to time and complained. Then either her grandson or I would take her hand and guide her as she shuffled along in her *zori*, muttering, remembering the bright room, the undrunk tea.

"I hate the dark," she said. "I've hated it since I was a little girl." Then: "Oh, look..."

Because we had rounded the bend and there lay the floating shrine, illuminated, hundreds of candles in their hanging cages casting their reflections against the lacquer.

Two acolytes bowed as we entered and then, this duty done, went back to the others. One of the priests waved a handful of fluttering paper over us then took off his black-lacquered hat and went back to the television we could dimly hear in the distance.

Our shoeless, *zori*-less feet slid softly over the lacquered floor as we entered the labyrinth and then paused to look. It was extraordinary, all of these open corridors lit by the wavering light of candles, which flickered in the light sea breeze. It was like being in a forest at night, and the lacquered rails were cool to the hand as we slowly shuffled from one corridor to the next, moving farther and farther out over the pale sand that caught the flames and sparkled in the light.

None of us said anything as we wandered through the corridors, our shadows falling first before us, then behind us as we walked. We stopped at the farthest veranda and turned to look at the floating shrine, black and silver, touched with orange and vermilion where the candles showed the lacquer. Looking in the other direction, the sea was black, with just a sprinkling of lights, Hiroshima perhaps, perhaps some nearer port. The great torii was invisible, standing there but hidden in the night.

I looked at my watch in the flickering candlelight. It was time. And then, just as the priest had said, as though by magic, I heard the murmur and the lapping. I looked down and through the spaces in the lacquered flooring of the veranda I saw the first silver line racing through. The tide was coming in.

We sat, our faces dark, our backs illuminated by the candles, as line after line of waves, all silver, all rushing, pushed themselves up the shallow beach and disappeared under us. Soon we were afloat, as though we were sailing on some enormous and illuminated pleasure barge. Thicker, deeper, with crests, the waves rolled under us. Their sound was now a roar as they dashed among the pilings and raced beneath us. One expected the shrine to rock, to begin its long voyage out under the invisible torii, out onto the open sea.

Then—and this the priest had not told me would happen, though he must have known, he who knew the ways of the seas and the planets—then one of the crests of the mountains lightened, and the great orb of the autumn moon appeared and at once the sea was a silver plain in front of it, with the great torii, standing deep in the water, casting its shadow toward us over the waters.

We were all silvered, our hands, our faces, and in this cold light the illuminated shrine turned warm, an ornamental cavern with red and orange lights. Beneath us the silver sheet now flowed endlessly, like a river. The tide was fully in and the moon was sailing higher and higher, growing smaller and smaller, some mighty balloon, some great eye, receding farther and farther.

The spectacle was over. We turned again to the shrine, now as familiar as one's own room after the celestial visions of sky and sea. Already the few tourists whom the lights had attracted were leaving, already the acolytes were at work extinguishing the candles one by one.

*   *   *

RETURNING OVER THE ROCKY PATH the old lady turned and—the first words she had spoken for an hour or so—said: "And how much did that cost you?"

"Not very much," I said, which was so. It had cost about ten dollars. Anyone could have the shrine illuminated; all you had to do was ask the priest in charge of the shrine office. The tide and moon were free.

"Well, it was very nice. I will never forget it," she said and, for once, did not draw her grandson's attention to any educational values the experience might have had. "There, see that shop there? I will now get us all some shaved ice."

While we were eating the ice, sweetened with synthetic strawberry syrup, our palates cold and our sinuses aching, she put down her spoon and said: "You like old stories, folklore, don't you? Very well, then, I will tell you the nicest I know."

She put down the spoon, pulled her kimono closer at the throat. Her grandson and I stopped eating and sat straighter. Then, as though ours was a picnic or a tea party, a pleasant, somewhat formal but unconstrained occasion, she cleared her throat, smiled at both of us in turn, and began:

"Once upon a time, after the last survivors of the Genji and Heike wars had fled, there was a beautiful young girl who lived in Shikoku. Every day she would draw water from the well and do the housework. One day, however, she forgot to draw the water and so it was night before she went to the well. It was a fine night, like tonight, and the moon was just as full as it is now.

"She bent over the surface of the water and there, far below, she saw a face looking up at her. At first she was frightened, for this was certainly a ghost. But as she looked she forgot her fear because the face was so handsome, and it looked at her with such longing. This, she told herself, is the ghost of a Heike warrior, long dead, and she gazed at him all night long.

"She had fallen in love with the ghost. Whenever the moon was full she went from her bed out into the courtyard and spent the night at the rim of the well, gazing through the depths at her handsome lover, who stared up at her.

"This went on for some time and she became thinner and thinner and finally had to take to her bed. She was pining away. Then one

286

day she died and her ashes were buried in the temple graveyard. People forgot all about her and her strange story.

"Then, many years later, something was the matter with the well and they had to clean it. They took out all of the water and went down to fix it. And what do you think they found at the bottom? Skeletons, armor, a sword? No, not at all. They found down at the bottom, where someone had dropped it long, long before, a large, old-fashioned mirror."

She stopped. Then she smiled. It was to me—not to a foreigner, not to an American—that she had been speaking.

Of all the things I saw, of all the people I met, on my journey, it is this I remember most clearly: this beautiful old woman sitting back, smiling after her story, her grandson slumped against her asleep, the strawberry-colored ice melting in the dishes in front of us, the light bulb overhead and, over that, the millions of stars in a fall night. If I close my eyes now, the scene returns, all of us sitting there on our shadows, the ghost of that ravishing story slowly disappearing, the boy breathing through his open mouth, the old woman pleased, happy. And yet I don't remember her face. I've often tried to remember what she looked like, and I've failed.

*   *   *

IN THE MORNING she was at the pier, hand in hand with her sleepy grandson with his hat down over his ears. They had come to see me off on the ferry that would take me back to the mainland.

"And now where are you going?" she asked.

"I don't know really. For me, this is the end of the Inland Sea."

"Of *this* Inland Sea, certainly, but why not go on to Kyushu?"

"What's in Kyushu? I've already been there."

"Oh, what isn't there? You haven't been if you can ask such a question. That was where it all began, in Kyushu. You like old stories, and you'll find so many of them in Kyushu that you won't know where to put them. That was where Japan was first made, you know; and that is where the giant monster cat of Nabeshima lives, and where the ghosts twitter like swallows. . . . Oh, you'll like Kyushu. Just take the train in the opposite direction, that's all."

"I want to go too, I want to go to Kyushu," the boy suddenly said.

287

"No, no. *We're* going back home today. You don't have any reason to go anywhere yet."

Waiting there in the mild autumn sunlight, I wondered aloud if I myself had any reason to go farther. Wasn't my journey done?

"Do you have any reason to go home?" she suddenly asked.

"No," I said.

"Well, then—that's as good a reason for traveling as anything I can think of. This is just the beginning."

Just the beginning. The Inland Sea was the prelude, the overture. Only now was the curtain opening—opening on the great island of Kyushu with its forests and mountains, its volcanoes, palms, pines, and bananas. Just by turning west and south, away from Tokyo, away from the snowbound province of Ohio, I could continue forever, following summer south.

"Be careful of the monster cat," said the boy.

"Oh, he'll be careful," said his grandmother.

The boat hooted, quivered, and the few early-morning passengers turned their faces toward the sea.

"Just remember to take the train going in the wrong direction, go to the left," she called above the noise of the engines.

I nodded and waved.

The boat instantly began wallowing at the pier and then moved slowly out into the strait. Soon there came the first salt breath of the open sea. Overhead a gull called.

They stood together on the pier, he black and small, she gray and small, and they both seemed the same size as the mountains rose around them. The great straddling orange torii waded into view with the whole floating shrine behind it, and the beaches moved in to create an island. The boy waved his hand once and I stood looking back at them until her silver hair became a point of light that suddenly vanished among the mountains and the forests.

Then I turned around and faced the sea.

*   *   *

I DON'T CARE if I never go back.

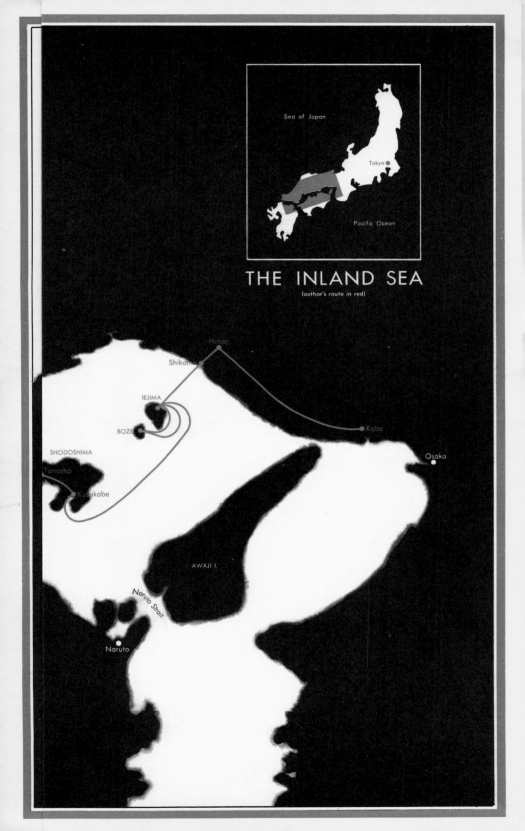

THE INLAND SEA

(author's route in red)

Sea of Japan

Tokyo

Pacific Ocean

Himeji

Shikama

IEJIMA

BOZE

SHODOSHIMA

Tonosho

Kusakabe

Kobe

Osaka

AWAJI I.

Naruto Strait

Naruto

Though I had earlier often passed along its coasts, my first extensive trip through the Inland Sea took place in the late summer and early fall of 1962, during which time I kept the journal that forms the basis of this book. Since then I have returned a number of times, acquiring other impressions, other bits of information, and some of these I added to the original journal. Later, in rewriting it as a proposed text for a magnificent collection of photographs of the Inland Sea by Yoichi Midorikawa, the same photographer whose work so handsomely illustrates the present book, I added more— things that had happened to me in other places in Japan (though they might well have happened in the Inland Sea), thoughts that had occurred to me fairly recently. That text, however, was never published. Now that another opportunity has arisen for publishing the journal, I have again added, rewritten, corrected. But the original journal still remains at the bottom of all I later put on top of it, hopefully in the way of enrichment.

The travels are real, the chronology is real, and the people are real, though certain details concerning them—myself included— have sometimes been changed for one reason or another. The places too are all real; they are there in the Inland Sea, within easy reach of the enterprising traveler. The history and folklore are also real—at least as real as they were when they reached me, filtered through the memories of the people I met and talked to.

Not only has a good amount been added, but a good amount has also been omitted. I have left out many long, dull days in what was a relatively uneventful trip. But I used those very days—and some long, dull days later on—to look back over the many years I have spent in this country (more than half my life) and to attempt, through the framework of this journal, an ordering of my thoughts.

One's thoughts about Japan tend to be contradictory. And this is fitting in a land where mutual contradictions are entertained with no seeming inconvenience. But the fact remains that the journal is now

289

being published for an English-speaking audience. While Japan has taught me, among many other things, that consistency is no great virtue, that, indeed, the quite consistent is the quite dead, I am nonetheless aware that one does not inspire confidence in the Western reader by fully demonstrating this attractive fact. Hence at times I have had to choose between past and present generalizations.

The issue has been further complicated in that I, no less than any foreigner living here, am naturally subject to that love/hate vacillation that ex-Ambassador Reischauer once called the Seidensticker syndrome. Though the phenomenon thus bears his name, this excellent writer and translator and friend enjoys no monopoly. It occurs with relation to anything we feel deeply enough about, and there are many of us who feel deeply about Japan.

My main problem, then, in finally presenting this journal has been what to sacrifice of my original ideas, particularly those with which I no longer necessarily agree. I have done what I think the Japanese would do. I have recast the more glaring, those that were sheer nonsense, I have mended the factually mistaken. I also called on my friends, and I should like to thank Sheelagh Lebovich, Eric Klestadt, and Meredith Weatherby for several careful readings of the manuscript and numerous suggestions for improving it, some of which I have incorporated into the book. Finally, I left the remainder of the original ideas precisely as they were. The reason is that they too are a part of the fabric, part of the emotional nexus, as it were, of that time and that self. This has its own validity and I did not want to disturb it.

Nonetheless, peculiar as some of these ideas might now seem to me or to anyone else who happens to be in a different phase of the syndrome, we must all remember that, as Helen Mears knew so well, for the Westerner Japan is a great mirror. In it we can see the land and the people clearly—but we can also see ourselves. And this, I think, is what this book is about.

290

The "weathermark" identifies this book as having been designed and produced at the Tokyo offices of John Weatherhill, Inc. Book design and typography by Meredith Weatherby. Text composed under the supervision of Serasia, Ltd, Hong Kong, and printed in offset by Kinmei, Tokyo. Photographs engraved and printed in gravure by Nissha, Kyoto. Bound by Makoto, Tokyo. The text is set in Baskerville 11 point with 2 point leading, with Baskerville for display.